A Sailing Surfer's Voyage
of Awakening

Swell

Captain
Liz Clark

Illustrations
by
Daniella Manini

patagonia®

Swell

A Sailing Surfer's Voyage of Awakening

FIRST EDITION

Editor – Sharon AvRutick

Book Designer – Mary Jo Thomas

Photo Editor– Jenning Steger

Photo Archivist – Sus Corez

Project Manager – Jennifer Patrick

Graphic Production – Rafael Dunn, Monique Martinez

Creative Director – Bill Boland

Creative Advisor – Jennifer Ridgeway

Illustrations – Daniella Manini

Publisher – Karla Olson

Printed in Canada on 100 percent post-consumer recycled paper

ENVIRONMENTAL BENEFITS STATEMENT
Patagonia Inc saved the following resources by printing the pages of this book on chlorine free paper made with 100% post-consumer waste.

TREES	WATER	ENERGY	SOLID WASTE	GREENHOUSE GASES
330 FULLY GROWN	154,357 GALLONS	148 MILLION BTUs	10,333 POUNDS	28,460 POUNDS

Environmental impact estimates were made using the Environmental Paper Network Paper Calculator 3.2. For more information visit www.papercalculator.org.

FSC
www.fsc.org
MIX
Paper from responsible sources
FSC® C016245

Hardcover ISBN 978-1-938340-54-3
E-Book ISBN 978-1-938340-55-0
Library of Congress Control Number: 2017958742

COVER Captain Liz and *Swell*. JIANCA LAZARUS
OPENING SHOT "When will you begin that long deep journey into yourself?" – Rumi. JIANCA LAZARUS
BACK COVER Anchor's down, surf's up. Ready for sea on my skin after three days of upwind sailing. JIANCA LAZARUS

In loving memory of
Dr. Arent H. 'Barry' Schuyler,
forever my sailing companion.
To my beloved father,
Russell J. Clark, for always
believing in me.
And for my wild soulmate,
Amelia the Tropicat,
may we meet again soon.

Contents

AUTHOR'S NOTE

I've come to believe that pursuing our dreams is as important to fulfilling our souls as it is to creating a better world. Doing so taps into a power greater than our own, allowing us to break free from perceived limitations. A path opens toward our highest Self and a daring kind of spiritual freedom and connectedness that could collectively transform the world. Each of us has a unique journey that is ours to claim. My hope is that by sharing both my inner and outer voyages on these pages, you will be inspired to listen more closely to the yearnings of your heart, to face your inner dragons, and to decide to choose love over fear, again and again.

Specific locations have been left out of this book because I believe the greatest inspiration comes not from a road map or waypoint, but from igniting the imagination to what is possible.

PAGES 4/5 "At sea, I learned how little a person needs, not how much." – Robin Lee Graham. JIANCA LAZARUS

PAGE 7 "If you have built castles in the sky, your work need not be lost; that is where they should be. Now put the foundations under them." – H.D. Thoreau. SHANNON SWITZER SWANSON

PAGES 8/9 "Adventure is worthwhile in itself." – Amelia Earhart. JODY MACDONALD

PAGES 10/11 All in, determined to learn the art of backside tube riding. JEFF JOHNSON

PAGES 12/13 "A good traveler has no fixed plans and is not intent on arriving." – Lao Tzu. SHANNON SWITZER SWANSON

PAGES 14/15 Climbing like a local after months of practice. CHRIS MCGEOUGH

PAGES 16/17 Broken autopilot, busted wind vane equal long hours at the helm. JIANCA LAZARUS

PAGE 18 Learning to sail in San Diego Bay, age eight. RUSSELL CLARK

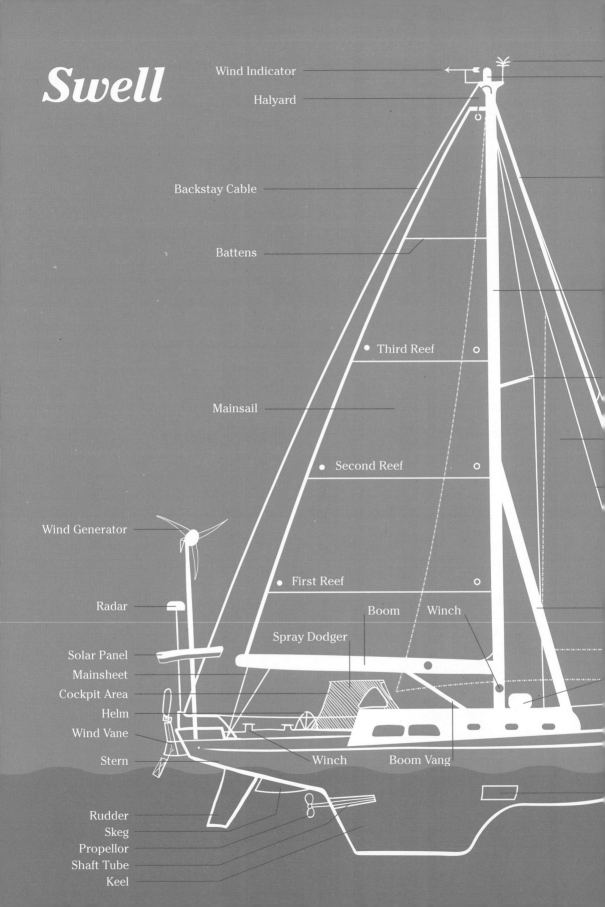

Swell

Wind Indicator

Halyard

Backstay Cable

Battens

Third Reef

Mainsail

Second Reef

Wind Generator

First Reef

Radar

Boom   Winch

Spray Dodger

Solar Panel
Mainsheet
Cockpit Area
Helm
Wind Vane
Stern

Winch   Boom Vang

Rudder
Skeg
Propellor
Shaft Tube
Keel

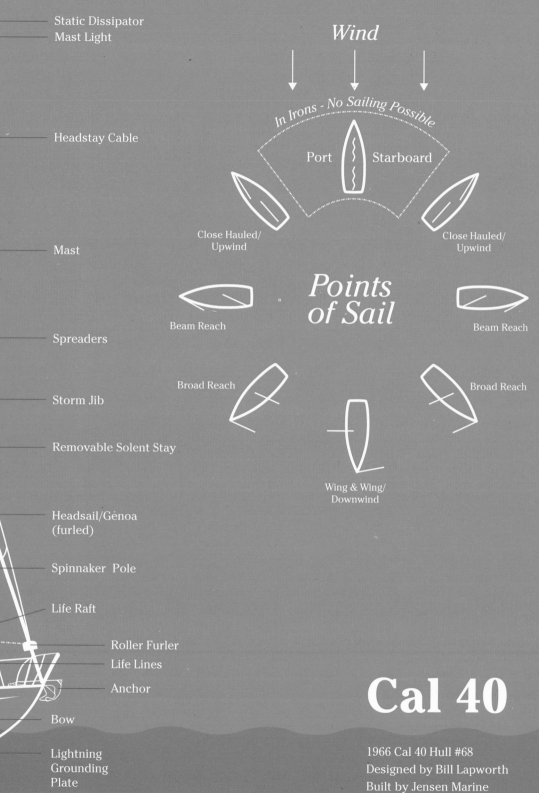

Static Dissipator
Mast Light

Headstay Cable

Mast

Spreaders

Storm Jib

Removable Solent Stay

Headsail/Genoa
(furled)

Spinnaker Pole

Life Raft

Roller Furler
Life Lines

Anchor

Bow

Lightning
Grounding
Plate

Wind

In Irons - No Sailing Possible

Port   Starboard

Close Hauled/
Upwind

Close Hauled/
Upwind

*Points
of Sail*

Beam Reach

Beam Reach

Broad Reach

Broad Reach

Wing & Wing/
Downwind

Cal 40

1966 Cal 40 Hull #68
Designed by Bill Lapworth
Built by Jensen Marine
in Orange County, California

La Capitana

Don't Give Up the Ship

It's still so close. Should I just go back?

Reflections bend and weave across the dark, surging sea. I sit on the aft deck with my legs hanging over the rail, looking toward the glowing coastline. It's nearly midnight, chilly and silent. *Swell* rocks gently at anchor at a small island just south of the United States–Mexico border. City lights halo San Diego and Tijuana. A mere thirty miles of ocean separate me from the safety of the wooden dock we were tied to a few hours ago. I wiped away tears after casting off *Swell*'s lines and watching a handful of my dearest loved ones gradually blend into the hazy winter skyline in our wake. Today is the thirtieth of January 2006, two weeks short of three years since acquiring this sailboat.

I blink with fatigue as I try to convince myself to feel excited and proud after the seemingly endless preparation. But my fear and anxiety don't want to negotiate. My inner turmoil seems written in the sky. To the north: light, familiarity, comfort, safety, family. To the south: dark, unknown, doubt.

I've been dreaming of this voyage all my life, but I'm a wreck of nerves. It's not rogue waves or pirates I'm worrying about—it's the thought of failure. *The horizons are calling. I want to sail away, surf remote breaks, learn from other cultures, find happiness and a better way to live in harmony with nature, but what if I make a stupid mistake? What if someone gets hurt? What if I'm not strong enough in mind or body? How would I ever get over the disappointment of failing myself and everyone who has helped me?* Dread rises, tightening my throat as I think about the countless people who have supported me in getting to this moment. I imagine myself hiding somewhere in the desert rather than facing them with the news that I've run aground or hit a reef. *Yes, I should go back and do some more reasonable sea trials before I sail off for good.*

A sea lion abruptly breaks the sea surface below my feet. He twirls and loops just under the water, spinning glittery ribbons of neon phosphorescence through the dark sea. He swoops and frolics, carefree and confident. My shoulders relax a bit.

Whirling eights and spirals, my visitor mocks my intense mood. "This is what you wanted," he appears to say—loop, swoop. "To live in the present … appreciate nature's simple wonders … feel free."

He comes up for a breath and stares at me, as if awaiting a response. *I know, I know … I can't go back.* The seasonal window to sail south is closing. I just have to do my best and take the challenges as they come. I'm petrified, but there isn't anything else I'd rather be doing.

The sea lion's bright trail dances off into the darkness.

"Don't give up the ship!" I call, imitating Barry during our goodbyes.

December 1989, Baja California

"It's time, Sweetie," Dad whispers, stroking my back. I roll out of my bunk and follow him past the engine room, into the main cabin of our family sailboat. It's 3 am.

He unfolds the chart for Baja and spreads it on the navigation table.

"So here's where we are," he says in a whisper, pointing to a small penciled X. "And here's where we're going."

He points to a small island off the coast. I blink my sleepy eyes.

"Let's measure the distance first," he says, handing me the dividers.

I spread the bronze tips and hold them to the side of the chart, adjusting them until they measure exactly twenty-five nautical miles, as Dad taught me. He then lines up the parallel rulers between the two points. I walk the divider tips along the rulers, making sure not to alter the distance between them.

"One, two, three, four, and a little more," I count softly.

"Okay, so what's four times twenty-five?"

I use a scratch paper to do the multiplication, carrying the two. I like math. "One hundred?"

"Very good, honey!" Dad whispers. "About a hundred nautical miles."

Then I align the hole in the compass rose over the X where we are on the chart to determine our heading, pushing the rotating arm to meet our destination.

"265 degrees?"

"Great, Lizzy! Let's get underway," he says, smiling proudly.

He slips my life jacket/harness over my head, buckles it, and kisses me on the forehead before we climb up the companionway stairs. Outside it's as dark as my haunted hallway back home. The seats are wet from the drizzling rain. I'm not scared, though. I'm always safe with Dad. The ignition buzzes as he turns the engine key.

Dad disappears into the darkness and I hear the mainsail sliding up the mast. On his call, I shift the engine into forward as he raises the anchor.

A few minutes later, he comes back with the flashlight gripped between his teeth, coiling the anchor snubber. "Are you ready for your first night watch?"

My hands are tingling. I feel nervous but important. A cold wind mixed with raindrops gusts under the canvas bimini. Dad pulls up the hood on my jacket.

"I'm ready, Daddy," I tell him. I am nine and a half years old now and my family and I have been doing overnight trips to Catalina every summer since I was a baby. Two weeks ago we left San Diego to sail through Mexico for the next six months.

"So remember, you are not to unclip your harness tether or leave the cockpit for any reason. If you have to use the head, wake me up, okay?" He points the bow out to sea. The glow of the compass light illuminates his handsome face as Endless Summer *pushes out into the night. He sets the autopilot, then lifts me up on the seat behind the wheel and hugs me.*

"Keep a close eye on the horizon in all directions," he continues. "If you see any lights or anything that seems odd, just wake me up. I'll be right here, honey."

"Okay. I will, Daddy."

He lies down on the cockpit bench. I look ahead and all around. For now, the horizon is clear. I touch my BFF half-heart necklace and think of home. Of Mattie and Trim, our golden retrievers, and gymnastics practice. Of eating oranges in the grove with my little sister, Kathleen. And catching crawdads in the canyon with my big brother, James.

The cold wind pulses across my ears. Scattered raindrops patter on the top of the canvas bimini. I squint into the dark night, exhilarated.

A week into the voyage down the coast of Baja, and we're still afloat. The arrival of a north swell abruptly rolls my crew and me out of our bunks early one morning. In the chill of twilight, Mark and Shannon haul up the stern anchor while I maneuver in reverse. Soon the compass points south again. The diesel grinds as the mainsail struggles to catch a light breeze. Once the sun beats out the morning fog, it glitters triumphantly on the calm sea to port. We are all in good spirits despite our rude awakening.

I met Shannon just before the trip, and I liked her immediately. She's a soft-spoken, scholarly blonde with dogged determination and a gorgeous smile. She listens attentively as I show her how to attach the main halyard to the top of the mainsail in order to haul the sail up the mast, or wrap the jib sheets properly around the winches. We have ocean love and adventure dreams in common, plus we both majored in Environmental Studies at UC Santa Barbara. And since she enjoys photography, I hope to use her photos in combination with my writing to sell some articles and find some sponsors. I'm determined to find a way to make enough money to avoid flying home to work when my savings run out.

I'm thrilled that Mark, a college roommate, is here, too. His steadfast friendship and constant humor helped me through three years of exams and young adult trials. I happily agreed when he expressed interest in joining us for the first leg of the voyage. Every time I begin to stress or second-guess myself, Mark's jokes ease the mood.

"We better not sink 'cause you know I can't swim, Liz," he teases as I nervously scan *Swell*'s rig.

A small pod of dolphins leaps toward *Swell* to play in the little wave that pushes off the bow. We watch from the foredeck as they surf and frolic, reminding me of the countless hours I spent as a kid sitting on the bowsprit of our family sailboat off the coasts of California and Mexico. My legs would dangle off the edge of the teak plank with the broad horizon before me—that's where I started dreaming about an extended voyage of my own.

I also witnessed floating trash and wildlife tangled in fishing debris, sparking my concern for the environment. Despite our family's financial struggles after returning from the voyage to Mexico, Mom saw me mailing the cash I earned from chores to Greenpeace. She gave me a "Save Our Seas" poster and a world map to hang on my bedroom wall. I drew arrows on the map to show the route I wanted to sail one day. Both the map and the poster came with me every time we moved, which was often. I looked up at them during junior high homework, after gymnastics practice, and between high school shenanigans. Even after a girlfriend introduced me to surfing at fifteen, and riding waves became a fanatical new passion, both my voyaging dream and environmental concern persisted.

As today's dolphins carry on west, I thank them for the visit, then head back to the cockpit to update the logbook. That afternoon, with daylight to spare, we near a series of boldly stratified bluffs with small waves rolling down the inside of the point. We unanimously decide to drop anchor and race to trade our winter jackets and warm boots for neoprene wetsuits and booties. Once the anchor is set, Shannon and Mark bolt to the foredeck to untie their boards, then paddle for the lineup.

They're halfway to shore when I finish squaring away the decks and leap over the side. The frigid sea washes away my accumulated angst. I'm at home in a four-millimeter wetsuit on my favorite shortboard. Strands of brown kelp wave at me with the surge of a swell. I smile and paddle for the break.

The surf isn't extraordinary, but today every glide feels like a victory. Surfing—my solace, my *numero uno*—took a back seat during the almost three years I spent preparing for the voyage. Fishermen in a panga wave as they whiz toward a cluster of brightly colored shacks that break up the endless tan-and-yellow Baja landscape. When the sun drops low, and the evening chill sets in, we catch a final ride and begin the long paddle back.

After a hundred yards, I look up. There's *Swell*, bobbing faithfully on her anchor, her hull's sleek, powerful lines aglow in the golden rays. Her beauty stops my breath for a moment. I can't believe it. *Swell* blurs as tears fill my eyes.

"I'm here!" I call to the sky. "It's real! Thank yo-o-o-u-u-u-u-u!" I'm not sure who I'm thanking. I don't believe in God, but this feels miraculous. There's salt on my lips and a burn in my shoulders. I'm paddling out, rather than in. I'm finally in my dream, awake!

The next morning the sun is out and the wind is right for our next passage south. I relish the crisp afternoon air while steering under full sails as we enter the wide mouth of San Quintín bay. Mark is in the galley making PB&Js and Shannon sits beside me in the cockpit, snapping photos of the multicolored sands and low grassy dunes off the port side. Suddenly I see whitewater fifty yards off the bow as a wave rolls over a shallow, uncharted sandbar. The depth gauge leaps from 150 feet to 20, to 17, and then 12 feet, as I make a jarring turn to starboard. My heart is in my throat, but thankfully our new heading brings us back into deep water.

Mark sticks his head out of the companionway with a purple stripe smeared on his shirt. "Geezus Liz, you could have just asked for extra jelly!"

I glance back to where I saw the wave, but now the murky green sea is calm, hiding the submerged sandbar once again. As we sail toward the south side of the bay to anchor, I nibble at my sandwich, heart still racing, thankful for the fortuitous timing. If that wave had washed over the bar only a few seconds later, *Swell* would likely be aground. Serendipity? Luck? Fate?

April 2001, Santa Barbara

My classes at UCSB are over for the day. The scents of low tide fill the chilly spring air as I walk out the dock in the Santa Barbara Harbor. After spending a semester studying abroad in Australia, the only way Dad could entice me to come home and finish college was by sailing Endless Summer *up from San Diego so that I could live aboard her in the harbor.*

Not only was the surf excellent Down Under, but I observed an underlying respect for nature in the small seaside community where I studied. On the contrary, I'm disillusioned by America's general disregard for the environment. It frustrates me that businesspeople only chase profits, while compromising our most vital resources—fresh air, clean water, and healthy soils, rivers, and oceans. Why aren't students required to learn about the natural systems on Earth that sustain our daily lives?

I walk past where the harbor patrol can see me, and then set down my skateboard to push the rest of the way out on the cement dock. I have to be at work in an hour. My girlfriend Katie picked me up before dawn this morning for a surf mission, so I need a catnap. Katie and I are a couple of kelp flies. The beaches can't get rid of us. We love everything about surfing—even the smell of our peed-in wetsuits, towel changing in parking lots, and the tar and seaweed that collects in our hair. The crowded lineups of wave-hungry surfers are the only bummer. That's what's so great about having a boat. Last weekend my friends and I took Endless Summer *up the coast to a spot without public road access. It was my first voyage without my brother or Dad onboard. We scored a long right under the coastal bluffs with no one around!*

Now I'm even more excited for my sailing dream. What could be better than waking up on the ocean, traveling the world, exploring for perfect waves with no crowds, and sailing away from this short-sighted society that's ruining the Earth?

When it's time, I pull on black slacks and a white blouse. I recently landed an afterschool job working on a handsome megayacht named Tamara, *docked nearby. This evening they are hosting an open house for influential people in Santa Barbara.*

Behind the bar on the aft deck, I carefully fill champagne flutes. I'm nearly ready to take off with my tray of glasses when a lovely elderly diva in a glorious fuchsia pantsuit approaches.

"May I have a glass, sweetheart?" she asks.

"Of course."

"Are you a student here in Santa Barbara?"

"Yes, I'm finishing up my degree in Environmental Studies."

"Oh! Then you must meet Dr. Barry Schuyler. He's one of the founders of that program."

I follow her with my teetering glasses over to a noble-looking elder gentleman, well-built and dressed in a handsome blue blazer with square, metal-rimmed glasses. His thinning hair is combed back cleanly.

"Barry, you must meet Liz. She's about to graduate from the ES program."

"Nice to meet you, Dr. Schuyler," I say. "Would you like champagne or an appetizer?"

"Thank you, my dear, I'm pleased with my wine," he says, lifting his glass. "Are you enjoying your studies? A few of my colleagues and I created the program after the Santa Barbara oil spill in 1969."

"Thank you for doing so. I'm loving it," I say. We chat casually about my favorite classes and about sailing. Then he pauses.

"Every September on the full moon," he announces, "I sail to San Miguel Island for the weekend with a group of friends and students. Would you care to join us this year?"

"Sure," I say without much pause, "I'd love to."

Swells and exams come and go. Nearly every weekend I compete in a surf contest somewhere on the California coast. The last one of the season is the NSSA Nationals and I manage to snag the win. I ponder a path toward professional surfing, but decide that my competitive thirst has been quenched. I much prefer the thrill of exploring for waves, like I'd done on summer breaks from school in Baja, Barbados, Costa Rica, El Salvador, and Hawai'i. Dad pays my tuition, so all year I can scrimp and save for traveling.

That summer I stick around to polish and clean on the megayacht in hopes of landing a permanent crew position for their upcoming voyage. September rolls around, and a week before my last quarter at UCSB begins, I'm surprised when Mom calls to tell me that a certain Dr. Schuyler from the Environmental Studies department just called to invite me on a sailing trip. I'm surprised; he hadn't even written down my name or number.

I don't know anyone else in the group. It could be awkward. But I've never been to San Miguel Island and hear it's majestic. I call him back and confirm that I'd like to join them.

Dr. Schuyler stands happily at the helm on our way across the Santa Barbara Channel. The boat is equipped with an autopilot and many able hands, but he clearly enjoys steering us toward the island in the distance.

When he tires, he sits down beside me. "Tell me, Lizzy, what are your plans after graduating?" he asks, without taking his gaze off the sea.

"I want to go sailing," I say. "I want to go on a long voyage across the Pacific, maybe even around the world."

He peels his eyes from the horizon for a moment and looks at me earnestly. "I also dreamed of an extended voyage, but between raising our four children, my career as a high school teacher and college professor, and writing my PhD thesis, I never went. Plus, my dear wife, Jean, much prefers horses to sailboats." He draws in a deep breath, and looks back out to sea.

"You, my dear, most certainly should go. Don't wait until life's responsibilities anchor you."

Mark, Shannon, and I sit atop massive sand hills on the far side of Santa Maria after making it six hundred nautical miles down the Baja coast. We admire the mountainous desert landscape encircling the large bay. The same wind that pushed us here created these voluptuous dunes. Gusts softly push sand up our ankles. *Swell* swings back and forth on her anchor on the far side of the sheltered bay. We're the only sailboat here. The long silence is rare for us, but from time to time Baja's stark natural beauty and undeveloped expanses hold us in a spell.

This desolate stretch of coast has provided plenty of challenges, but I'm learning every day. The first test of my mechanical savvy had arrived the morning after nearly hitting the sandbar. Ready to raise anchor, I turned the engine key, but nothing happened. I tried again: nothing. After half the day thumbing through manuals, troubleshooting, and nearly electrocuting myself, I placed a satellite phone call to Mike, my mechanic friend. He helped sort out the mystery of the neutral safety wire, and we continued down the coast.

Blustery offshore winds on that passage called for constant sail changes—reefing (lowering) and raising both the main and headsails as the wind fluctuated in strength. It made for good practice, but one gust overpowered *Swell*, pinning her down on her side when the jackline—a fixed line that runs the length of the deck—got sucked into the roller-furling winch. Hours later, we straggled into our destination, frazzled and wind-chapped, with only a few rays of daylight to spare. But to our delight, a thick northwest swell was arriving, too. Waves peeled into the horseshoe bay, and some friends we'd planned to meet waved madly from their campsite on the point. The surf pumped and bonfires raged for an unforgettable three-day rendezvous.

We dodged lobster traps and long-line buoys on every passage, executed several tight, tricky double-anchor maneuvers, plowed through breaking waves on harrowing dinghy landings and launches, and escaped a near collision with a Carnival Cruiseliner. Mark and I panicked one evening when a bright light on the horizon appeared, until we realized it was Mars rising over the sea, not a northbound ship.

Amidst the firsts and follies, I have started to understand how *Swell* sails and anchors. Even though neither have much sailing experience, Mark and Shannon gracefully mitigate my high stress and respect my overly rigid rules—like requiring hourly updates to the logbook on watch duty, and, no matter the weather, wearing a harness clipped to the jackline to go out on deck underway. Despite fatiguing watches, culinary challenges on passage, limited opportunities to bathe, cramped quarters, pulling ropes and wrestling sails, my crew has remained positive.

Still seated together on the dune, I break our thoughtful silence by slipping a handful of sand down Mark's pants. He chases after Shannon and me, and we all roll down to the bottom, choking on sand and laughter. After dashing into the cold sea to wash off, we pack up our gear and head for the dinghy. On the way, I come across a perfect, saucer-sized sand dollar on the low tide flats. I pick it up and stash it in my bag to send to Barry from the next port. Now that my nerves are settling, I'm beginning to comprehend the enormity of what he's done for me.

June 2002, Santa Barbara

I tire of staring at the ceiling in my brother's apartment and roll onto my side. The clock in the kitchen reads 1:30 pm; I am still horizontal. I've been in the States for almost a month, after sailing away as crew on the Tamara *back in December. To my shock, the megayacht turned out to be owned by a commune of sorts, and the seventy-two-year-old leader of the more than fifty members hoped I would join his on-board harem of seven child-bearing "wives." I jumped ship in the Bay of Acapulco, happy to join a solo captain I knew on his thirty-four-foot sailboat. For four months, Rick and I sailed south looking for surf and adventure (and we found plenty), but at the same time he discouraged me from helping sail the boat, preferring I cook or clean. He whittled away at my confidence and I came home convinced that I'd never be able to captain a long voyage on my own.*

My dream is broken. A tear rolls down my face. I feel so lost. My friends are starting at corporate jobs; just that thought makes me feel numb.

Since the election of George W., I'm more and more disappointed with the direction the United States is headed. I mean, refusing to comply with the Kyoto Protocol? Dismantling the Endangered Species Act? Gutting the Clean Air and Water Acts? I want off this bus. But how? I'm completely out of money.

Despite my pitiful state, my brother has welcomed me graciously. My things are in the back of my car, so as not to clutter his small apartment. As he leaves for work each morning, James endearingly pats my head as I remain on his couch, staring vacantly up at the ceiling's thick beige drywall spackle.

"Why don't you go down to the beach today, Lizzy?" he encourages.

"The surf is small," I muster.

"You know, getting a job isn't all that bad. You can still have a life outside of work."

I can't rally a reply. Silent tears run down my face and I squeeze his hand tightly, hoping he feels how much I appreciate his care. He kisses my hand before heading for the door.

A dreary month goes by before I finally walk into the lobby of the Santa Barbara Yacht Club for Fourth of July festivities with some friends. Dr. Barry Schuyler and his wife, Jean, stand in the entryway looking distinguished.

"Lizzy! Good to see you, my dear!" he says, smiling, then casually proposes something extraordinary: "I'm looking for someone to sail my boat around the world. Would you be interested?"

My stomach drops and everything gets quiet for a moment. I wish to scream, "Yes! Of course!" but my uncertainty holds me back.

"Thank you, Dr. Schuyler, but ... I'm not sure I'm ... cut out for it," I tell him, the words sticking in my throat.

"Stop by my boat sometime. She's in Marina 1, slip I-23. A small sloop called Freya.*"*

A few days later I'm back on my brother's couch, now fixated on the retired professor's proposition. Was he serious? Give me his boat? There's got to be a catch. I must find out! I finally drive down to the harbor. Dr. Schuyler is standing on the dock beside his boat when I arrive. It's the same kind of boat that my childhood heroine, Tania Aebi, had sailed around the world at eighteen years old. I'm instantly intrigued.

"Hello, young lady," he says politely. "Did you reconsider?"

"Hello, Dr. Schuyler, I did."

"Please call me Barry. Come aboard and sit down. Let's discuss."

The tour of Freya *doesn't take long because she's so tiny. But she's clean, cozy, and organized. We sit in the cockpit and he lays out his idea. He explains that he and Jean are involved in all sorts of meaningful work with community charities and nationwide NGOs. But now at almost eighty years old, he finds that his longtime dream of voyaging still haunts him. He wants to live vicariously through someone else's sailing adventure. The next best thing to living the dream himself would be to help someone else do it.*

The proposition seems too good to be true; I must give it a shot.

After a discussion with Barry, my father approves, and plans are hatched. Barry writes up a list of my pretrip duties—very reasonable things like apprenticing with a sailmaker, a rigger, and a marine mechanic, and studying major ocean currents and wind patterns. I happily agree to write him letters and keep in touch from various ports around the world. He will help financially to get the boat ready for safe ocean travel, but after that I will have to figure out how to fund my voyage.

My depression dissolves almost instantly as my sailing dream comes back to life. Barry and Jean invite me to live with them until I get back on my feet. I soon land a job as a bartender at a restaurant overlooking the harbor, and spend my off-days sailing and tinkering aboard Freya. *Barry and I attend a ham radio course together, in hopes of keeping in touch via radio once I sail off. I take* Freya *up the coast and gain confidence captaining her short distances. She's fit to my size and strength, and I soon feel more optimistic about my potential as a captain.*

But on the way to San Miguel Island from Cojo Point late in the summer, I take a wave over the stern off the notorious Point Conception. The cockpit is pooped and I'm terrified, bailing seawater as it pours down into the cabin. After this happened in only medium-sized seas, I start feeling nervous about making open-ocean passages in Freya. *She's so small; I can't even stand up straight inside her tiny cabin. I will hardly have room to bring a surfboard or a friend. This isn't quite how I envisioned the dream.*

When I express my concerns to Barry, he understands—and a week later, he's back with a new proposition. He tells me that if I find a bigger boat and raise some money, he'll match the funds to enable me to purchase it.

My father, who just closed a business deal, is instantly willing to pitch in, and we soon find a new boat, just a few rows down from Freya. *It's a 1966 Cal 40—a type of sailboat that Barry himself has owned, loved, and knows to be seaworthy. He assures me we can have a rigger set her up for my slight, but muscular five-foot-four inches and 110 pounds. When I see the boat the first time, I stop in my tracks: A rainbow arches over her.*

On February fourteenth, 2003, Barry signs the paperwork to make me an elated sailboat owner. The retired professor and the young dreamer are now set to empower each other toward the same horizon-chasing dream.

The northwest wind blows cold and constant on *Swell*'s stern quarter, making for a frigid 3 am watch. It's our last night at sea before arriving in

Cabo San Lucas. I pull my beanie low over my ears and praise the biting tailwind as I watch the speed gauge bounce between six and eight knots. Mark and Shannon have already fulfilled their night-watch duties. Leaning against the teak washboards, I soak up the scene around me.

The nearly full moon is high in the sky, illuminating the mountainous southern Baja silhouette to port. The winged-out mainsail and white edges of the deck glow in the silver light. The low whistle of the wind and rush of water past the hull are sweet music compared to the noisy rattle of the diesel motor. Only eighty more miles until we reach the cape.

My solitude frees time to think. It's still so surreal that I'm actually here aboard my own little ship. It seems all too improbable—too extraordinary to pass off as luck. In hindsight, I can see how the string of adversities helped lead me here: I cursed the disappointing job on the *Tamara*, but thanks to that evening serving drinks on her aft deck, I met Barry; and despite the disheartening sailing trip with Rick, the experience taught me exactly what needed to be done in order to outfit *Swell* for my limited strength and size. I still don't know how I'll manage once my savings run out. I honestly haven't had time to think about it.

March 2003, Santa Barbara

Barry estimates it will take about a year to prepare the boat for the voyage and assembles a team of local experts to help. I spend my days working alongside Mike the marine mechanic, Marty the rigger, James the electrician, and Bennet the sailmaker, learning all kinds of tips and tricks about tools, glues, resins, metals, hardware, rope, sail material, knots, wood, backing plates, wire, and ways to build, fix, troubleshoot, customize installations, and transform what was old and rotten into something strong and durable. Four to five evenings a week, I bartend at a restaurant in the harbor, squirreling away my tips for the voyage.

Barry and I meet in the parking lot of the Santa Barbara Yacht Club once a week, where we walk arm in arm up to the dining room on the second story. We stand near the window for a moment and look quietly out at the sea; I feel our mutual dream on my shoulders. After we're seated, he pulls out a manila folder containing an assortment of pertinent article clippings, and a small stack of books with the pages carefully marked. We read through the items while he regally sips white wine. We both intend to keep things simple, but it seems no matter how hard we try, overhauling the boat for the voyage becomes more and more involved. The list of refit "to-dos" and purchases quickly expands. When our food arrives, we dive into discussions of current projects and dilemmas.

The outfitting process becomes all-consuming. We often dig into one repair, only to find three more. Each decision is a compromise in a forty-by-eleven-foot space. The boat will be my home, my transportation, and life-sustaining capsule. If I want to carry more water, I have to sacrifice a second fuel tank. Building a small navigation table means losing the port-tack sailing berth. Which do I bring, a spare mainsail or my beloved 5'9" squash tail surfboard? The choices seem infinite and there is never one simple answer.

Where safety is concerned, do I need an EPIRB and a life raft? Manual and electric bilge pumps? A storm drogue and storm sails? Life jackets? Fire extinguishers? A flare gun and flares? A saltwater still? A backup GPS? Overboard bag? Is the electrical system grounded properly? How will I receive weather information? Is there redundancy in all the major systems? Is my tetanus shot current? Do I need a strobe light? Jacklines and harnesses? A bilge alarm? First aid kit? Underwater epoxy? What about a lightning rod? Emergency scuba gear? Bolt cutters for cutting away the rig if it falls?

Barry helps me keep focused. We know that the boat needs a sound hull, strong standing rigging, and a reliable engine. He has her hauled to assess the underside. The leaky deck rail is ripped off and glassed over. Mike checks over the engine, reinforces the rudder shaft in case of a collision, and donates a stronger boom that's been sitting in his workshop. The rigging cables need replacing, so once the boat is back in the water, Mike teaches me how to measure, cut, and fit the new wires. I haul myself up the mast to replace them one by one.

Marty makes dozens of changes to adapt the boat for my size and strength. He carefully rerigs the inner workings of the new boom with heavy purchases to make sail adjustments easier, and equips the boom's exterior with small winches and sturdy blocks to aid in reefing. He reworks and upgrades the components at the mast head, installs high-visibility navigation lights and a removable Solent stay for a storm jib. He meticulously reinforces every possible point of weakness in the rig, replaces all worn-out halyards, sheets, and hardware, and also teaches me useful knots and clever leverage tricks. Self-tailing winches are installed in the cockpit and on the mast.

For long-distance voyaging, a self-steering wind vane is fixed onto the stern. Bennet fits a spray dodger and sun shade in the cockpit. The main windows are replaced; hatches resealed; and a long-distance SSB radio, VHF radio, GPS chartplotter, and new navigation lights installed. James adds a small watermaker, and bigger deck cleats, too. The mainsail and furling genoa are in decent shape, but the bow anchor needs new chain and rode. Plus, this kind of voyaging requires a stern anchor setup, backup anchors, extra rode, extra chain, shackles, swivels, line leads, and chafe guards. There won't always be a local chandlery or someone to call to make repairs, so

I also need spare parts, equipment manuals, and tools to fix and maintain the vitals. Our projected year of preparation stretches into two.

For living on anchor, James installs an extra water tank, and a new battery bank with a clever setup of solar panels that integrate a small davit to help raise and lower the dinghy's outboard motor for passages. Water and fuel pumps are added, along with interior lights, a refrigeration compressor, and a 110-volt power inverter for charging camera batteries and laptop computers. He builds a new switchboard with monitors to display battery and charging levels, and replaces most of the boat's old wiring and fuses. The cooking stove is still in good condition, but the propane storage has to be moved from the foredeck to accommodate the new life raft. My carpenter friend, Jaime, builds a permanent navigation desk with shelves. On a weekend visit from my father, we plumb in a stowable shower on the aft deck and a macerator pump for the holding tank.

My "deal" with Barry becomes a subject of controversy in the harbor. Some question my capability, others argue over refit solutions. Many claim I'll never leave. It's a constant challenge to orchestrate multiple projects, navigate egos, and disregard doubters, but Barry's confidence in me never falters.

"What do you think about self-defense?" Barry ponders one afternoon. I pause and think for a moment. A gun? No. Mace? Couldn't hurt. Pipe wrench? Machete? Bow and arrow? Nunchucks? Voodoo dolls?

"Martial arts classes could be a good idea, my girl." I add it to the list.

Another day I ask him, "What about Swell*?" In spite of the seafaring superstitions around renaming a vessel, this boat's name has already been changed numerous times. I feel a new one will be nice, in honor of our quest.*

"Swell ... Swell ... hmmm ... it has a nice ring to it, reminds me of Slocum's Spray. *And it certainly holds meaning for your surfing pursuits."*

"Plus meaning happy, good. And to grow and expand."

"True," he ponders. "And you won't have to explain it. I like it. Swell *it is. When shall we rechristen her?"*

Two and a half years pass in a blur of boat work and bartending before departure finally nears. Lying on my back, I stroke my brush over the last exposed corner of the forward cabin, completing the final coat of paint on Swell's *interior walls and ceiling. I rest my head for a moment, staring up with satisfaction, then crawl out to look at the clock. Only six minutes to get to the restaurant!*

I plunge my brush into the cup of thinner and sprint up the dock to exit the heavy steel marina gate. Dashing for my car, I extract some cleanish work attire from the mess of clothes, boat parts, receipts, and surfboard fins scattered over the backseat, then look around to see if anyone is watching. All clear. I drop my jeans and pull on my work pants, peel off my paint-stained T-shirt, and slip the wrinkled restaurant uniform over my head. After swiping deodorant under each arm, I close the car door and take off running toward the white, two-story building in the northwest corner of the harbor.

"Lizzypants!" my boss Mikey calls from behind the bar as I stride through the double doors on the second floor.

"I finished the interior paint today!" I tell him, simultaneously informing the patrons at the far end of the bar.

"You smell like it, too," Mikey says with a smirk. "We need limes cut and there'll be food ready for table 250 in about ten minutes."

"And I need another margy, Lizzy," Jimmy says, smiling from his favorite seat at the north end of the bar. "Same glass."

I love my coworkers, the regulars, Barry, the boat experts, and this harbor community, but the pressure to leave is mounting. It's already a week past the date I'd told the local newspapers I would set sail. I slice limes into drink garnishes, and think about how much I've learned: I can now switch out a drill bit in seconds flat and drive a screw without stripping it. I can make a mean martini, and also mix epoxy and drill through stainless steel. I've witnessed that with the right tools and a little creativity, almost anything is possible. Still, I wonder if I'll be able to solve new problems once the masters are in my wake?

I dart down to the kitchen to pick up the food order, then set it down in front of one of our less charming regulars.

"Shouldn't you have sailed away by now, Liz?"

I pour his beer, and manage a half-smile as I set it in front of him. The mounting fear behind my confident façade is the reason his question bothers me. Though I know that Swell's *new systems are designed for my strength and size, we haven't had time to actually test them at sea yet. What if I can't handle her long boom and large mainsail in strong winds? Will I be able to lift an outboard with the davit? What if the doubters are right?*

And then departure day arrives. I drive up to Barry's home to say goodbye and find him in his small, boat-like office off the garage, where he's penning a letter to a friend. Rolls of charts hang from the ceiling and a well-organized library of nautical books and environmental references fill the bookshelves.

"Well, my girl, it's been quite an adventure already! I bid you the fairest of winds and the finest of company. You will be dearly missed."

"Likewise, Barry, I'm going to miss you so much."

"As the great Emily Dickinson said, 'Parting is all we know of heaven, and all we need of hell,'" he says with a wink. I smile, tears filling my eyes as I struggle to find words to express my gratitude.

"I sure wish I could come along." He smiles mischievously and follows me to my car with his walker.

I hug him tightly and look into his fiercely twinkling eyes. "Thank you for everything."

In a ceremonious cadence, he repeats his usual parting words. "Carry on, my dear. And don't give up the ship!"

My crew of friends and I only go twenty-five miles south to Channel Islands Harbor in Oxnard that day. With fewer visitors and less distraction, James, Marty, and I spend another grueling month finishing up the installation of the electric autopilot, mounting the spinnaker pole at the mast, reinforcing the anchor cradle, and more.

The next two months in San Diego are even busier. I try to relax and enjoy the holidays with my family, but the lists and uncertainties make it nearly impossible. I had motored nearly the entire two hundred miles from Oxnard because of slack winds, so I've still had virtually no practice sailing Swell. *But waiting another nine months until the next sailing season seems too long, and I know that nothing major has been overlooked.*

With my dad's unwavering help, I make the final push. Only details remain, but there are still so many things I need—from a dinghy and outboard motor to more medical supplies, an outboard bracket, charts, cruising guides, fishing and diving gear, and a proper quiver of surfboards. Camera gear, binoculars, zincs, jerry cans, oil filters, a soldering kit, fiberglass repair materials, caulking, bung plugs, flashlights, lee cloths, and courtesy flags. A few good luck charms couldn't hurt!

The day before my departure, I sleep at my parents' home instead of aboard Swell. *I dread the dawn. This is it. Remaining projects or purchases can be accomplished along the way. I have no more excuses. My crew is ready. The boat is stocked with food and topped off with fuel and water. A small group of friends and family cast off the lines, and I maneuver* Swell *out past the same docks where I learned to sail on an eight-foot sailing dinghy.*

An orange glow gradually appears on the eastern skyline silhouetting the mountains while *Swell* continues steadily south. Mark pops his head out of the cabin around 6:30 am and Shannon shortly after. We reminisce about our 800 miles of southbound adventures.

As the late morning sun ascends, the air hints of warmth for the first time. We gladly strip off the stinky jackets, boots, and beanies that we've lived in for eighteen days. When the iconic arch at the southernmost tip of Baja comes into view we hoot and high-five, pull down the sails, and shove each other into the open sea for a celebratory swim.

I don't tell them how relieved I am to have made it here, or how much their supportive company helped me get through that intense first leg. I'm sure they know.

I maneuver *Swell* among the parade of fishing and tour boats streaming out of the mouth of the port of Cabo San Lucas, and belly her up to the fuel dock. Mark and Shannon hop off with the lines. The *señor* in charge looks at Mark.

"*¿Quieres diesel, amigo?*" (Do you want diesel?) he asks.

"*Pregunta a la capitana*" (Ask the captain), he says, pointing to me.

The man looks at me, then back to Mark. "*¿Ella?*" (Her?) he questions to be sure. Mark nods.

"*¿Capitana?*" he asks me.

"*Si, señor,*" I reply for the first time without reserve. "*Diesel. Llena el depósito, por favor.*" (Fill the tank, please.)

1,580
Nautical Miles Traveled

Livin’ the Dream

Oh, Mexico!

Shannon spots the waves. “Right there,” she says pointing, then hands the binoculars to me.

The surf peels down a palm-lined point beneath dusty brown hills as the first big south swell of the season fills in. We jump up and down with excitement, then continue south to find the nearest protected anchorage where we can safely leave the boat. Around sunset, I steer into a small bay behind a breakwall, while Shannon pulls down the sails. It’s been a long, hot passage with several complications.

As the sun rises the following morning, we shovel oatmeal into our mouths and stuff our dry bags with sunscreen and a change of clothes. We opt to leave the dinghy on deck and paddle our surfboards ashore, and soon we emerge from the sea through bathers and beachgoers.

We huff and puff uphill to reach the main road, and just when we do, a Doritos delivery truck pulls over. A middle-aged, mustached driver sticks out his head and asks, “*¿A dónde vas?*” (Where are you going?)

“*Al norte*” (North), I reply. We are determined to get to the point we spotted yesterday.

“*Vamos*” (Let’s go), he says. “*Me llamo Armando.*” (My name is Armando.)

Armando places our boards in the back among boxes of chips and I'm reminded of the warm, generous hearts of the Mexican people. I'm grateful to my mom for her insistence that we all study Spanish as kids on the voyage through Mexico. After a brief stop at the local gas station, our jolly escort goes out of his way to drive us down the long dirt road to our destination. Armando pulls out a laminated photo of his children as we bounce past a small strip of palapas and stilted bungalows. He stops just a skip away from the reeling, overhead lefts.

"*¡Gracias, Armando!*" we call as he pulls away. Surfers perched at a restaurant nearby crane their necks, curious to see who's getting out of the truck. We walk toward them, a little nervous.

A smiling expat leaps to his feet to introduce himself. "Hi girls. I'm Pablo!" he says enthusiastically. "Where'd you come from?"

"We're anchored down the way," I reply. We sailed in yesterday."

"Oh! We saw you sail by. Lovely boat. *¡Bienvenidos!* (Welcome!)" He grins and fidgets like a kid. He's nothing like most of the grumpy expats I've met on surf trips. I'd like to talk to him more. But it's hard to focus on the conversation while I'm being hypnotized by the waves funneling down the point.

"Do you know where we can safely leave our bags while we go for a surf?" I ask.

He leads us around the back of his friend's house nearby and even gives us some surf pointers. "Walk to the top of the point and hop in the current at the river mouth. Once you're out there pick a lineup on land because the current is moving fast. Most of the guys will drift too deep and if you pay attention you'll have all the sets for yourselves," he encourages. "Go have fun!" I hang on his every word, feeling lucky we'd found a new *compadre*.

Shannon and I spend the morning gorging ourselves in the surf. Like mosquitoes in a room full of lightly clothed gringos, we just can't help ourselves. Several hours later, we both wash in with limp arms and wide smiles. Pablo orders up frozen banana-mango *licuados* (smoothies), and we lie in the sand in the shade of the restaurant's palapa. He first came to this area in 1979 at twenty-three years old, chasing empty waves. When his travel buddy went home, Pablo stayed, fell in love with wild Mexico, and "learned how to be a Mexican."

I've hardly sucked down my tantalizing drink before the empty waves rolling across the inside sandbar catch my attention. I begin to twitch and squirm on my pile of sand, attempting to convince myself that I need shade and rest. But when another set washes across the bar with no one on it, I run for my board, rub on more sunscreen, and sprint back up the point.

I'm mad with joy and creativity—so in love with surfing, the warmth, the freedom of my new life, and the victory of each small improvement in my surfing skill. Shannon takes photos from the beach. I practice my backside foot placement, bottom turn to off-the-lip, cutties, and grab-rail drops.

After the second session, Shannon and I walk the beach to check out the impressive Michoacán beach scene. We have arrived at the height of *Semana Santa*—Mexico's equivalent of spring break. The little town's usual occupancy has quadrupled. Three and four generations of families share food, sun, and laughs. Platters teeter with mountains of fresh fruit, guitars are strummed, and *cervezas* passed. It's difficult to distinguish one group from the next; it appears customary to stop under anyone's shade and have a snack. The sense of *familia* spreads well beyond the borders of the beach blankets.

After some bodysurfing and a mini siesta, we're back at the restaurant, smiling through each mouth-watering bite of *enchiladas con mole* washed down with refreshing *jugo de sandía* (watermelon juice). The horizon bleeds out into a thick layer of red-orange. Since Mark flew home more than a month ago, we've hosted a couple other fun crewmates, but I'd caught bronchitis, sprained my thumb, and 300 miles of coast were plagued by red tide and swarms of jellyfish—impeding us from using the reverse osmosis watermaker and making it complicated to swim and bathe. A lightless Mexican Navy ship nearly ran us down and *Swell* got stuck on a sandbar while navigating through a river mouth. Yesterday, Shannon's personal EPIRB safety device fell overboard, and as I attempted to turn around and get it, I wrapped our fishing lines around the prop. So we are appreciating the new tide of good fortune today.

"Well, Snaggs," I say, "we better start walking back before it's too dark to catch a ride." She earned her nickname because she caught on to everything so quickly, and because she was also prone to catching herself on things.

"Look," Pablo chuckles. "Here come *la policía* (the police) on their evening rounds. I'll ask them to drop you girls off on their way south. They're friends of mine. You can leave your boards here with me if you'd like for tomorrow?"

Snaggs and I ride off in *la policía*'s truckbed. Officer Luis clutches his machine gun beside us as the little town on the point disappears into the darkness. As we accelerate down the main road, the cool wind whips our hair and soothes our sunburns.

They deliver us to the jetty near *Swell*, where we hop out, giving copious thanks. We clamber out onto the large rocks, strip down to our swimsuits, seal our dry bags, then leap into the black abyss on a rising surge. Some teenage boys fishing off the rocks look on in disbelief.

Swell's anchor light sways in the distance. We swim slowly through the blackness dragging our dry bags, giddy from our dreamy day. As we approach the middle of the bay, we try not to think about what might be lurking below and instead focus on the surreal glittering lights all around us: The sky is packed with winking stars, the lights of the pueblo sparkle across the surface of the bay, and glowing flecks of phosphorescence trail our movements through the dark sea. *Swell*'s white hull finally appears from the shadows and we haul our iridescent-dappled bodies up the side, then hit our bunks as quickly as possible, looking forward to doing it all again *mañana*.

Sea Wings

Swell's genoa luffs noisily, struggling to catch the light following breeze. "Today is the day, Snaggs," I say to Shannon. "It's time to attempt to set the spinnaker pole." Between swells and new crew, we continued to hop south through the polluted ports and charming bays of mainland Mexico. We're halfway down the coast of Mainland Mexico now, sailing toward the famous surf break at Zicatela, Puerto Escondido.

"You mean that big pole on the side of the mast?"

"Yep," I nod. Marty the rigger had talked me through the process before I left, but I hadn't found the courage to try until now. Setting up this long pole perpendicular to the mast will give the corner of the genoa a firm point of attachment to allow it to catch more wind. We need to go faster in order to make Puerto Escondido before dark.

I drag out the designated lines and talk myself though the steps. I remember he said something about "triangulating with three lines so that the beast of a pole can't get out of control." That means one line going forward, another going aft, and a halyard to hold it up.

It takes me several tries to get the lines positioned correctly. The halyards are tangled, then I route the fore and aft lines wrong. Shannon braces herself against the cabintop, steadying the pole while I jump around getting the lines right.

Finally, I crank on the winch, and the pole rises into place while Shannon holds the lines, bridling it fore and aft. We tie them off when it's reached the right place and haul the genoa out again. The pole holds it out perfectly, and with the full mainsail to port, *Swell*'s sea wings are spread wide open.

"We did it!" Shannon cheers.

"Yea! And we've gained almost two knots!" I exclaim. Snaggs goes down to make sandwiches, while I make an entry in the logbook to recount the momentous event. After lunch Shannon takes the watch and I lay back and doze off, head in the clouds.

Day by day, I am learning to captain *Swell* more proficiently. I'm constantly reading equipment manuals and finally figured out how to use the

SSB radio to download weather forecasts. Between planning and prepping for passages, we explore for waves, try local restaurants, and meet new friends. We sure get a lot of attention as two young women. Most of it is positive—dinner invites, special tours, questions, and curiosity—both from locals ashore and people on other sailboats in the anchorages.

"Cruisers" is the accepted title given to people living and traveling on small boats for extended periods of time. Some have taken a sabbatical from work; for others, it's a permanent lifestyle. We see the same faces often, as most boats are heading south and share the same window of time to get to safe hurricane-season destinations. Most cruisers are much older than Shannon and me, seeing as it takes resources to buy and maintain a boat. There are occasional "in-betweeners," in their thirties and forties, often with kids aboard, and a few male "single handers" here and there. But the majority of cruisers are retired, salt-of-the-earth couples who never intend to return to land and know every trick in the cruising book—from covering their eggs in Vaseline to make them stay fresh longer, to pirating the latest electronic charts, and knowing which clothespins actually hold drying clothes on the lifelines. He'll always have advice about fixing things and she can sew curtains and cushions and whip a delicacy out of a few simple ingredients.

People go cruising for various reasons. Some relish the everyday "sunset happy hour" that starts at 5 pm on one or more of the boats in a harbor. There is usually an open invite as long as you bring your own booze. Others, like the scuba divers and shell collectors, or surfers like us, do it to enjoy their watersports or hobbies. Many just love sailing and the ocean, and living free and disconnected from society. They all have stories to tell, some louder than others. At almost every bay, a cruising wife—likely dying to talk to someone other than her husband—organizes a potluck get-together, spreading the word via the VHF radio. Whether the potlucks are on the beach or on one of the boats, these eclectic events are the social fabric of cruising life. As diverse as they come, cruisers are almost always helpful, good-willed, and frugal. There is one golden rule—always do your best to help another cruiser in need—because inevitably at some point, you'll need help too.

I feel lucky to have Shannon aboard; she's straightforward, ready for anything, and laughs at my jokes. Sailing with others means being together twenty-four hours a day without many comforts and with lots to accomplish. You quickly learn each other's personal habits (for better or worse), and must seek compromise between everyone's different needs and wishes. Boat life lacks immediacy and privacy, so hangups, quirks, and weaknesses are rapidly exposed. An "elephant in the room" can sink the ship. There's no TV, no Internet, no picking up some take-out when you're hungry. But Shannon and I inhabit this space well together. There's a forward cabin with a v-shaped berth, a tiny head with a hand pump toilet, a central cabin area with a narrow bunk, nav table, and galley, and then two aft crawl-in berths—the smaller serving as storage and the bigger as Shannon's bunk. Three or four aboard can be fun for a stint, but two feels a bit more spacious.

On passages, we now trade watch duties with a simple nod. On watch, vigilance for boat traffic, weather changes, fishing buoys, and equipment issues is obligatory. While off watch, we read, listen to music, spot sea life, snooze in our bunks, make food, fix things, or take photos. Shannon steers *Swell* while I get the anchor up or down, and helps furl the sails as we come into harbor. We're reading Rachel Carson's *The Sea Around Us* aloud at night and discuss the coastal pollution, development, and other environmental issues we observe.

Swell's little galley stove boils tea and oatmeal in the mornings, and cooks up rice and fish, curry, or quesadillas in the evening. Opposite the stove and sink, the rectangular lid of the fridge doubles as a countertop, making every foray within an act of juggling half-made sandwiches or chopped veggies above while scavenging for perishables piled randomly below. While it seems things would be so easy to access in such a small space, it quite often requires some bodily contortion and patience. Each storage compartment becomes its own little universe, and the extraction of one simple item, like a tool or pan for cooking, can require taking everything else out too.

Even with our little watermaker functioning, freshwater use is strictly limited. Using the device requires constant filter changes, cleaning, and energy. So we wash dishes with salt water pumped by foot in the galley sink. To bathe, we leap off *Swell*, climb into the dinghy to soap up, rinse off in the sea, and can usually afford a brief freshwater rinse under the little shower spigot on the aft deck.

Making calls on the satellite phone is crazy expensive, so unless there's an emergency, contacting home at sea happens via short text emails we can send and receive through *Swell's* SSB radio. The bulk of our communication happens in port. We spend hours in Internet cafés calling home, sending emails and photos, and networking to sell photos or articles. Barry and I are mostly in touch via email, because the ham radio he installed at home has grounding issues. He's been forced to purchase his first computer, in spite of his "incurable allergy to electronic devices." I enjoy writing him about the voyage happenings about twice a month. Then I edit these letters to use as updates on my website. It's great to see how people are enjoying them. A surf forecasting website is even reposting them! And now Patagonia, the clothing company, is interested in sponsoring me with gear!

When we arrive at a port, we're required to check in with the local officials and then we usually provision for food, fuel, and the propane used for cooking, plus make necessary repairs. We do laundry, too, when the opportunity arises. If we're lucky, it's at a new friend's house or a Laundromat, but more often we stomp and scrub it clean in buckets when freshwater is available ashore. So "dirty," as applied to our clothes, has become a relative term. Practical is much more valuable in this lifestyle than stylish, so you wear things until you can't stand the smell or sight of them.

New surf spots, language barriers, and local bureaucracy are intimidating at times, but we've had nothing but positive experiences with the warm-hearted Mexican people. Not only have we been given rides and offered fresh fish, but people are always happy to help. The general *mañana* sentiment means the locals are not too hurried to talk with us. They walk us down the street to make sure we find our destination, and repeat their words slowly enough that we can understand. Although to us, the disparities between rich and poor seem great, families are tight and work hard to support each other. They cheerfully accommodate our *gringo* needs, even when it has nothing to do with earning them any money.

On the way into Puerto Escondido at sundown, Shannon and I wrestle the spinnaker pole back into its cradle. Once the anchor is down, we decide the only reasonable thing to do is go ashore for ice cream. Luckily the bay is calm enough to beach the dinghy. This isn't always the case. Our participation in nightlife has become selective since it often means anchoring the dinghy off the beach and swimming in through the surfline to get to shore. We'll show up to dinner invites or *discotecas* salty and sandy, with a dripping dry bag in tow.

We walk the length of the town to stretch our legs, winding along sidewalks packed with vendors selling corn on the cob, tacos, traditional woven goods, whirling plastic doodads, portrait sketches, and mini wood carvings. Upon spotting an ice cream shop, we duck inside. Snaggs and I are easy to please—ice cream, some surf, a few cute guys to flirt with, and a decently calm anchorage. In that order.

We sit outside on the curb licking our quickly melting delights. A group of young kids play in the street nearby. One of their *pelotas* (balls) comes flying our way and an adorable chubby girl comes racing after it. She stops short, seeing Shannon's ice cream cone, and reaches out to signal that she wants some. Shannon caves and hands it over.

Little "Gordita," as they call her, inhales what is left as a wide-grinned boy comes running up and hucks his feet over his head in an awkward cartwheel. I pass him the rest of my cone, get up, and cartwheel myself. The girl then bounces Shannon a ball. Shannon chucks it to me. Soon the road around us erupts into a playground of rocketing *pelotas*, sprawling brown limbs, deliberate collisions, speedy footraces, dance moves, and unbridled yelps. It's like the whistle for recess has blown and Shannon and I revert to our days on the blacktop.

After an hour of dodging tourists, twirling kids, and flinging *pelotas*, I look over to see Shannon dancing in a misshapen circle of squirming kids, holding hands and singing with glee. I'm not sure who's having more fun—us or them? We begin to tire, but they don't. We need an escape plan.

"More ice cream?" I propose, thinking of Barry and my father's generosity. Shannon nods.

I get permission from their onlooking mothers, who've been sitting on the sidewalk, taking in the show while selling handmade crafts. They nod unanimously. We herd the kids into the ice cream parlor, and the head count doubles as children up and down the street catch on to the deal. Even Juanito Chiquito, who couldn't have been more than two years old, is lifted up by his sister so he can pick out a flavor. They walk out one by one, ice cream princes and princesses flaunting their tall, cold scoops. Snaggs and I go for round two, and then sit back on the curb where we started, surrounded by our new fleet of young friends licking, laughing, and wiggling beside us. Gordita is pinned at my left hip, alternately dipping her spoon into her scoop then mine.

A Fillet of Humility

Knife in hand, I hunch over the taut body of the medium-sized tuna we caught on our passage. *Swell* is tied to a dock for the first time in months, and it's nice to have a flat open space to clean our catch. Just as I begin to make my first cut, a lanky forty-something *gringo* walks up and leans casually against a nearby dock box.

"Nice catch," he remarks.

"Thanks," I reply, not even looking up. I'm not enthused about having a spectator. He doesn't catch my hint, though, and launches into a detailed fish story. *Roger that, amigo, you're the boss, now please let me fillet my fish in peace*, I think.

He carries on and I roll my eyes while preparing to make the first cut. I was up all night fighting a three-knot current and an angry bee swarm to get here. I'm tired, and hungry, and not in the mood to chat right now.

My knife isn't sharp enough, and my impatience is making it harder. I massacre the first fillet, finally hacking it off the carcass. Then I struggle to grip the skin to remove it from the meat.

"You know," he says, pausing his storm story.

I knew this was coming.

"If you cut the outline of the fillet first, and leave the meat connected to the bones, it's a hell of a lot easier to pull off the skin."

I continue peeling and pulling at the skin of the first fillet, struggling to hide my irritation. He keeps right on with his stories, jolly as ever. "My parents weren't sailors, you see ..."

I try hopelessly to tune him out, flipping the fish over to start on the other side. My foul attitude aside, I decide to try his technique. I slice across the backbone first, then from the head down to the stomach, and so forth, finishing with the fillet completely outlined.

"Perfect. Now pull the skin back starting from the head," he says.

It peels off perfectly in one piece.

"Thadda girl," he smiles, then turns and walks down the dock.

My exasperation dissolves quickly into guilt. I had been so cold and disrespectful, hardly even looking up at him. I finish the cleanly cut second fillet and run to catch up with him.

"Here you go." I hand him the fresh hunk of meat. "Thank you for the tip."

Light in the Dark

It's 3 am. I'm sitting on the bow in total darkness, my harness clipped securely to the mast like a baby's umbilical cord to its mother. The moon has set. I can't really make out the horizon, but the steady sound of *Swell's* hull cutting through the calm sea provides some orientation. The darkness is freckled with twinkling stars and planets, clusters of lights from land, and thick blooms of tumbling phosphorescence in the bow wake. I can't stop staring. There's something about the scene that brings all the mysteries of life to mind.

What the heck are we doing here on this tiny speck in the void? What is life about? I ponder.

The mainsail rustles, filling and slackening in the light offshore breeze. The warm, dry air carries whiffs of dust and burnt trash from the coast of Guatemala. As I scan and squint for lights from other ships, I have no answers, but feel certain that I am where I am supposed to be.

We were lucky to bump into Pablo in Puerto Escondido, our expat buddy from farther north, who quickly advised us to change out our shortboards for the biggest boards we had, and lose our leashes so as to lessen hold-down time at the heavy beach break. He even gave Shannon a big-wave board. Thanks to his tips, we caught some unforgettable rides, although I was frustrated because I never managed to get a tube. When the surf got too big we rounded up a few local Mexican surfer girls, picked up Katie, my surf buddy who had flown in to join us, and sailed to a remote surf spot outside of town. We enjoyed the time like sisters, but being around such confident women had quietly reminded me of my own insecurities.

The dark night and solitude coax my inner shadows to the surface. I've put off facing them for as long as I can remember, always finding an excuse. I have never felt pretty or desirable enough. I fight with the ugly parts of me on the inside, too—I can be terribly greedy, impatient, and self-centered. I'm too sensitive, too reactive, too quick to judge. And when my bouts with depression arise, the sadness blots out everything and the world becomes almost unbearable.

My parents' faces come to mind. I always tried to make them happier but nothing ever worked. I feel their pain as my own. The uncomfortable silences, the sorrow I don't always understand, the sound of another beer being opened, a door slamming, hidden tears, the smell of cigarettes, alcohol, regret, misunderstanding. The distant looks in their eyes. The feeling of being alone even when they were near. My throat swells. Hot tears well up in my eyes. I quickly wipe them away.

Knowing these feelings can return with only a slight trigger renders me weak and vulnerable. I have to face my own flaws, slay these emotional monsters, and give up trying to change Mom and Dad. Now I'm here, living my dream. There are no excuses for being unhappy.

Pssssssssshhhhhhhht, pssshhhht. Something surfaces for a breath nearby.

Glowing torpedoes rocket toward us from the starboard quarter: dolphins! They light up the sea around *Swell* with their trails of phosphorescence, surfing the bow wake and looping back for more, bringing light to all this darkness

Million-Dollar Views and Fine Dining

Yet another tropical thunderstorm engulfs *Swell*. After four months without rain through Central America's dry season, the falling water is a welcome change. Large drops pelt the decks as Shannon and I sail from Nicaragua into Costa Rican waters after two soggy days at sea. Unlike Nicaragua's stick-straight coast, Costa Rica has thick fingers of land that jut out into the sea, creating a haven of deep, forested bays. We approach the entrance to one of them, hoping for protection from the west wind and sloppy seas.

Waking the next morning to blue skies, we set off with ambitious plans to hike to the top of a nearby mountain through the wild national park area. It's an all-day affair with DEET, machetes, cameras, mud, and fire ants. Thanks to Shannon's fierce trail-blazing skills, we make it to the top.

The silence on the peak feels sacred. We sit and take in the 360-degree view of the high hills and jungle slopes. *Swell* is just a tiny speck in the grand bay below. Gratitude mixes with sweet fatigue. I quiet myself and try to hear what the tiny puffs of wind are whispering.

We finally emerge from the foliage at sea level to find the dinghy stuck in the silty mud of low tide. We jump in the sea fully clothed to await the rising tide and wash off our filthy shoes, clothes, and bodies.

When the dinghy floats free, we head back toward *Swell*, noticing a new neighbor anchored just to our port.

"They're awfully close," I remark.

Shannon wrinkles her nose in agreement. We study the faded white fishing panga with its neon blue rails, and the name *Angelo* scrawled across the side in slightly smeared magenta script. Three men lounging in the afternoon sun immediately hail us as we draw near. They introduce themselves as Efrain, Manuel, and Geronimo, and ask if we have a light bulb to replace the dead one in their flashlight.

"*¿Les gustan ceviche? ¿Quieren venir a cenar con nosotros?*" (Do you like ceviche? Want to come eat dinner with us?)

I look at Shannon. We are both starving.

"*Sí. Gracias. ¡Hasta pronto!*" (Yes, thanks. See you soon!)

Back aboard *Swell*, we scrub ourselves of the lingering mud and DEET, then scour the rather barren food bin for something to bring as a side dish. We grab the last pack of Oreos instead.

"Is this a good idea?" Shannon asks.

"Do you want me to bring the Mace just in case?" I reply.

"Couldn't hurt."

It's dark when we row toward the panga.

"*Hola, amigos*" (Hello, friends), we call.

"*¡Vengan!*" (Come!) They welcome us aboard, taking our bow line. We climb over the rail and into the makeshift cabin. Wet and worn wooden slats cover the bare hull forward of the two raised fish holds in the aft. A small relic of a radio dangles by a wire from one of the two-by-fours holding up a blue plastic tarp to provide shelter from the rain. From its tiny speaker, a man's voice belts out a Mexican love ballad accompanied by dramatic horns. We offer them an extra flashlight I had aboard *Swell*, since I didn't find a replacement bulb. The light is put to use right away as Manuel fishes a packet of Tang out of a dark compartment.

As rain begins to softly fall on the tarp above, we exchange pleasantries. They set their nets earlier and will pull them first thing the next morning. Geronimo passes us a plate of fresh ceviche to share. A thunderclap cracks above, and it begins to pour. It doesn't faze the three *amigos*. Efrain, the captain, is tall and thin, and appears to be the oldest—maybe in his thirties. He speaks little at first, except for sporadic one-liners that neither Shannon nor I can catch, but send the other two into cackling hysterics. Geronimo, "*El Rey de los Indios*" (The King of the Indians), as he calls himself, is thick, short, and jolly. He speaks the most English, and gladly takes on the role as translator when it's necessary. Manuel is younger and a bit shy.

To our surprise, and despite the hideous weather and lack of cooking conveniences, Efrain whips up delicious seafood fried rice on a one-burner kerosene stove. They pile our shared plate with more ceviche and serve up the powdered juice with ice. Ice!

The rain heightens into a deafening fury, barraging the tarp inches overhead. We get used to the lingering smell of dead fish, and our new compadres turn out to be great company. We eat two plates each and talk into the night about life, love, music, and politics as if dining in a fine restaurant. They may be fishing illegally in these waters, as we understand the whole area to be a national park, but it's clear that they are trying to get by on their catch. Efrain has two children at home to feed.

They top off the delicious meal with steamy hot cocoa. We break out the Oreos and when Geronimo lifts his cocoa, we push our warm plastic cups together in a final toast cheering, "*¡Salud, amigos!*"

Snaggs and Gadget

After five months moving *Swell* down the coast of the Americas, Shannon and I motor south on our last passage together. She is ready to chase new dreams, and a boatyard in Costa Rica awaits our arrival for *Swell*'s haul out tomorrow. There is normal wear and tear to address, the waterline needs raising, and after a recent lightning scare, I want to add a grounding plate under the hull.

Gazing at the thick tropical forest ashore, I'm reminded of how much we've accomplished together. At an average speed of five-and-a-half knots over 2,500-some nautical miles, our perspectives have molded as gradually as the landscapes have changed. As Southern California's busy blacktop transformed into the desolate dunes of Baja, we withdrew from attachments to our cell phones and schedules. Below mainland Mexico's arid mountains and palm-lined coasts, we were reassured of the goodness of everyday people, yet simultaneously troubled by the trash on beaches. Against Nicaragua's striking volcanic skylines, we witnessed the ache of poverty and grieved social injustice in a community where young girls carried water to their homes from a local well, while a rich American developer, who had seized oceanfront land with promises to aid the local community, teed off on the fenced-in golf course at his new marina-resort. As Costa Rica's steamy green jungles took over the coast, we tested our self-reliance and celebrated perfect surf all to ourselves and unexpected friends arriving with provisions, then farther south felt conflicted about the impacts of the booming ecotourism industry.

The transformations, both personal and in the coastal geography, came at a natural pace—a new smell in the air, a disturbing dichotomy to wrestle, a different bird in the sky, a new Spanish vocabulary word, an increase in sea temperature, or an incident highlighting something we needed to work on within ourselves. Seeing other ways of life makes the world feel more spacious. And traveling at this pace has given us time to take it all in and figure things out. A marina manager in Mexico had showed us how to siphon gasoline from a jerry can to a tank without getting our breath involved. I learned how to dive down and replace the zincs on the propeller. I successfully changed the engine oil on my own, shot my first fish with a speargun, and managed to wire in small cabin fans. When the windlass stopped pulling the anchor up, a clever cruiser named Clyde taught me about the inner workings of its motor. I can now sharpen knives, splice rope, and tie a one-handed bowline.

Shannon's main duty has been to take photos, but her strength of character has fortified me through equipment failure and operator errors, stress about money, hull scrubbing, an ex-boyfriend who showed up unexpectedly, stuck anchors, bumping nightclubs, and failed crushes. Only Snaggs, in her yellow bikini, would think to pull out the guitar when the Mexican Navy boarded *Swell* with drug dogs. The officers quickly abandoned their search and took turns strumming songs for us. She came up giddy after our close encounter with a bull shark and swam out fearlessly into massive surf to take photos. Her deep Christian faith never wavers. We don't discuss God, as I'm resistant to religion, but it's easy to tell that she feels supported and confident through the toughest moments. To be honest, I'm jealous; I can only wonder how good that kind of connection feels.

I read our position off the GPS, while Snaggs jots it into the logbook as we assess the distance remaining on our overnight passage. The sun drops into the sea to starboard and I feel a surge of nostalgia as my time with Snaggs comes to a close. Soon orange and pinks swallow the sea and sky.

"Well, Snaggs, can you believe we made it this far?"

"Yes," she replies. "You're a good captain, Gadget." I'd earned the nickname for my unwavering preparedness and perpetual fixing and fussing over gear.

"I couldn't have done it without you. It's not going to be the same."

"Don't worry, God watches out for the brave."

I smile and look down. "I hope you're right."

Keep Laughin'

I feel a little dizzy looking up at the curved underside of *Swell*. Now that I am faced with the job of sanding and painting her below the waterline, she seems enormous. The tall grass itches my ankles. Or maybe it's just irritating my nasty no-see-um bites? The little devils devour any exposed skin at dawn and dusk in this swampy Costa Rican boatyard up the river.

I climb back up the ladder. I have been pecking at each project all day but getting nowhere. I look down again at my to-do list: Aside from sanding and painting the bottom, raising the waterline, and grounding the hull in hopes of diminishing harm from a lightning strike, I need to insulate the refrigerator box, fix the stereo, install more fans, and remove the foul, old holding tank from the forward cabin. Plus, the bilge needs cleaning, the starboard running light isn't working, and the floor needs a few fresh coats of varnish. I think this heat is making my brain swell, because I can't figure out where to start.

If I can just replace the stereo, at least I'll have music while I'm doing the rest of the jobs, so I remove the dead one and carefully match each of the colored wires to their coded replacements on the new one, crimping them together with butt connectors, and heat shrinking each one. After screwing it back into its brace on the wall, I flip the switch on my electrical panel and push the stereo's power button.

Nothing. Not even a flicker.

"Urrrrggggggggg," I grunt and roll my eyes, pushing the power button over and over, hoping it will magically turn on. I give up and pull out some headphones and my iPod. Okay, moving on.

The running light seems the next easiest item. So I gather my tools and a ladder and head to the bow to pull it apart. I clean up the wiring and change the bulb, then go to test it. It flashes on for a moment, then dies. Deep breath. Slight despair. Enormous irritation. I inspect for an electrical short and find nothing obvious, so I shift a pile of stuff to clear a place to sit down among the chaos of tools, supplies, and snacks in the cabin. They all seem to glare at me as if to say, "Do something!"

Sweat dribbles down my face. The heat seems so thick I almost have to swallow the air to breathe. Mosquitoes buzz my ears. I'm simply miserable. It's weird without Shannon here. I'm not quite sure what to do with myself.

Surf! That always makes me feel better. I grab my turquoise twin fin and my surf bag and make my way down the ladder, across the river, and to the bus stop down the street.

The waves look about chest high, occasionally bigger and peeling off at various peaks down the sandbar point a few miles south. The wind is a little onshore, but it's worlds better than dealing with *Swell* at the moment. A smiling, wrinkled old Tica woman selling green mangos on the road to the beach motions for me to leave my bag with her. I buy a mango, and we chat for a while, then with a parting "*Pura Vida!* (a common Costa Rican expression and salutation), I sprint across the hot black sand and paddle out through the soupy brown water and sit alone at the top of the river mouth. A few small drops and turns are all it takes to lift my spirits—but between sets, the project list clouds my mind like a bad hangover.

Wandering down the road a few hours later, I hope a bus or taxi will appear. A few men catcall from their trucks while other cars pass, loaded with families out for Sunday activities. I keep walking in the direction of the boatyard, switching my board from arm to arm to keep the blood flowing. A clearing appears with a lone tractor parked alongside the road. A black Tico man in his midforties sits in the driver's seat.

"Watcha doin' walkin' here?" he asks with twinkling eyes and a Caribbean twang.

"Heading home," I reply. "Whatcha doin' up on that tractor?" I stop and squeeze into the shade of the tractor's enormous tire for a moment.

"I'm watchin' it. Get off at six. I'm Charlie. Who are you?"

"I'm Liz."

"You alone?"

"Yep."

"You married?"

"Nope."

"Why not?"

"I dunno, haven't found the right guy, I guess?"

"Look girl, you betta find yourself a husband now, or else you gonna get old and nobody's gonna wanna look atcha then," he says with a chuckle, baring a sparse array of teeth. "You wanna marry me?"

"Naw, thanks though, Charlie."

"You see … is 'cause I is old and ugly," he replies, throwing his head back and unleashing a great, unchecked flood of laughter. I laugh, too.

"Thanks, Charlie," I say, getting back to my feet. "I needed a laugh."

"Girl, you betta learn how to keep laughin'… Ain't no utha way to survive."

I reach up and shake his big callused hand, then wander off down the road again. Keep laughing. Keep laughing.

Captain and the Kid

I wake with a pain in my stomach and leap out of bed, but before I can make it to the rail I projectile vomit across the aft deck. I must have caught a bug while surfing in the polluted water. I haul out my medical bag, but I'm too weak to shuffle through the overflowing baggies and scattered pills inside. I sweat and shiver feverishly all night in my forward bunk, Charlie's advice echoing in my mind between vomiting into a bucket precisely every seven minutes. The next day, I feebly make my way to the pay phone near the marina office and dial home.

"Hello, Dad?" I say, my voice cracking.

"Hi, sweetie! What's going on?" I'm instantly soothed by the sound of my father's voice.

"I got sick. And the projects ..." I burst into tears. "I don't know where to start, Dad. I can't do this!"

"Well, I'll come help!" he announces cheerfully and without pause. "I don't have much going on with work this week. I'll catch the first flight possible."

Hope lightens my chest. "Really?"

"Yeah, I have plenty of frequent flyer miles. We'll make it fun!"

The dismal yard comes back into color. The next day I feel better, and hop on a bus to visit the nearby junkyard to scavenge a piece of scrap copper sheeting we can use to fashion a grounding plate. Next, I take the bus into town to purchase supplies for the other projects. Aside from riding waves, there's nothing I love more than working with Dad, except when he's a bit too "well-oiled."

Dad has an excessive affinity for beer-drinking, but he doesn't like to talk about it. Whenever I try, he changes the subject. Since his entrepreneurial pursuits kept him traveling constantly, no one ever wanted to bring it up on the rare days he was home. He always provided for our financial needs, although his pioneering ventures in cancer technology and treatment were often unstable. Dad needed to drink to relax, so the elephant in the room was permanently adopted by the Clark family. Some days it was only five or six beers, but other days it was an eighteen-pack. He and Mom often argued on those nights, and she'd usually have a few beers too, likely to help her tolerate his intoxication. It had become a situation that was easier for me to bear from afar.

Despite the long plane flight and a two-hour drive from the capital, Dad's eyes are twinkling when he steps out of a taxi at the boatyard three days later. I leap into his arms and propose a day of sightseeing and beach-going before we launch into the projects.

"But we only have six days, Sweetie! What's first on the list?" he asks, rubbing his hands together enthusiastically. Dad enjoys manual work and never fears diving head-first into a project. I prefer to study them for a while, so together we make a good balance of calculation and action.

For the next six days, we work from dawn to dusk. He recounts stories of following his Grandpa Dawe around on plumbing jobs and family home-building projects when he was a kid in Los Angeles, learning how to do a little of everything handy. In addition to being a jack-of-all-trades and a devoted father, Dad is a free thinker, an artist, a risk taker, and a visionary. He's endlessly generous, often intense, and unstoppable when determined—a wildman with an aptitude for articulation, spontaneity, and making the everyday fun. But he doesn't like to bend, and when he gets frustrated, his hot temper explodes into foul language and fits. Unfortunately I inherited this volatile side of Dad's disposition.

While fighting off clouds of those vicious no-see-ums, we sand the hull and add two lovely blue pinstripes at the height of the new waterline. We devise a plan for grounding the mast, and Dad passes me tools while I lie on the floor of the head with my upper body shoved under the toilet to blindly bolt a cable to the base of the mast. Then we both cringe as I drill a hole through the hull's thick fiberglass to connect the cable to the bronze plate we've attached to the hull. When that's finished, we deal with my little refrigeration box that won't stay cold, fitting together blocks of foam insulation to go inside it. Then finally we prep and tape off *Swell*'s underside, and roll on two thick coats of antifouling paint. When I beg for a break, Dad powers on, always wearing his great, unwavering smile. We return to his little hotel room every evening, looking like two worn-out coal miners.

On day five, we brush on the last touch-ups of bottom paint as the yard guys prep the rolling sling that will carry *Swell* back to the sea. I squeeze Dad's hand as her pristine hull hits the water again. We tie her off to a nearby mooring and then head to the bar for dinner and a celebratory beer. Dad has been so good about not drinking too much this week. We order our food, then walk across the street to watch the sunset for the first time since he arrived. Murky brown waves churn against the rocky strip of beach awash in trash and debris. Guilt surges over me; Dad came all the way to Costa Rica and he hasn't seen a single palm-lined beach or waterfall. He hasn't even been in the ocean.

"Wow, it's so beautiful!" he says. It's just like him to relentlessly see the good side of things. "I've had such a wonderful time, Lizzy."

The next morning, we wake early. A lump lodges in my throat as I call a taxi to pick him up. The driver arrives, and I fight back tears when I load his bag into the trunk. He pulls me close, holding me tightly for one more precious hug.

"I love you so much, Sweetie. When you get overwhelmed, just remember what your grandmother would say: 'Life's hard by the yard, but a cinch by the inch!' You can do anything. I'm so proud of you."

I'm stuck searching for the proper words to thank him as I reluctantly let him go. He climbs in the cab and I watch it disappear down the long, straight road, my tears unleashing. He's always been so good to me. I just wish he would be as good to himself.

Danger! High Voltage!

It seems darker than usual as *Swell* plows south again. I blink into the unending blackness, unsure whether my eyes are open or closed. Dark, dark, dark.

An eerily warm breeze grazes my cheeks, but I focus on the sweet evening song of the gecko that crawled aboard in the boatyard three months ago. His melodic chirps help me ignore the sense of foreboding that has become a regular part of night watches during Central America's rainy season. Thunderstorms are expected. After more than a dozen close calls with cascading bolts both at anchor and underway, it seems like calling it "lightning season" would be more appropriate.

My recent guests and I have ducked and dodged our way through nightly thunderstorms in order to surf Costa Rica's wave-rich coastline during its most consistent wave season. Other sailors call me crazy, laying low in a protected place for the five or six months of the wet season. It turns out surfing and sailing are not always as compatible as I'd hoped.

Often a region's best wave season doesn't coincide with its safe sailing season. Swell-exposed coastlines that are great for surfing generally offer fewer safe anchorages, or unbearably rolly conditions for a monohull. Just finding rideable waves along a stretch of open coast is hard—it requires getting close enough to shore to read the surf from the back. This adds distance and time, fairly impractical at *Swell*'s modest speeds, not to mention dangerous with my basic navigation equipment. When I do find a wave, I have to find a place to safely "park" *Swell* before I can even think about surfing. It's clear that surfing can't be first priority; safety and survival more frequently call the shots. Add the timing of weather and swell, each country's complicated entry and exit procedures, provisioning and maintenance, crew schedules, and Internet café hours. Surf time quickly evaporates.

But when all the ingredients do come together, it's pure magic. So even after several frightening near misses with lightning, here I am again, pressing my luck on one more surf mission. I've always been stubborn. My Auntie Julie Ann always says it's because I'm a Taurus. My desires often outweigh reason, especially when surfing is involved.

Fatigue steadily weighs on my eyelids as we enter Panamanian waters. I head below to wake my latest crew.

"Jake … Jake … I'm getting tired, can you take over for a while?" His lids flash open to reveal his wild, emerald green eyes.

"Hi Lizzypumpkin. Of course," he replies. He smiles that mischievous smile that drew me to him back in Santa Barbara shortly after Barry's proposal. We shared a fun love story, full of sea adventures and surf chasing. Jake was nonstop exuberance and charisma. Hanging with him was never boring. His thirst for living on the edge often got him into trouble, but I couldn't resist his lion heart, self-deprecating humor, and courageous will. He never tried to contain me, supporting me unwaveringly toward this voyage, as he pursued his own commercial fishing dream.

We rented a small studio together to get off our boats at the end of the first year of *Swell*'s refit, and spent two fantastic weeks there making meals and enjoying a bit of land luxury. But Jake had impossible luck. If there was a one-in-a-million chance of something going wrong, it would. One day he came home looking white as a ghost, saying something about the State of Hawai'i finding a DUI on his California record while he was on probation. I was surprised because I'd hardly ever seen him drink. He was in trouble, he explained, and drove off the next day with panic in his eyes. He spent the next six months in state prison on Kaua'i, and he wrote me a letter every single day.

Left alone in the studio, with all of his belongings, I mourned him. But I was scheduled to be heading down the coast on *Swell* by the time he would get back, so I began to detach myself from the whole situation. I met a charming carpenter in the surf at Hammond's Point, and his great humor and fun-loving spirit helped me forget about the pain of losing Jake so abruptly. My new friend helped build a nav station aboard *Swell*, and he encouraged me through the intense final stages of *Swell*'s preparation. I adored him too, but my heart was already out to sea. The story with Jake felt unfinished, though, so when he offered to fly in and join me for a couple weeks, I couldn't say no.

After an hour's sleep, I wake to the sound of fat raindrops pelting the deck. The noise quickly escalates into a deafening torrent, and I push up off the settee and climb up the steps. Glancing at the radar screen on my way up, I see a massive squall blacking out the entire eight-mile radius of the radar screen!

"Is this normal?" Jake asks.

"Eeesh, this doesn't look good," I mutter, surveying the flashes of lightning on the horizon all around us. I had recently heard about a couple whose boat had sunk underneath them in minutes after a lightning strike blew a hole through their hull. I sure hope that grounding plate works.

It seems to be closing in on us from every side. I try to steer us where the radar shows a small gap in the storm, but my efforts are in vain. The sails hang limp in the swirling, convectional air.

"Don't touch anything metal!" I warn, as the bolts bear down closer and closer. Thunderclaps rumble commandingly as white claws of lightning rip down all around us, illuminating our harrowing reality. I duck below to unplug the radios in a panic, my fingers trembling as I yank out their cords.

"So this is your idea of fun?" Jake asks, aghast. We huddle together, trying to avoid touching anything metal, puny and powerless against the

raging sky. My body tenses with each flash of light, bracing for the deafening thunderclap that follows. Jaw clenched, I dig my nails deeper into
my calves with each incomprehensibly powerful rumble.

"This is bad," I whisper.

"Well, if it's any sign of what's to come, your pet gecko just abandoned
ship!" Jake reports, wide-eyed. He wraps his arm tightly around me.
The fiercely independent part of me doesn't want his support, but this
could be it, I'll take it! The dreadful minutes linger on until three bolts
shred the sky just above us.

CRACK! And again. And again.

The thunder hits our chests with visceral force. The third bolt strikes
the water just a boat-length away, exploding the surface into a tower of
whitewater dressed in the full spectrum of the rainbow. The radar blacks
out and the chart plotter flashes a question mark, then goes blank.

I moan with terror and clutch Jake. Silent tears stream down my face.
Never have I felt so humbled by nature's power, so raw, unbridled, and
unpredictable. I brace for a direct hit, but the next bolt strikes farther
north. We both sit in silence for a long time, as the storm starts to break up.

"You okay, Captain?"

"I changed my mind," I stutter. "I think I want a white picket fence and
a golden retriever."

The Decision

Ear infections have plagued me for several months now. I think the
problems started from surfing in the polluted waters near the boatyard.
I've tried everything—a potpourri of antibiotics, even by injection, and
all the home remedies in the book: ear cones, garlic, grapeseed oil. I even
borrowed a hair dryer. Antibiotics help temporarily, but as soon as I stop
them the infections flare up again. Local doctors are baffled. Jake is leaving tomorrow and he's worried about me. Both my ears are swollen and
painful. I can't surf, I'm fatigued, and I can barely hear.

I decide to accompany Jake up to the capital of Costa Rica where he'll
catch his flight home. After goodbyes, I go see a specialist, who looks inside
my ears with a small video camera that projects the image onto a screen.
It's a jungle in there! She determines it's some kind of rare fungus and uses
a tiny vacuum to clean them out, then prescribes me some antifungal ear-
drops. I'm to stay out of the water and rest for at least three weeks. With
the holidays coming, I decide to fly home and be with my family to heal.

Swell is safe at a dock with friends watching her, so I can rest at my
parents' new apartment in Point Loma. My hearing and balance gradually

come back, but my body feels strange. My period is late, and my breasts are sore. I think back to that fateful morning when Jake's bad luck surfaced again—a condom broke. I need a pregnancy test.

Two pink lines on the urine test stick find me facing a decision I hoped I'd never have to make. I tell my mother right away, and Jake too. They both want to support whichever decision I make. I'm appalled by the thought of ending my voyage. I haven't even been gone a year. I'm just gaining momentum; stopping my dream now seems unthinkable.

A few days later I'm at a private clinic in Los Angeles where my mother and the compassionate doctor reassure me that having an abortion doesn't make me a bad person. All the controversy and stigmas connected to it weigh heavily on me, though. But I remind myself of what I know to be true in my heart: It's not the right time … I'm not ready… I still have so much work to do on myself.

I curl up on the passenger seat on the drive home, tears streaming silently down my cheeks. It will be my deepest, darkest secret. My mother strokes my arm. I'm unspeakably grateful for her support through this. Nonetheless, I slip into that familiar dark place. I don't get out of bed for days, don't accept phone calls, and hardly eat. Nothing even has taste.

When I finally feel ready, I get myself down to the ocean, where the smell of the sea and the blue of the sky helps lift me out of the sadness. I submerge myself in the cold water, wallowing in the slimy kelp strands. No wetsuit. The cold stings me back to life.

I have my health back, and my sailing dream awaits. But it's not just about my own dream anymore. I feel recommitted to my voyage as a way to empower others to chase their dreams and raise awareness about pressing environmental issues. Now I'm on this journey for something bigger than me.

4,505
Nautical Miles Traveled

Buena
Manifestación

Positive Vibration

The last hints of daylight tuck below the western horizon as *Swell* motors out of the wide gulf, headed out on an overnight passage. My newest crewmate, Heather, takes the first watch. Upon her arrival two weeks ago, we bused overland to explore the Caribbean side of Panamá before readying *Swell* to head south along Panamá's Pacific coast. Heather scans for other boats while I scurry around transforming *Swell* into passage mode as the coast fades into a strip of sparsely scattered lights.

Heather and I met behind the bar in Santa Barbara. During our first shift together, the petite brunette with Bambi-like brown eyes proved patient, hardworking, quick-witted, and caring. Over the following two years, we became like sisters and survived being hit on by stubbly, unshowered fishermen and pining regulars by cracking jokes and rolling our eyes at each other when someone got out of line.

About an hour into her watch, I'm putting away the dishes when Heather comes down the companionway, pale and wide-eyed.

"Ray's here," she says, "He's right outside."

"What do you mean?"

I can't understand. It's completely dark out and we're already well off-shore. I hurry past her up the steps and see Ray, the wily fifty-something Volkswagen salesman-turned-cruiser standing in his dinghy and hanging onto the lifelines as we drag him along at five knots. We had crossed paths in several anchorages, where he'd clearly developed a crush on my new crewmate, *but I can't believe he followed us all this way!*

"What the hell are you doing way out here? You scared Heather!" I say sternly.

"Just thought I'd remind you girls, Panamá is to the left!" he says, tossing his head back and exploding with hyena-like laughter.

"Get outta here, you creepy ol' pirate! We don't need your help!" I shoo him off in a fluster; he disappears into the dark behind us.

I had hoped for a smoother start to Heather's first night watch, but thankfully, lecherous older men are something she's quite skilled at navigating. She has an incredible capacity for grace in the face of insisting drunks, picky snobs, and now, brash sailors. It doesn't matter that she's never sailed before. Whether it's dish-washing or onion-chopping, algae-scrubbing or fish-filleting, hitchhiking or ten-hour bus rides, Heather is game. She has a knack for self-control and a persistent positivity that I hope will rub off on me.

Central America's lightning season is finally over and I'm excited to get moving again. We're both thirsty for nature, more self-awareness, and a better understanding of what life is about. She has just been through a difficult relationship, and on the tail of my traumatic decision and ear problem, we're both healing.

We slowly hop our way down the coast and through the undeveloped islands off Panamá, reading spiritual and self-help books voraciously along the way.

"Why don't they teach us this stuff in school?" I ponder aloud while reading the illuminating ancient Toltec wisdom in *The Four Agreements*.

"I know, and how to breathe, calm our minds, and meditate!" Heather adds, breaking for a moment from the book of yogic philosophy she's studying to become a yoga instructor.

As we go ashore one morning, a local man fishing from a small pier greets us. "*Hola. ¡Buena manifestación! Me llamo Gerardo.*" (Hello. Good manifestations! My name is Gerardo.)

Upon returning from our walk, Gerardo invites us for a meal. We both get a good feeling, so we follow him to his simple tin-roofed shack in a rugged corner of jungle and mangrove. Compared to how we've both grown up, he has very few material things, but his calm demeanor and overwhelming generosity show another sort of richness. He feeds us fresh fish and coconut water, pointing to his toucan and monkey amigos in the nearby trees while light rain falls majestically. Although he speaks little, his peaceful presence and simple living move us to question our modern "needs" and lifestyles.

"*¡Muchas gracias!*" we call out as we head home. "*¡Y buena manifestación!*"

We discuss our books and insights while preparing meals, wandering beaches, watching sunsets, and making passages between the endless coves and islets. The fresh air and wilderness feel cleansing and curative. Panamá's ten- to fifteen-foot tidal fluctuations are a new challenge, but Heather never makes me feel rushed. We remind each other to see the beauty in the present to avoid dwelling emotionally in the past and look for the upside in mistakes or perceived failures. We wonder about meaningful coincidences, the unlimited possibilities of "manifestation," and how to flow with, rather than force, what life presents.

I'm not wired to flow; I often develop stiff ideas about how I want things to go, and then have a tantrum if they don't pan out. This first year at sea has shown me that if I insist on having everything my way, I'll spend most of my time miserable. Equipment failures drive me insane since things break almost as steadily as I repair them. Forcing passages nearly always gets me into trouble with bad weather. And I often waste energy throwing my arms up in frustration about illogical bureaucratic rules or "unfair" circumstances.

I know I must work on being more positive—more flexible when the wind shifts and willing to see water in the carburetor as a chance to learn. I won't last long out here if I don't. So far, the ocean has been a gentle teacher, and I've only had some minor slaps, but I know I need to stop making the same mistakes.

I launch a conscious effort to go with the flow. Soon we're awed at a long, open-faced wave we find while exploring by dinghy. I push Heather, a beginner surfer, into a perfect head-high set on the longboard, and she rides it for a hundred yards while I cheer all the way. One evening ashore, we're attacked by sand flies while Heather leads a yoga session. After collapsing with laughter, we decide to go fishing instead and end up catching dinner. When the wind wakes us up in the night, and forces us to leave our anchorage, I bite my tongue not to complain, and the next morning we find ourselves in a gorgeous empty bay where we dive with rich sea life and cartwheel along wild beaches.

As we begin to feel part of the wildness around us, we climb trees, bathe in the swirling fluorescent sunset sea, pee off the stern under the moonlight, and sleep outside under a sky of winking stars. Nature restores, soothes, and heals. While attempting to harvest coconuts, catch fish, forage high-tide lines, and make mud baths, we talk through our recent adversities and begin to feel new strength and clarity.

When the full moon rises over a jungle island backdrop one evening, I call out "*¡Buena manifestación!*" then howl at the gorgeous golden orb.

"*¡Buena manifestación!*" Heather exclaims, howling too. "It's perfect! Gerardo's phrase sums up everything we've been talking about! Positive thoughts create positive experiences!"

I wake up the next morning feeling the need to make peace with people I've wronged and spend a day writing apology letters to friends, ex-boyfriends, and family. Heather studies her yoga books in the cockpit while I type madly. All our recent discussions are helping me see my own faults, and I feel I need to clear out the negativity in my past so I can start again with a fresh slate, living from a better set of principles.

We continue south, and one morning in a deep sheltered bay about halfway down the coast, a local man paddles out to *Swell* in his dugout canoe. While we exchange batteries and DVDs for fruit, the wind switches and swings *Swell* over a shallow sandbar. Soon there is a second canoe. An adorable young family needs first aid supplies for their toddler. While searching around *Swell* for their requests, I don't notice the tide is dropping out fast. Our visitors head for shore just as *Swell*'s keel hits the sand. It's too late; I'm panicked and stressed and pissed off while the hull begins to lean over as the water drops out from under us.

After a foul half hour, the lightbulb goes on: this is a perfect opportunity to try to change my perspective. I take a deep breath, remembering how Barry described his numerous boating follies as "learning experiences." It's only sand below us; the tide will rise again. Heather keeps her cool, and I can't help but smile as she attempts to make breakfast on a 65-degree angle. She climbs up the tilted cabin from the fridge to the sink, and we crack up as the water flows sideways out of the faucet, spilling down onto her legs.

I decide to make use of the next few hours to clean the port side of the hull. "At least I don't have to hold my breath!" I call up to Heather while the stereo blasts Bob Marley's voice, reminding me to keep a good vibe.

As January slips into February, we continue to play like kids in the wondrous island landscapes, embracing simplicity and cherishing the natural world around us.

After dropping anchor at a small island one afternoon, we tandem-paddle the longboard to what appears to be a deserted beach. We haul the board up above the high-tide line and skip off down the shoreline to stretch our legs after a long day of moving *Swell* south. We don't get very far before a short, balding *gringo* in a dress shirt appears from the trees in a fluster.

"This is a private beach. You are not welcome to walk here," he growls at us.

I try to reason with him, but he shakes his head and scrunches his face. I feel my blood beginning to boil.

"How's it going to hurt anyone if we just walk near the water's edge?"
I sharply question.

Heather softly steps in. "It's okay, sir, we didn't mean to bother you,"
she says. "Lizzy, let's go for a swim instead."

Heather is clearly way ahead of me in this game. I back off, and we turn
away. We've only made a few steps when he calls out, "Well okay, you can
go for a walk, as long as you stay near the water."

He stomps back into the trees. We recommence our walk and I contemplate my hot temper and how quickly the man had changed his tune
when Heather had simply complied. All the new concepts we're learning
are simple, but breaking my ingrained patterns isn't.

It's Not Magic, It's Maintenance

The hard-edged outlines of skyscrapers appear slowly out of the pale,
low-lying haze as *Swell* fights the last few upwind miles toward Panamá City.
My head aches with exhaustion from the prior night's passage. Heather
and I, plus spontaneous additional crew—Brad, a surfer friend from back
home—had battled stiff, shifty headwinds and short seas around the infamous Punta Mala while playing a perverse game of hide-and-seek with
the constant stream of supertankers exiting the Panamá Canal.

I didn't shut my eyes all night. A rush of adrenaline kicked in every time
we'd spot an approaching tanker. I would squint at the new set of lights on
the horizon hoping to make out their course and speed before they were
on top of us. The mixed seas and darkness played with my confidence.
I woke Heather or Brad several times to confirm whether I was seeing
red or green lights to determine whether the ships were going east, west,
or coming straight at us. We'd figure it out just in time to tack off, speed
up, or slow down so as not to be run over by the enormous steel beasts
moving at an unrelenting twenty knots.

After catching a dorado, dodging twenty-two ships, making seven
tacks, and constantly trimming sails for the shifty winds—I'm wrecked.
As our projected morning arrival stretches to midday, my lids and limbs
grow heavier, but the searing noise of planes and helicopters keeps me
alert as the city comes into focus. We wince at the harsh sounds and
currents swirling with trash. At last we haul down the sails and nudge
Swell in among the 100 or more sailboats packed into the little brown
bay at La Playita de Amador, a small island connected to the city by a
causeway. Flags from around the world wave at us from the boats—
Poland, Austria, Germany, Australia, Ecuador, England, France, China,
Sweden, South Africa, New Zealand, Hungary. This is the crossroads of

east and west, and it's high season for cruisers, like me, readying to sail toward the South Pacific.

Our outer island vacation has abruptly ended, and both Heather and Brad have planes to catch. I'm sad to see them go, but I'm feeling the pressure to tackle the repairs and projects that have sprouted like weeds aboard *Swell*. With its bountiful availability of parts and provisions, Panamá City is a perfect place to prepare for my upcoming passage. I'm learning that good preparation means doing everything possible to solve and prevent problems *before* going to sea. I've honed my sailing skills in the nearly 4,000 miles hopping down the coast, but the islands of the Pacific are now calling, and to take on the greatest stretch of open ocean on the planet, *Swell* must be prepared for anything.

I transform the cabin into project mode, spreading my tools across the bunk in the main cabin for easy access and starting a frenzy of list-making. I need to install extra water storage in the forepeak, check the rigging, repair my headsail, patch the dinghy, fix the leaky faucet, clean the hull, inventory the food stocks, look over my safety gear, write the next blog update, reply to emails. Neither my outboard nor my generator is working properly. The list makes me swoon, but I indulge myself by buying a wide variety of cheese and chocolates.

"A cinch by the inch," I tell myself, thinking back to Dad reminding me of my grandma Julia's saying.

First, I want to install extra freshwater storage to allow me to carry twenty more gallons of emergency water for the passage across the Pacific. I've got to be prepared if the watermaker stops working. While thinking my way through how to plumb it into the existing system, I dive under the sink in the head and notice a trickle working its way down the bare fiberglass near the thru-hull for the toilet pump.

Come to think of it, water has been slowly filling the bilge for over a week. I've heard the automatic pump working from time to time, but I blamed it on the leaky manual toilet pump that is begging for new O-rings. It's now obvious that the leak has another source.

So I set the water project aside and spend the rest of the day in the tiny opening under the sink trying to determine the leak's source. First, I try to tighten all the fittings and reclamp the hose to the barb. What should be a simple process takes hours because of the cramped space. I don't have the room to get enough leverage to pull, twist, and yank on the various fittings and hoses.

By late afternoon I've finally retaped and retightened the fitting junctions and connected the hose with an extra clamp. I turn the lever of the valve with anticipation, and … drip, drip, drip. I sigh. My spectators under the sink—scattered soap bars and toilet paper rolls—look on impartially while the leak resumes even more aggressively than before.

That evening, I forgo bathing and clear a place on the cabin sole to lay a cockpit mat among the scattered tools. I dip a spoon into the peanut butter jar, take a bite of cheese, and break off a large square of chocolate, mulling over how to fix that damn leak.

At 8:00 the next morning, I turn on the "cruiser's net," which is held over the VHF radio for sailors in the bay to ask each other questions, expose bargains they've discovered in the city, and try to sell, trade, or buy things from each other.

While seasoned sailors on the net warn of exorbitant food prices and limited boating supplies in the Pacific, I dive back into the sweaty, dark cave to take everything apart that I had so carefully reassembled the day before. I've got to stay positive and try again. I inch my body deeper inside the hole and manage to reach my fingers around the backside of the valve. Ah-ha! I feel a sliver of a crack. Using the vice grip, I carefully turn it around and see a vertical split in the cheap plastic valve where it threads onto the thru-hull.

I chime in on the radio net to ask if anyone knows where I can buy a replacement. A cruiser replies; he has an extra valve on board in bronze and drops it by later in the day, refusing to take a penny for it. He even talks me through the process of installing it.

"You will need to plug the thru-hull from under the hull with a tightly-fitting wooden bung plug," he explains. "That way the ocean won't come flooding in while you switch out the cracked valve."

After half a day of procrastination, I find a proper size plug, fish the hammer out of the tool bag, and shove earplugs deep in both ears. Standing at the rail of *Swell*'s port side I look down at the murky brown water. Foamy swirls of pollution and rainbows of oil decorate the surface. I sigh and jump, hammer in hand.

Underwater, I feel around for the opening to the thru-hull and pound the plug into the hole, then hurry back on board for a rinse. Back in the compartment, the valve backs easily off the threads while I pray my plug will hold. Not a drop of seawater enters. I wrap the threads in plumber's tape and screw on the new bronze ball valve, smiling like a hero as I crawl out of the hole.

"I did it! I did it!" I sing, grooving to my own little victory dance.

All that's left to do is put the hose back on the fitting. I boil up some water and soak the old hose in the pan of hot water to expand it, swab it with grease, and then shove it onto the bronze barb with all my strength. The hose stiffly refuses to slip over the lip of the fitting. I push and pull and twist it with every last drop of my strength, begging and fighting to get it on, but it doesn't cooperate.

After two more rounds of hot water and wrestling, I accept defeat. I had celebrated too early. The sun is setting. I'm dirty and exhausted. My tough, self-sufficient outlook crumbles as Dad's famous words ring through my head, "Sometimes there's no replacement for brute strength." I sigh and push the tools aside to make room for a cockpit cushion once more, curl up despondently with my pillow, and wonder who on Earth I can beg to crawl in that hole and help me?

The next morning, I decide to head for the Honda dealership in the city with my broken portable generator. Public transportation is cheap but frightening. The Red Devil buses hug corners like they're in the Indy 500 and taxi drivers use their horns in place of their brakes. Nothing short of a miracle finds me safely at my destination, and, to my relief, they fix the minor glitch in no time. Back at the dock, I load the generator into the dinghy, and pull the outboard starting cord. I pull again, and again. Nothing. I pump the fuel ball, check the air valve, pull the choke. She won't go.

"You too?" I say to the motor, rolling my eyes. I let it sit for a few minutes, then pull a few more futile times. A young guy appears with a group of charter tourists and they load into the dinghy beside me.

"*¿Todo bien?*" (All good?) he asks before they pull away.

"*No funciona el motor*" (The motor isn't working), I reply feebly.

"*Espera. Vuelvo pronto.*" (Wait. I'll be back soon.)

When he returns, he ties my bowline to the back of his dinghy, and drags me out through the obstacle course of sailboats back to *Swell*.

"I'm Marcos," he says, while tying my line to *Swell*'s stern.

"I'm Liz. Thank you again for the tow."

"Any interest in selling that outboard?" he asks, pointing to a little backup Nissan outboard my Dad had given me before leaving. It had clung to *Swell*'s stern rail all the way from California without a single use.

"Yeah, sure. If you can give me a hand with a little project, the outboard is yours."

"Deal." He smiles.

Marcos arrives on the scene a couple days later and quickly wins the battle with the hose under the sink. He offers to help with anything else I need, bringing a gust of progress to the stagnating half-finished jobs. He's a sweet Colombian guy in his early twenties, who captains local charter boats and seems to break all the Latin male stereotypes. He's soft spoken, thoughtful, uncannily chivalrous—and clearly skilled aboard boats. Before lunchtime he helps me complete the plumbing puzzle for the water bladder installation and solves the outboard mystery with a few quick tweaks to the carburetor. I breathe a sigh of relief as boxes on the lists are ticked off right and left.

I thank Marcos for his help and assure him I can take it from here, but he's in no hurry to leave. So I pull off the engine cover because the oil needs changing. He pokes around the engine while I suck the old oil out with my drill pump.

Suddenly he looks up at me gravely, "Your motor mount, *está roto!*" (it's broken!)

"No." I shake my head stubbornly. "It can't be!"

He guides my hand to the rear of the motor, running my fingers lightly across the severed mount's jagged steel. I scrunch my face in disappointment. This means a whole new project, a major one, and I fret about my schedule and my new crew—girlfriends Kemi and McKenzie—who are already waiting on me to have *Swell* ready.

"*Mira* (Look), the one on the other side is the same," he adds. I'm stunned.

"Don't worry, I can help."

Over the next two weeks, Marcos stops by to lend a hand when his other jobs allow. We devise a pulley system from the boom to lift the motor enough to remove the broken mounts. Each time I hit a roadblock he has a solution. He's confident and resourceful. I think he likes me, but I dare not go there. His calm, angelic aura makes my inner turbulence all too clear. He needs someone less complicated, plus I'm not looking for permanence; it's been too much fun feeling free and mingling with anyone I please. I can tell he understands. Not once has he pushed the subject.

Between projects, I catch up on emails, writing obligations, and other Internet chores at the TGI Fridays on the far end of the causeway. They offer free Internet and a cheap lunch special that includes dessert. Sometimes I order an extra fudge brownie sundae to ease my stress.

Although my letters to Barry and website updates are all about the fun surprises and many sea miles I have logged, a great portion of my voyage has been awash in exhausting schedules and daunting expectations I've placed on myself. My spare time is spent writing blogs, replying to emails, and contacting magazines and potential sponsors. The hard work has paid off with a handful of features in major publications, and now both a surf forecasting site and a surfing magazine are publishing my updates. I was even named one of five of *Surfing Magazine*'s "World's Most Committed Surfers." In spite of what seems like significant marketing successes for my supporting companies, one day while sitting in the shiny red booth, I open an email from my only financial sponsor, explaining that they are cutting back their marketing funds. They have no budget for my voyage in the coming fiscal year. I'm gutted. The thought of soliciting a new sponsor on top of everything else bursts my stress capacity.

"How will I get by? I can't manage all of this!" I lay my head on the table beside my turkey sandwich as my mind spins anxiously. I'm sure

Barry would help, but I refuse to ask. The deal was that after leaving, I would figure out my own finances.

When I can't possibly drink another soda water refill or hear another B-52's song, I kick my way back toward Playita de Amador on my skateboard under the orange streetlights of the causeway, gazing at the city skyline to the south. I find stairs to bump down or slopes to trim across while the north wind blows in my hair—a desperate attempt to mold my current reality into something like wave-riding after two months without surfing or even swimming.

By the end of the month, I've accumulated enough hours at TGI Fridays to get paid overtime, although I still hadn't come up with a way to earn a little money. Marcos and I wrap up the final projects. Along with the outboard, I offer up cash and anything else I think he might need, but he refuses everything but the outboard.

"No. No, thank you, Liz. I just wanted to help you toward your dream. I dream of sailing to the South Pacific too one day, but now is not my time. It's yours."

My new crew, Kemi and McKenzie, return from their overland surf excursions, sun-kissed and brimming with stories of surf and adventure. Both die-hard surfers and seasoned travelers, they had no trouble being flexible to give me the time I needed to deal with the explosion of projects and preparation.

After several provisioning runs, Marcos drives us all up to the tourist viewing point of the Panamá Canal at Miraflores Locks to marvel at this unbelievable engineering feat. A man's voice pours out of a loudspeaker with dates and facts about the Canal as tourists gather to witness the massive locks opening. After describing all that goes into keeping the Panamá Canal functioning, the man announces, "You see, folks. It's not magic, it's maintenance!"

I smile to myself as the locks open for a transiting ship—I can relate!

The Colombians Are Coming!

Before saying goodbye to the Americas, there's time for one more Panamanian adventure. South swell season is here, and I'm dying to catch a few waves before the long Pacific crossing.

A voice comes over the VHF radio as McKenzie and I approach a forested and picturesque bay, three weeks after finally leaving Panamá City. After an epic first stop for surf, Kemi had to head back to Mexico for work.

"*Swell, Swell*, this is the *Lost Coast Explorer*, do you copy?" I recognize the voice of one of the guys from the charter yacht we had met while surfing on another island earlier that day.

"Yes, *Lost Coast Explorer*, this is *Swell*. I copy you," I call back.

"Hey Liz, I'm calling to tell you: Do not go to the beach across the channel," the crewmember warns emphatically. "Some Colombian drug-runners are at large on the island. They were being chased by the Panamanian Navy today and ran their boat aground on the beach there. They fled into the jungle and while one of our crew was on the beach he narrowly escaped being kidnapped. Come over for dinner after you get anchored and we'll fill you in on the details."

The buzz about the Colombians is at full-tilt when McKenzie and I arrive aboard the old fishing trawler that had been converted into a deluxe surf charter vessel. Captain Chris and the *LCE* crew are hosting paying guests from California, Brazil, and beyond, but they make us feel wholly welcome. The large table of men step on each other's renditions of the dramatic chase over dinner, but McKenzie and I are distracted by the melody-in-your-mouth, multicourse meal that keeps pouring out of the galley. We nearly fall out of our chairs when it culminates in an ice cream–covered peach cobbler.

From what we gather, the *LCE* had anchored off the beach for a surf earlier in the day. One of the guests broke his leash and his board washed ashore. As he recovered it, one of the suspected fugitives had run at him, whether to grab his surfboard or to capture him to hold him hostage, no one knew. In any case, the guest got away just in time.

Neither McKenzie nor I know what to make of it all, but we nod in agreement when they insist that we come for breakfast in the morning. "We should all surf together for safety," they reason. Okay by us. We'll happily find out what's for breakfast and ride their speed boat across the channel to the best surf spot around.

To be honest, I'm not worried about running into the fugitives. So far, I've used what I envision as a bubble of positive energy to keep clear of dangerous people. I refuse to let my mind play out scary scenarios that could happen—I simply can't. Locking the cabin at night would make it hot and stuffy, so I never do it, and, so far, I've had no thieves or intruders. I don't carry weapons—other than a flare gun, Mace, and some bear spray. I try to do good things for others, and I'm quick to surround myself with good people in a new port. I take obvious precautions like avoiding being out alone at night, and I often wear oversized clothing so as not to attract unnecessary attention to myself. I try to move away from sketchy people or situations before anything escalates.

When the sun peeks over the mainland the next morning, we are already bouncing across the channel toward the beach break full of coffee and pancakes. Any notion of danger quickly melts away as the island comes more clearly into view. Towering green mountains ease into a thick forest of coconut palms spanning for miles in both directions.

The trunks of the front row of palms lean way out over the wide strip of beige sand.

The island has never been inhabited by humans, and exudes a noticeable, vibrant energy that I haven't felt in other places. It feels divinely in harmony. A tranquil little estuary reflects the colors of the sunrise and the pinks, reds, and greens of the flowers and foliage lining it. Morning rays illuminate the large logs washed up around its edge. A pair of scarlet macaws squawk and chase each other above the tree line.

The beach break, too, is a heavenly work of nature. The swells seem to wrap in from both sides and reunite into hollow, thin-lipped, A-frame peaks that peel off, up and down the long stretch of sand like the sketches I used to draw on the borders of my schoolwork. McKenzie and I squeal with delight and leap into the warm sea. We spend the morning grinning at each other between sets from our own personal peaks. At one point, we meet out the back and sit together shaking our heads in disbelief. A crewmember is even waiting outside the sets in the boat with a cooler full of ice water and sandwiches.

"We are totally spoiled," McKenzie says with a smirk as she shakes her cute blond dreadlocks out of her eyes. We both look up as a luscious A-frame comes feathering toward us.

"I'll go left," I say.

"Perfect! I'll go right," she replies. We split the peak, drawing turns all the way to shore.

After gorging ourselves on waves that morning, we decide to sit out the afternoon session and relax aboard *Swell*. Peacefully whiling away the afternoon, we recount moments in the surf, write in our journals, and dismiss any real threat from the drug-runners, until suddenly we hear a panga pull up outside. One of the *LCE* crew calls out, "Get your anchor up as fast as you can! The *Lost Coast* is leaving! See that boat? The Colombians are coming!"

McKenzie and I fall speechless. After considering the situation for a moment, I reply, "Well, there's no point in trying to outrun them in *Swell*. They'll be here before I even have the anchor up."

"Well then, grab your most valuable possessions and come with us!"

Stunned and in disbelief that a scene this serious might actually be unfolding, we bumble around *Swell* shoving our passports, cash, diaries, and other odd material affinities into a backpack, lock *Swell*'s entry, and climb aboard the panga. The dark vessel bears down on the bay. We hear the *Lost Coast* throw its engines into gear, but we speed away much faster in the panga.

I look guiltily back at *Swell*, feeling like I've abandoned my best friend, as the vessel in question enters the head of the bay. Tension builds. The *Lost Coast* turns north, and the Colombians turn north. *Lost Coast* goes south, and the other boat follows suit. McKenzie and I grip each other and the rail and prepare to witness a horrific nautical showdown.

As the Colombians finally overcome the *Lost Coast*, I can hardly bear to watch. I brace for gunshots, but all at once both boats stop, their anchors plunging abruptly seaward. Captain Chris's voice comes over our VHF radio.

"It appears we are being boarded ... It's not Colombians, it's the Panamanian Navy, undercover."

Swamped with relief, we circle back to learn that the navy had come out disguised as a drug boat, in hopes of coaxing the fugitives out of the jungle. When they saw us surfers flee and *LCE* try to do the same, they couldn't help but find the behavior suspicious. No one had bothered to make radio contact until the situation had reached full panic.

In spite of the explanation, the navy conducts a thorough search of the *Lost Coast*, and then four officials want to do the same aboard *Swell*. The mood leaps from gravely serious to serious disbelief when they discover it's only McKenzie and me aboard. They ask me to fill out the required captain's paperwork, but seem less interested in searching *Swell* than learning how we'd managed to get ourselves to this remote locale without any men. As they debark with smiles and handshakes, the commander gives us his personal phone number with a wink—in case of any nautical emergency, of course.

In the days to follow, the saga continues as the undercover officials hunt for the missing men ashore. Their vessel remains anchored off the beach break, and we pass by daily en route to the surf to hear the latest news. When they capsize their aluminum tinny in the waves one day, we help out by providing masks and snorkels so they can find their machine guns washing around in the impact zone.

All the while, the crew of the *LCE* adopts McKenzie and me as part of their daily routine. On the fourth morning in the bay, we fail to stir for breakfast, and awaken to air horns and wake circles until we crawl sleepily into the panga with our boards. Our last day together is my twenty-sixth birthday, and after another fun day of surf and a lavish chocolate cake aboard the *LCE*, the Panamanian Navy crew shows up, bringing news that the fugitives have been apprehended. Captain Chris invites them aboard and we all celebrate together.

Cold Beans and Submarines

The gang of heavy gray clouds that has circled us all morning finally closes in. *Swell* feels more like a submarine than a sailboat as the rain pours down so heavily that sea and sky blur together. We run about catching rain in any vessel we can find to hold water. The poorly functioning watermaker contaminated our drinking water supply a few days prior, and we are desperate for some salt-free refreshment. We fill the buckets, water bottles, teapot, jerry cans, pots, and pans. Once the tank is topped off, McKenzie grabs the soap, and we strip down to bathe in the falling torrents. The cool drops pelt our naked bodies. We open our mouths and lie back on the deck. There could be no lovelier shower than this—no sweeter faucet than these clouds, nor fresher air, nor broader seascape. I'm alive! Thank you, heavens!

We are seventy-five nautical miles out on the farthest offshore passage either of us has ever taken. When the *Lost Coast Explorer* continued south, McKenzie and I pored over the chart to choose our next destination, spying an isolated little island about 400 miles offshore, renowned for hidden pirate treasure and abundant sea life. After sorting through the piles of damp swimsuits and rotting provisions, we prepped for the passage: calculated the distance, stowed the surfboards, hoisted the outboard and dinghy, ran the jacklines, tied down the jerry cans, readied the fishing lines, checked the engine fluids and belts, raised anchor, and headed for sea.

It was daunting to point the bow straight west, but with McKenzie as crew, I knew I was in good company for the challenge. We'd met on the Big Island of Hawai'i years before, when she'd accidentally backed over my surfboard in a sandy parking lot. Miraculously the board came away unscathed, and it turned out she was my sister's friend. When she emailed asking if I needed some crew with photography skills, we planned a date for her arrival. Aboard *Swell*, McKenzie and I had clicked like ruby slippers.

McKenzie shares my delight in new experiences, no matter how good, bad, or bizarre. She's tough, independent, and dangerously witty. Her easygoing attitude, lack of time constraints, and well-traveled confidence make her an ideal voyaging companion. Plus, she's four-star behind the camera, willing to haul and schlep, pull or tie any rope, and she is and probably will be the only person ever to make a quiche aboard *Swell* underway. I've thoroughly enjoyed watching her annihilate Latin male egos in the surf with late drops on the biggest waves of the day. Our unspoken agenda is simple: surf hard, learn hard, laugh hard, and seize each day.

Hours after our deck showers, the rain hasn't let up. I had been so focused on the surf, I realize that I hadn't checked into the typical winds and currents along our route, nor received a recent weather report. We're committed now, so I hustle through wet sail changes due to the light, shifty headwinds.

The rainwater is finding its way into more than just our water containers. It leaks down the mast and onto the cabin sole; it drips from the corners of the front hatch onto the forward bunk. It creeps in from around the portlight seals. The humidity permeates our pillows and blankets. It feels like we could wring water right out of the air.

"I feel like fly tape," McKenzie writes in the logbook. By the second day, the sticky dampness is becoming intolerable. We attempt to cover the leaky spray dodger and bimini with a plastic tarp, but the water still finds its way in.

By evening, the rains slacken, but sharp headwinds fill in where it leaves off. We're now close-hauled, heeling way over, and beating into a stiff, short chop. In an attempt to distract ourselves from the rodeo ride, McKenzie clutches her way below to heat our teapot of fresh rainwater for some tea. "The stove won't light!" she calls up.

"Did you turn on the propane switch?" I ask.

"Yeah, it's on."

I crawl to the back of the cockpit and open the propane locker. The pin on the pressure gauge hangs limply at zero.

"No! How?" I wonder aloud. We lost all the propane.

I hear the lighter clicking again and again, hoping for a miracle. Our wet butts and bunks and the bucking headwind slop have shortened our morale, but now, no propane? It can't be! We assume our soggy positions in the cockpit in silence. It's McKenzie's turn on the high side. She fights the steep incline of *Swell*'s heeling with all four limbs while infuriating drips of water spill down on her head. I just had the pleasure of the same experience, so I understand when she soon retires to the "cocoon"—our shared sea berth below. I stay on watch on the "throne"—the soggy stack of cushions on the leeward side of the cockpit where gravity holds us up against the lower side of the cockpit's teak washboard.

The wind builds steadily overnight, turning the sea into an army of wave soldiers insisting that we are headed in the wrong direction. Every time we launch up over a wave and crash down into the next trough, it feels like a bomb detonating under the hull. I remember Barry warning me that his Cal 40, *Antara*, "had a tendency to slam quite fiercely going to windward." As the conditions deteriorate, we consider giving up on our destination.

"There won't be anywhere to get propane until we make it to the Galápagos!" I shout to McKenzie from the cocoon. "Which is another 500 miles south from Cocos Island!"

"But we're almost halfway to Cocos!" she shouts back from the throne.

"Yeah, and the guidebooks make it sound magical!" I call back. We decide to deal with another day or two of misery for the delight we hope to find upon arrival.

Throughout day three, moving around *Swell* is a cruel game of human pinball. We white-knuckle our way around the cabin, generally just to exchange places between the cocoon and the throne for watch duties. To add to our dismal state, we are now under siege by salt water instead of rain. Each time *Swell*'s hull collides with a wave, spray launches skyward, catches the wind, and showers over the deck. Nothing it touches ever fully dries and we've long since run out of dry clothes and the motivation to change.

As morale slips further, I flash back to an Army survival class I had taken at UCSB. The gruff officer, who had only one volume of vocal expression—yelling—had warned us of a grave condition called "dampass."

"It's something to avoid at all costs," he had loudly cautioned. "Once you've got it, there's no going back. It's a sure sign that you are losing to the elements."

His words echoing in my mind, I muster the effort to fish a bottle of baby powder out of the cupboard in the head and pour it down my soggy pants.

"Yes, that's better." I whimper, passing it to McKenzie.

From then on, during watch exchanges we meet between the bunk and the cockpit, pulling out the waistbands of our foul-weather gear to shake excessive amounts of powder down our festering, damp pants. Temporary relief from the wetness and timely one-liners from McKenzie keep our spirits afloat while trying to pee or trim the sails or locate something to eat on a bouncing forty-degree angle. Even simple tasks—like brushing our teeth and digging the cream cheese out of the reefer to eat with the crackers—seem way too hard.

As the miles to go reach less than seventy-five on our fourth morning at sea, those damn headwinds stiffly persist. The cabin has long since exploded with loose objects, wet clothes and towels, charts, wrappers, odds and ends. The forward hatch is an intermittent waterfall. Along with dampass, our bodies are sore and bruised from the constant tensing, clutching, and collisions.

Midday, I start the motor to help *Swell* hold some momentum into the waves since we hope to make landfall by dark, but just as I sit down on the throne the alternator belt begins to squeal. I clench my jaw in denial.

"That's a lovely sound," McKenzie says, straight-faced. She has perfected survival through sarcasm.

I submit and go below, stumbling across the cabin to fish out a couple screwdrivers, a pry bar, and a twelve-millimeter socket wrench. I haven't finished unscrewing the screws that hold the engine side door shut before nausea sets in. Disregarding my gurgling stomach, I pull off the access door, and inch into the hole beside the warm Yanmar. I loosen the nut on the alternator slider, slip in the pry bar, push the alternator firm against the belt, then tighten down the nut. My face tingles and flushes as the hot, stinky diesel smell threatens to send me to the rail.

Heat! An epiphany surfaces through my queasy haze. I back out of the hole, and make for the bin of canned food. After locating some refried beans, I peel off the label, and pinball back toward the engine compartment to place the can in an innocuous spot, then refit the engine's side door. Gripping my way back up to the cockpit, I turn the engine key to start her up again. No more squealing!

Half an hour later, I remove the can from the engine compartment, pass it up to McKenzie in the throne, then make my way to the high side with a can opener and two spoons. We pass the lukewarm beans back and forth, eating out of the can. A propane-less upwind delicacy.

After the much-needed nourishment, I pull out the logbook and zoom in on the GPS to check our progress. Our soggy, flattened butts beg for mercy. I stand up in between dousings, holding onto the stainless rail on the spray dodger, and squint ahead.

"There it is!" I scream. "Land ho-o-o-o-o-o!"

"Who you callin' a ho?" McKenzie smirks.

We exchange excited grins as the island's steep stone cliffs grow out of the sea. The sun drops behind the island on our approach into the crescent-shaped bay, but we can see a waterfall spilling from the south side of the cliff heights, straight into the sea! Gorgeous!

The next morning we leap in the sea, then launch the dinghy, and row ashore, eager to feel solid ground. Broad-leafed trees reach out over lush undergrowth and we follow a footpath across the island, arriving at a park station hours later. The ranger is surprised to see us, but invites us in for lunch and explains the work they do to protect the national park's surrounding marine reserve from illegal fishing. He offers us a ride back to our bay in his patrol boat since it's along his afternoon route.

We get home as the sun is setting, and row the dinghy over to the waterfall across the bay to indulge in our first lather since the rain shower on deck four days prior. Using the oars, I hold the nose of the dinghy under the falls, while McKenzie delights under the thick, cool flow of fresh water. We switch places so I can rinse, then drift nearby to soap up, massage our scalps, and shave our legs as the clouds above the cliff turn highlighter pink. Already, we're sure the discomfort to get here was worth it!

As we're rowing back toward *Swell*, a man waves us over from one of the scuba diving excursion boats anchored in the bay. We are not about to refuse a hot meal when the captain invites us aboard for dinner, so we load up at the diver's buffet and top off with ice cream while Captain Christian tells us about the best spots to freedive to see hammerheads, mantas, and turtles. He even downloads detailed weather information from his satellite to help us plan for our next passage. And more, upon learning of our propane problem, his cook loads us up with a bag full of juices, breads, cakes, and cheeses, since they're headed back to the mainland the next morning.

Back aboard *Swell*, we're dazed by the marvelous surprises and generosity the day has bestowed. While writing quietly in our journals, a voice comes over the VHF radio.

"Calling the only sailboat in the bay, this is the *Arkos*, do you copy?" McKenzie and I look at each other and then at the radio. I drag my tired body up off the seat cushion.

"This is the *Swell*, Arkos, we copy you," I reply.

"Is this Liz? I've heard about your voyage. We were wondering if you ladies would like to come check out our submarine?"

We both raise our eyebrows and repeat aloud to each other, "Check out his submarine!?"

"That's one hell of a pick-up line," McKenzie laughs.

"You think he's for real?" I return.

"Come on, get dressed, Liz. I mean you might only get asked that once in your life. I'll row." I pull on some clothes, and even though it's nearly 10 pm, we row toward the well-lit trawler at the other side of the bay.

"Hi. I'm Jesse. And this is Mick and Giles. Welcome aboard," says a tall, dark-haired guy about our age. He takes our line and helps us out of the dinghy. They show us around and then finally unveil the prized yellow submarine, which is offered to the paying scuba divers aboard as a special side excursion. We're informed it can descend to 800 feet.

Jesse disappears for a moment, then comes back with two cups full of chocolate ice cream.

"I'm sure it's been a while since you had this," he says, passing them our way.

"Well actually ..." McKenzie starts in. I quickly pinch her arm and talk over her.

"Yeah, no freezer aboard *Swell*! Thank you!" We're in heaven.

After some cleaning and repairs aboard *Swell* the following day, we head off on a freediving adventure. McKenzie dons her long, sleek freediving fins and slips into the sea. I get the dinghy anchored and soon join her. She's a mermaid underwater. I follow her graceful lead under ledges, around rocks, and through the busy underwater scene. Sharks! We see smaller black- and white-tips down near the reef, a group of silver-tips being cleaned by tiny shrimps, and then an unidentified eight-footer who scares a squeal out of my snorkel when we nearly bump into each other.

As we move out over deeper water, a school of eight to ten hammerheads glide past. McKenzie's fearlessness keeps me from shooting back toward the dinghy for safety. Soon we're both kicking toward them, totally in awe. Next a hulking bigeye tuna powers through the sea below us, along with a flashing school of jacks, and then, out of the depths, we spot a giant manta! The enormous ray glides by, performing an act of underwater flight so graceful that I become acutely aware of my awkward limbs. Its wings curl slowly upward, exposing their white undersides before descending again in what appears like slow motion. I dive down to watch as she soars out of sight with one wing flowing up and the other down in a yin-yang-like image that stamps itself into my mind. I want to be more like a manta—strong, but graceful and poised—soaring effortlessly through life.

On our way back toward *Swell*, we stop by the *Arkos* to say hello. Jesse and Giles soon return, towing the submarine back from a dive. When the sub guests have departed, Mick, the head pilot, leans over the rail and calls, "Hey girls, if we go right now, we can do a quick dive in the sub before the sun sets. What do you think?"

"Me … uh … us … what? Submarine … now? Yea!" we stammer.

The Glory Is Forever

After getting whooped by more headwinds and a tenacious crosscurrent for another five hundred miles and five days south, McKenzie and I pull down the sails as *Swell* hovers over the equator. We make an offering to Poseidon and leap ceremonially into the bottomless blue before carrying on into the Southern Hemisphere. The headwinds and spray grow colder overnight, and at dawn we spot the northern end of the dry, volcanic island of San Crístobal, Galápagos. The chilly effects of the Humboldt Current add to the historic archipelago's mystique. We watch morning fog hunching in the lowlands and cloaking rocky outcroppings along the shoreline while wrapped up in our winter jackets. I stare at the rocky, wild island and can't believe I actually sailed myself here—the location I'd chosen for my sixth-grade assignment, "A Destination I Want to Visit."

We are sure our good fortune with kind sea neighbors has run its course by the time we reach the bay at Puerto Baquerizo Moreno. But the next day we're invited to tour a Venezuelan tuna ship. I've always thought of these purse-seiner operations as evil—being a big cause of the decline of the oceans' fisheries. It is hard not to marvel at the huge tuna-killing vessel's internal processing and storage systems and the helicopter on the top deck used to spot the giant tuna schools that they can capture in a single day, but the massive holds full of frozen fish unsettle me. Thousands of motionless tuna eyeballs of all sizes stare back at me, even haunting my dreams that night.

Over dinner, the friendly fishermen show us photos of their families, and elaborate on the fun they'll have with their kids when they return home.

They are good guys, just trying to make a living like everyone else—cogs in a global economic system based on oil and growth and pushing for the harvesting of more and more resources, faster and faster, before the other guy gets to them. The general lack of respect and understanding of our connection to nature with which European men colonized the world has perpetuated a greedy, me-first mentality that keeps a few rich profiteers finding faster, more efficient ways to catch tuna, clear forests, extract oil, and propagate industry without regard for the health of the ecosystems on which they capitalize, much less the finite nature of our planet. Progress they call it. But as Barry and I would often discuss, humans depend on Earth's fine-tuned systems for survival, so "progress" that pushes nature out of balance does not truly advance us. But then, I'm no eco-angel either; I gladly accept the ten gallons of diesel they offer me. I'm part of the problem too.

On the subject of economics, after all my financial stress, I've hardly spent a hundred dollars since leaving Panamá City. As McKenzie preps for a journey to Machu Picchu, we score a few more waves and make friends with the local sea lions who like to sleep (and poop) in our dinghy. And when I'm sure there cannot possibly be another sweet surprise, there he is.

He arrives late, stepping assuredly into the warm light that spills from a bare lightbulb dangling over our table at the little open-air restaurant in town. He stands there for a moment, illuminated. A black headband holds wild brown curls off his tanned face and thick stubble. He sits down, joining us with his two Spanish friends for dinner. We had all met earlier that day at a surf break just west of where our sailboats are anchored.

I'm not sure whether it's the headband or his striking green eyes and strong jawline, or the aura of freedom that surrounds him, but my heart instantly backflips. Gaspar is the captain of a modest little thirty-five-foot cutter, *Octobasse*, and has been sailing solo for four years out of Spain. "The Glory Is Forever" is scrawled at his bow into the McDonald's-yellow stripe running the length of the hull. His friends had flown in for a visit.

There hasn't been a man in every port, although there certainly could have been. My independence intimidates some, but seems to intrigue most. I'm always keeping a sharp eye out for "the one"—the man who I hope to someday sail off into the sunset with—but in the meantime, I've kept it interesting with plenty of dates and local forays. Back home, I always refrained from anything that might earn me a "promiscuous" reputation, but moving from place to place so quickly removes that worry and makes it easy to keep things light. There's no better way to see the best of an area in a short amount of time than with the help of a friendly local—preferably a cute surfer around my age. There was the charming surfer cowboy in northern Mexico, the pro surfer in Puerto Escondido, the hot rasta surfer on the Caribbean side, the California yes-man I met surfing in Costa Rica, and the beautiful black guy I met out dancing in Panamá City. He surfed too. But this … this feels different.

McKenzie flies off on her next adventure. She uses the slim remainder of her travel savings, but after almost three lucky months with her, I'm certain she'll be fine. Time and again, we were shown the good-hearted spirit of everyday people. Time and again, our risks were rewarded, and it seemed as if someone or something was watching over us.

With a few days alone before the arrival of my next crew—my mother—Gaspar and I get to know each other.

Despite his good looks, he's more about function than aesthetics. I like his callused hands, sharp knives, able body, and charming Spanish accent. He's a few years older than me, and gave up his sailing sponsorships after two years at sea for more freedom to move about as he pleased. He picks up odd jobs in various ports—a project for whale conservation in Chile, shark tagging on Easter Island, bartering or laboring where he can. He sailed all the way to the South Pacific, and then decided to sail back against the trade winds to visit Central America. We've crossed paths in this horseshoe-shaped bay, heading in opposite directions. I try not to think about the unfortunate timing, and allow his dark curls, sea wisdom, and carefree approach to voyaging captivate me.

There's little hope. I fall hard and fast. Neither of us resists, despite the fact that on the day we met he told me that he'd just fallen in love with a girl on Easter Island. After a few days together, I dismiss that information as inconsequential. My blazing heart incinerates all logic. I'm flat-out sprinting into a future together—voyaging, surfing, and exploring the world. It's going to be all the freedom and adventure *plus love*! What could be better!?

"I found you, my little rider. I found my woman," he whispers in my ear as we slow dance in the cockpit of *Octobasse* under the stars. I melt into him—safe, cherished, whole, but also free.

The blissful days with Gaspar blur together. The enchantment of the Galápagos adds to our love-heightened senses as we run hand-in-hand through hills of towering cacti, hang out on the rocky shoreline with marine iguanas, freedive with sharks and sea lions, and cross our eyes like the blue-footed boobies. Instead of motoring the dinghy back to *Swell* after a day's excursion, we drift across the bay letting the cool evening breeze push us out into the anchorage, wrapped in each other's arms under the open sky as the lights of town flicker in the distance.

"*Te amo, Lissy. Te quiero* (I love you)," he says. I question nothing, allowing myself to drift fully and freely on a sea of love—adoring, unarmed, present. I refuse to think about the fact that we'll soon be sailing away from each other, or that it's already late in the season for me to cross the Pacific. I prefer to ride out this delicious love high—people-watching in town together, basking in the sand side-by-side after a surf, making out under the stars.

When my mother arrives, she too is quickly smitten by the Spaniard. We follow Gaspar and the *Octobasse* to the next island, and Mom is perfectly happy relaxing aboard *Swell* while Gaspar and I row off to the "Love Canal." As he rows between the narrow passage in the cliffs, sea lions cuddle and sun themselves on the nearby rocks, seemingly concurring that love is all there is.

As the date Mom and I set for our departure nears, I feel a surge of trepidation, not knowing when or if I will ever see my Spanish lover again. The thought leaves me breathless. "Love like this isn't a mistake," I write in my journal. My lip quivers between sentences. "The universe will bring us together again if it's meant to be."

On the last morning on the island of Santa Cruz, Mom helps me scrub the algae off the anchor chain and stow the dinghy. As we finish up the final prep, Gaspar swims over and looks over my rig one more time. He finally approaches where I stand on the foredeck, and delicately pushes a dangling lock of my hair back behind my ear. He lifts my chin so that my eyes meet his. "Head south-southwest until you find *el viento* (the wind)," he says sternly. "Pay attention to your ropes for chafe. *Hablamos en la radio* (We'll talk on the radio) at 8 am and 6 pm *todos los días* (every day). *Te amo* (I love you), my little rider."

"*Te amo*, Gaspy," I reply. Tears drip down my face—for happiness, for the pain of separation, and for the gratitude I feel at having shared these precious moments. I look down. He gently lifts my chin again and breaks into his favorite Ketama song.

"*Cantale conmigo, Lissy … No estamos locos. Sabemos lo que queremos. Vive la vida igual que si fuera un sueño …*" (Sing with me, Lizzy. We are not crazy. We just know what we want. Live life as if it is a dream …)

I can't help but smile. He leans in for a last kiss, then dives into the sea. Before swimming away he calls, "Remember, the glory is forever, Lissy! I love you! *¡Adiós, Mama!*"

6,514
Nautical Miles Traveled

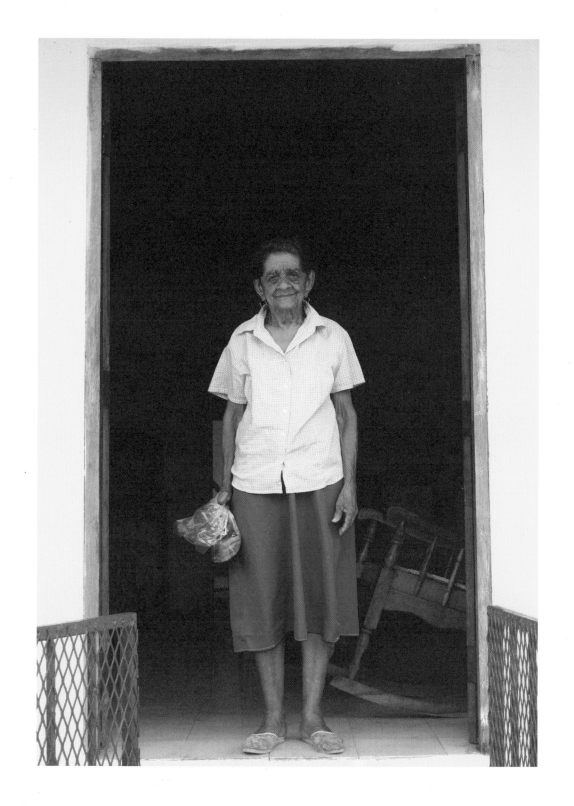

Blue Mountains Constantly Walking

Mom and Me Take on the Sea

It's no average day aboard *Swell* as we motor through a boundless mirror of glassy seas. Now that romance is in my wake, my mental horizons are clearer, and I ponder the incredible: My mother has signed up to join me in crossing the largest expanse of open ocean on Earth! On that thirteenth day of June 2007, as the islands of the Galápagos shrink into the distance behind us, our destination, the Marquesas Islands, lies a daunting 3,300 nautical miles to the west.

Two months prior, I received an email from my father. Both he and Barry had been worrying ever since I'd announced my decision to cross the Pacific alone. I didn't have any friends lined up for the trip, and after gaining confidence sailing *Swell* with crew, I decided that I was ready to try sailing solo. The subject line stated, "Crew for your Pacific crossing." I opened the message and read, "Your mother wants to go with you. She is very serious. Love, Dad."

The next day I found a pay phone ashore in Panamá City and dialed my mother's number, telling myself not to be disappointed if she'd already changed her mind. A lump rose in my throat as I heard her sweet hello over the street noise.

Before she could say anything, I spilled my anxiety into the receiver: "Mom, don't worry, you don't have to come, I'm sure I can do it alone."

"I've made my decision and I'm sticking with it," she assured me.

So now, two months later, my mother—the fairest of fair-weather sailors, who was often uneasy when we sailed as a family—sits beside me in the cockpit, sunning her legs and gazing seaward as we motor south through the flat equatorial waters in search of the trade winds. A lone minke whale surfaces to the north, while a pod of common dolphins leaps toward *Swell*. We make our way to the bow to watch them play.

My father introduced Mom to sailing during their teens. She enjoyed a pleasant day sail with light breezes, but began to distrust the sea when our family was caught in a serious gale off Baja in 1989. Sitting on deck with a good book on a tranquil summer day in Catalina, tied securely to a mooring—that was her ultimate idea of boating—so it's hard to believe that she is choosing to be out here with me. I'm elated at the thought of spending so much time together, but anxious imagining what might go wrong. We don't always see eye to eye.

On dawn watches and in quiet moments during my eighteen months at sea, I've thought a lot about my relationship with Mom. I'd been rebellious and distant during my teenage years, and later so focused on my surfing obsession and sea-travel dream that I took her steady love for granted. Our differences often made understanding and appreciating each other difficult.

She found solace in tranquility; I found it in adrenaline and action. She could never quite understand why I filled my plate so full; I judged hers as too empty. I always had her unconditional love and blessings to pursue whatever made me happy, but she didn't always agree that wild abandon was the best approach to my goals. After a nonstop streak of back-to-back evenings out with friends or perpetual surf adventures, I would end up sick, exhausted, hysterical, or sometimes all three. She'd say she told me so, and I'd be annoyed because she was always right.

So I can't help feeling grateful that Mom is leaping way out of her comfort zone and putting her life in my hands to accompany me on this passage. In addition to some serious quality time, she'll get a real taste of the life I've chosen. For better or worse, there will be no one to distract us, no phones to answer, no surf to chase, and no other obligations.

Swell motors through the slick seas, sniffing out the wind. We are gaining about a knot from the South Equatorial current. Long-period swells billow underneath us like massive neon-blue sheets. I still can't imagine winds that blow endlessly west. Thus far, I've only experienced localized coastal wind patterns. But I remember learning how surface winds in the tropical Pacific flow westward and toward the equator as the "trade winds." Mom and I are currently in the region where the northeast and southeast trades collide—and the air has nowhere to go but up, creating the infamously windless "doldrums." Luckily, we have enough fuel to continue motoring south.

"What is that annoying squeak coming from inside the port quarterberth?" I whine.

"I don't hear it," Mom replies. "That's one of the great parts of aging, honey. But geez, these swells are awfully rolly!"

We meet eyes and burst into laughter.

"Mom, it's completely calm!"

Wind finally tickles the sea surface on the dawn of day five and a few hours later the southeast trade winds sing across our ears. Mom helps me set the spinnaker pole, and once we get the sail in place, *Swell* begins to skip across the iridescent blue. We've carved out our roles and rhythm a bit: Mom helps with cooking, while I handle all the sailing and watch duties. She fell asleep on watch our first evening out—succumbing to the new moon darkness—so I have decided that since I wanted to try to do this passage alone, I will handle the sailing responsibilities as if I were by myself. Mom will be here to provide her loving company and lend a hand if I need it.

As we gaze proudly up at our full sails for the first time on the passage, the jib halyard suddenly parts. We watch in horror as the headsail slides smoothly down the furler track and into the sea. I bolt up on deck in a panic, tripping over my harness tether. I try not to leave the cockpit area without wearing my harness attached to the jackline (especially while Mom is here!). When I reach the bow I tug at the massive, dragging sail ballooned full of seawater. I can't let it break free—we have no spare! But my forces are puny against its great weight. So instead, I rush to pull down the mainsail and slow the boat before the submerged genoa breaks away.

With the mainsail down, I run a halyard to the head of the sail, but discover that the spinnaker pole must come back down because the two halyards are tangled. I can feel Mom's worried eyes on my every move as the bow bounces and rolls under my feet.

"Hang on tight, honey," she repeats.

Once the pole is secured on deck, I crank hard on the winch, relieved to see the sail inching out from under the hull. A minute later I'm able to yank the bulk of it onto the foredeck. After two hours of tedious line untangling and sail wrestling, the genoa rises back into place on a spare halyard, the pole goes back up, and *Swell* takes off like a racehorse again, surfing steadily into the troughs of the following seas. Amazingly, the sail is not damaged, but a large blue tattoo of bottom paint smears across it as a reminder to inspect for halyard chafe before a long passage, as Gaspar urged.

High Seas Surfing

On the morning of day seven we are perfectly on course and making great speed in the steady winds. I tidy up the cabin and whip up egg sandwiches with avocado, cheese, and sweet chili sauce as we suffer through the *French for Dummies* audio CD in an attempt to show up in French Polynesia with at least some basic vocabulary. Halfway through the nasally man's lesson, the wind spikes. The seas increase sharply, and a wave rolls into the cockpit, sending Mom howling below.

I try different strategies throughout the day to stabilize our ride, but the growing swells and strengthening wind continue to make it challenging. By dusk, we are reefed down to a sliver of a storm jib and I've altered our course to take the swells directly astern. Even then, we're barreling down the steep ramps of water like a school bus with no brakes.

We manage to get some grilled cheese sandwiches onto our plates for dinner, but getting them into our mouths is an entirely different story. We juggle our grip between the plates, forks, and cups that all slide back and forth and sideways on the little nav table with each roll and heave. In the event that we need something out of reach, Mom must hold everything at once while I traverse the three difficult feet for a napkin or hot sauce. Once we make it through the circus of a dinner, I pull out the computer, check our latitude and longitude, and scan the propagation chart for the frequency with the strongest signal for downloading emails and weather charts, then turn on the Sailmail modem that connects to my single side-band radio. I'm pleased as it buzzes and clicks and successfully downloads the messages, but then cringe reading Dad's email aloud:

"Ladies. I have some bad news. The swells are going to get bigger and steeper over the next five days. Hunker down and heave to if you have to. There's an unusually large storm off northern Peru that is sending wind and swell your way. You shouldn't see anything over thirty-five knots or twenty feet. Love you both so much. You can do this. Love, Dad."

We look at each other bleakly. "Five days?" Mom asks. After studying my other weather sources, I solemnly confirm.

"I'm going up to check our course, and do some sail adjusting," I tell her.

"You are not going out there!" Mom replies matter-of-factly.

I try to hold back my smirk. Our captain-crew and mother-daughter roles are confusing. We both laugh. I hug her and assure her I will be okay.

She crawls into her bunk in the forepeak for the evening, and I hear her mumble something about "wishing she could be airlifted out" and that "this is where they should have sent Paris Hilton for punishment." Ha!

The night is long and mostly sleepless for me. Every time the white-water crests of the waves crash and roll along *Swell*'s flanks, she careens down a blue-water wave face and spins into a tail slide, tossing our bodies one way and then the other as the hull retaliates. Cups clang, teak joints whine, halyards slap, cargo groans, and the sea roars loudly past my head, reminding me that less than an inch of fiberglass separates us from all of that wild water.

Day nine finds us more resigned to "living in a washing machine," as Mom calls it. Sarcasm becomes sporadic relief from the constant, inescapable bucking and lurching. The swells remain tightly packed and confused, with fingers of the thirty-knot winds running wrinkles up their massive faces. Every step is a gamble, as the floor constantly falls and twists beneath our feet. Snacks become meals and our already basic hygiene further slackens. When just going to pee is like a bad trip through a fun house, showering and tooth-brushing lose their normal priority.

That afternoon I stand on the aft deck watching the swells with frustration, my body braced between the solar array and the backstay. Some swells come at us from the south and wedge into intimidating peaks behind the stern. Others sneak across from the north, sending *Swell* bucking to port and complicating the determined lines of westbound water. My limbs go numb and I lose my breath when it appears the next wave will break right over us. I grip the backstay tighter as the stern rises and *Swell* see-saws as the water mountain moves underneath us. I plead with the sea to calm down as the next lurking giant approaches—please, for Mom!—but its face is twisted, scattered, and unavailable for discussion.

Like lost tourists on a busy New York City sidewalk, we do our best to go unnoticed, maintain the flow, and stay out of the way of that powerful flood of indifference. Mom complains little but refuses to come out of the cabin—the "roiling sea" is just too frightening. She spends most of her time on the starboard half-berth in the main cabin, bracing her legs against the nav table, brow furrowed and eyes locked on the pages of the ironically named *Carefree Crossword Puzzles* book. The woman on the cover is wearing a white one-piece, sprawled across a lounge chair at the beach under a white umbrella. I want to be her.

"What large diving bird has only four letters?" Mom asks as the boat careens into a trough. I'm totally impressed that she can focus on all those little letters; the mere thought makes me nauseous. I'm not much help with the crossword puzzles, as I reel between frustration, seasickness, fear, and thinking about the Spaniard. I haven't heard from him for days. The hours bounce on like a bad dream we can't wake up from, and I'm forced to let go of my vision of our dreamy mother-daughter cruise.

On the morning of day thirteen, the aquatic carnival ride calms slightly. I alter our course back to the rhumb line, then attempt to get the wind vane self-steering pilot working. The electric autopilot continues to steer like a champ, but I fear burning it out by running it all these days without a break. The wind vane—if I could figure out how to use it—is made expressly for long passages like this and operates solely with the push of the wind. I've read the manual a dozen times, and go slowly through each step, but every time I set its steering pin, *Swell* rounds up to port. I give up and steer by hand for a while, enjoying surfing her down the open ocean peaks. When I finally turn the autopilot back on, I pay out the fishing line for the first time since the swell spiked, and lie back on a cushion. Gaspar appears on the inside of my eyelids. As I doze off we are diving through underwater caves holding hands.

"*ZZZZZZzzzzzzzzzzzzz!*" Fish on! I reel in a lovely bigeye tuna, then clean and fillet the gorgeous red steaks.

That afternoon, I'm back in dreamland when something strange happens: stillness. My eyes flash open in a panic from a nightmare that we've run aground. I jump up to find we are moving along at seven and a half knots with full sails. The demon swells are gone!

"It feels like we're floating on a cloud!" I shriek.

"It's the strangest sensation!" Mom calls from below, and now, for the first time in five days, she comes up into the cockpit. We embrace at the glorious respite. Relief. Appreciation. Hope. Mom sips on her precious last beer, and I launch eagerly into a three-pan seared tuna dinner as *Swell* glides smoothly past the 1,500-nautical-miles-to-go mark. Halfway there.

Sea Spell

Once the awful swells have passed, the days begin to blur behind the distorted lens of sea travel. After two straight weeks at sea (three times as long as I've ever gone before), the sensation of timelessness is unlike any I have ever known. This expanse of blue seems infinite, and it feels as if time has no beginning or end. Landfall is still far away, meaning there's no hurry to do anything, and no hour of the day holds any particular significance over another—especially since I've stopped trying to contact Gaspar on the radio. Mom and I just sleep when we feel tired, eat when hungry, and move when the body demands.

The trade winds blow with intense purpose—nothing like the manic swirls of convection in Central American waters. In every direction our view is an endlessly dynamic canvas of blues and whites. All day long, innumerable indigo windswell peaks, driven by the force of the trades, push west across the sea surface. Whitewater toppling from their crests looks like the wind's shoes sprinting west. Plump white tufts of clouds trot through the unbounded azure overhead. On and on and on. All of us headed west.

The blue-water scene is so hypnotizing that my usual high-speed demeanor is lulled into a persistent lethargy. Without a reef to hit for a thousand miles in any direction and winds so reliable that the sails rarely fuss for attention, there isn't motivation to fight it. I shuffle about in a peculiar haze. One afternoon, I intend to straighten up the cockpit, but instead find myself lying on the heap of cushions with my head partially over the rail, content to watch the purply-blue swirls of our wake radiate outward from the push of *Swell*'s hull.

Mom has hit a similar stride. Other than reeling in our next meal when the line squeals and beholding the sun's colorful traverses of the horizon, we float through the days between conversation, sunbathing, a bit of cooking, and cuddling.

Looking out over the seamless blue, there is absolutely no indication of our current place in history. I'm reading Melville's *Typee*, and over one hundred and fifty years later, his description of this same ocean passage couldn't more perfectly match our daily observations.

"Every now and then," he writes, "a shoal of flying fish, scared from the waters under the bows, would leap into the air and fall like a shower of silver into the sea." As I look up from the page toward the horizon, the fanatical little water-walkers shoot out all around us, right on cue.

A day later, I pick up *Typee* again while lying on the bunk in the main cabin, after finally tiring of watching the food hammock swing back and forth above me. In Melville's next passage, he describes a "blatant languid spell" that cast a sort of "disinclination to do anything" over him and the crew during their twenty days through the trades. "Everyone seems to be under the influence of some narcotic," he continues. "Reading was out of the question: take a book in your hand and you were asleep in an instant." That's as far as I get before my eyelids fall like little anchors and *Typee* spreads across my forehead to block out the daylight.

Vision in the Clouds

On day fourteen the full moon arrives. We watch her glorious golden roundness rise from the sea behind us as we savor cabbage salad, spaghetti, and the sunset. After dinner, Mom washes the dishes while I chart our position and make notes in the logbook. I kiss her good night as she heads for her bunk in the forward cabin, then grab my headphones and iPod, slip into my harness, and head out on deck to be with the moon.

As I sit leaning back on the mast, the night scene takes my breath away. The tall, puffy cumulus clouds look like statues in an evening sky gallery—spotlighted by soft, silver moonlight. The sea is dressed for the occasion in stunning black sequins. The infinite sparkling moonbeams make it difficult to take my eyes off her. I'm underdressed in my underwear and inside-out T-shirt, so I let my hair down to feel a bit more elegant. The seascape before me is as clear as day, but without the harsh rays of the sun I can just keep staring. I turn on my star-gazing playlist and sway with *Swell*'s rhythmic downwind gallop. I haven't heard from Gaspar in more than a week and have been troubled by his silence. Tonight I don't want to think about him. The surrounding scene feels sacred, like visual poetry. I want to be present.

Beethoven's *Moonlight Sonata* plays into my headphones. There's glory all around me, and yet that damn Spaniard keeps creeping into my head. I feel so empty not having any news. I want to mentally swim in these glittering moonbeams, I want to give all my attention to Mom and *Swell* on this passage, but I constantly wonder where he is and why he hasn't been in touch. Warm water wells in my eyes and I close my lids to push the tears out. There's so much to be happy about, but I feel a chronic anxiousness. Am I enough for him? Maybe I'm not pretty enough. Maybe if I had bigger breasts or girlier clothes he would have written. I wipe my cheeks, take a deep breath, and look out over the mercury-coated sea.

Floating above I notice something extraordinary. I blink and rub my eyes, but it's still there: The perfect figure of a woman sprawls across the sky in the clouds. This isn't just the kind of cloud form where it looks like a rabbit for a moment and then quickly morphs into normal clouds again. This is different. She is perfect. Exquisite from her flowing hair, to her round chin to her petite ankles. Lying on her back with her arms folded behind her head, she stares peacefully up at the entire universe. Her naked body is as anatomically correct as if Michelangelo himself had sculpted her.

I shake my head and stand up. But she's still there, floating over me as deliberately and undeniably as the moon. She smiles casually toward the heavens, bathing in the decadent moonlight. Am I really seeing a woman's flawless form in the clouds? Will she mutate into a hamster or a bulldozer in a few more seconds? Will she leave as soon as I move to wake Mom?

I'm motionless … I hardly breathe … but she doesn't go away. Minutes pass, then all at once, I understand why she is there. A clear notion emerges into the forefront of my thoughts.

"You are more than enough. You are divine—as beautiful and grand and limitless as I. There is nothing to worry about. Be present. Be patient. Treasure this precious time with your mother for healing and growing."

Emotion washes over me, and more hot, silent tears flow down my cheeks. As a tomboy growing up in a culture that values women mostly for their physical appearance, I have never felt beautiful enough or comfortable with my unique femininity. In fact, I associate femininity with weakness, so I have fostered only the traditionally masculine aspects in myself—the ones that make me a good surfer, a capable captain, a problem-solver and go-getter. But I long to feel more balanced in my feminine skin. To be softer and more accepting of others and myself. To stop beating myself up for not looking like the women in beauty magazines. The cloud goddess has reassured me that it's possible and that there is much more going on here on Earth than I understand. Am I somehow truly a divine part of it? All I can think to tell her is, "Thank you." I repeat it a few times under my breath as she finally dissolves into the other clouds. Then run to grab my journal and sketch her form so that tomorrow I won't wake and wonder if I had only dreamed her.

Blue-Water Bonding

On day seventeen we are thrilled to see the miles-to-go number on the GPS drop below 500. I write in the logbook, "This endless river of blue is simply incomprehensible. We cannot imagine finding a speck of land among it. We're down to canned food and sporadically blurt out food cravings just for the mouthwatering torture of it—rosemary mashed potatoes, freshly picked blueberries, handfuls of arugula, chocolate mousse, cheesecake! I can hardly stomach another stale Ritz cracker or canned green bean. But on the bright side, we've had a lot of time to talk."

I've learned more about Mom in the last week than in all my years before. Born only thirteen months after her sister, she was "likely an accident," Mom says. She came into the world fighting for life as a tiny two-pound preemie and spent her first five weeks in an incubator at a hospital in downtown Los Angeles. Her alcoholic father usually waited in the car when he brought her mother, Myra, from Gardena for visits. Twelve years later, Myra divorced him, and moved Mom and her sister and older half-brother into a small apartment in Downey.

Myra had come to California alone in her mid-twenties. One of nine children raised on a small subsistence farm in Virginia, she stopped going to school after the fifth grade, for lack of transportation. When she tired of living on a riverbank with a boyfriend, fishing and shooting rabbits, she headed west with dreams of a new beginning. Working in local convenience stores, she did everything in her means to feed, clothe, and educate her children, but offering emotional support eluded her, as it was something she herself never had. In great contrast to my privileged childhood, Myra's limited income and work schedule made extracurricular activities, holidays, travel, and extravagances rare, and Mom was never encouraged to dream or explore her interests. Her father died of a heart attack when she was only sixteen.

Mom met my father in junior high. He fell in love with her mischievous, fun-loving spirit and wooed her through high school on dates to drive-in movies and bay cruises in *Fleety*, his fourteen-foot day-sailer. Although they attended separate colleges, Dad couldn't let her go. They were married at twenty-one and moved to San Diego, where Dad started law school. His first law practice was successful, and they bought a barely habitable structure on a lot with an ocean view. They rebuilt the old heroin den into a lovely cedar-sided beach home, and seven years after their wedding, my brother, James, arrived. My sister and I came two and seven years later.

Mom and Dad plunged joyfully into parenthood, but their own emotional needs often went unmet. Neither having been raised by parents in a loving relationship, they didn't quite know how to nourish each other emotionally. Even when money was no longer an issue, and they were settled in a beautiful ranch home on ten acres a few miles inland from the beach, they still couldn't seem to connect deeply. Dad turned to alcohol; Mom was medically labeled with "depression." Dad soon put law aside for real estate, but when his investments suddenly evaporated, they decided to take the family on a six-month sailing trip to Mexico. Afterward, Dad was offered an entrepreneurial position developing cancer centers. After losing both his father and Mom's mother to cancer, this new work offered significant meaning. He started flying all over the country, often leaving Mom on her own to take care of us kids.

For the first time I see Mom not just as a parent, but as a friend and a human with an entirely different story than my own—and I'm surprised to learn that her tender, sensitive soul is, in fact, so much like mine. I've always seen our relationship from a child's one-sided perspective. I'm sad, realizing that she had never lived her own dreams—nor was she ever encouraged to dream at all—before dedicating herself to motherhood.

"Mom, I'm so sorry I never took the time to know you better," I cry while stroking her legs on the bunk beside me, suddenly overwhelmed with guilt for a lifetime of wishing she was more like the other PTA and soccer moms. Forgiveness cracks open a long-shut door in my heart. I wish now more than ever that I could heal all her inner wounds. "I never understood you until now."

"Oh honey, it's okay. Please don't worry. Look, we're here right now together. I never dreamed I'd be doing this! I am living your dream with you. This is probably the most amazing thing I'll ever do." she says sincerely. "You gave me the courage to cross this ocean. Plus, I haven't smoked a single cigarette since we left. Maybe I'll finally quit this time."

I kiss her cheek. I'd been trying to get her to stop smoking for as long as I can remember. I shed some happy tears and we hold each other for a long time.

As the miles-to-go slip away, I notice how we wipe the counter in the same circular strokes, incessantly interrupt each other, and even react with the same kinds of faces. My hands are exact replicas of hers. I've completely stopped pouting about the Spaniard, and I'm cherishing the intimate time with Mom. I couldn't be happier when she wants to reel in our catch when a fish strikes, tie knots, and help trim the sails. We hold hands basking in the afternoon sun, crack up over Scrabble games, and speak in foreign accents to entertain each other.

Surprise, Surprise!

In the dark morning hours of our nineteenth day at sea, I'm roused from slumber in the cockpit as I feel *Swell* accelerate. I'm now accustomed to light, short sleeps between scanning the horizon and making sure all is well. With the slightest change in motion or sound, I'm instantly awake. As I sit up from the cockpit cushion, a fat raindrop lands square on my forehead. I haul my blanket down into the cabin and shuffle around sleepily looking for my rain jacket. Before I can get an arm into the sleeve, the rain is coming down in a roar. Another gust shoves into the sails. I scramble to pull my harness back on over the jacket.

For more than a week, moderate trades have pushed us along gently. I always put a reef in the mainsail before nightfall, but with the benign conditions the last few days, I'd decided to leave the sail full last night in hopes of gaining a few extra miles toward our destination.

As I clamber out of the cabin, *Swell* wobbles through another surge of speed. We're overpowered and I need to get the mainsail down immediately. I clip my tether to the jackline and make for the mast in the clobbering rain as the next gust drives *Swell*'s nose hard to port and twists the hull over onto her starboard rail. I'm nearly to the mast when my harness tether stops me like a dog on a chain. The tether clip is stuck on a stanchion post because *Swell* is heeled so far on her side. The gust won't let up. It pins *Swell* farther and farther over. The spinnaker pole and headsail submerge into the sea as the starboard rail sinks down into the black water.

"Liz-z-z-z-z-y-y-y-y!" I hear Mom scream from below in terror. My mind freezes as I fear the worst. I cling to the rail on the cabin top, hugging the nearly vertical deck. The warm ocean water climbs eerily up my shins as *Swell* lies over, contrasting with the cool rain pelting me from above. Each harrowing second seems endless.

"Hang on, Mom!" I manage to call out. The gust finally lets up. Hundreds of gallons of sea rush off the decks as *Swell* gradually rights herself. I crawl aft to untangle my tether, then lunge at the mast, releasing the halyard and yanking down the mainsail with all my adrenaline-pumping might. The squall has nearly passed by the time I secure the third reef and make it back to the cockpit to find Mom at the wheel, wide-eyed, steering into the blackness with the autopilot alarm blaring.

I reset the autopilot with trembling hands and we sit down among the wetness, holding each other for a long time.

"It was my fault. I should have reefed before dark, and I should have been on deck at the first sign of the squall instead of going below for my rain jacket. I'm so sorry you had to go through that."

"It's okay," she says. "We're okay. And you'll know for next time."

We snuggle up on the soggy cushion for the remaining hours of darkness as *Swell* barely makes three knots under our heavily reefed sails. That's enough excitement for one night.

Thankfully the following days breeze by uneventfully, until at five in the morning on day twenty-two, I open my eyes to see the silhouette of a lone black noddy perched on the solar panel, gazing ahead calmly as if he's taken over my watch.

"A bird!" I exclaim. Land must be near! I sit up to scan the horizon as the dawn's rays begin to halo the eastern seascape.

"Mom! Come quick! There's an island!" I yell down into the cabin. She crawls out of her bunk to join me in the cockpit. We rub our eyes and squint, but the tiny dark smudge of land ahead remains. We beam at each other, almost speechless. I wrap my blanket around us and we watch the sun slowly rise out of the sea, digesting the surreal moment.

Around midday the winds slacken and we're bobbing along at an agonizing three knots. The island remains a small lump in the distance. Our stomachs growl, but neither Mom nor I can bear the thought of another canned food meal. We're so close, I can almost taste the fresh fruits and warm French baguettes the guidebooks describe. Mom digs around in the refrigerator box for a while. I hold my tongue. The batteries are low on charge and she's letting out all the cold air. Back at home, she loved to joke with me when I'd stand at the refrigerator door, staring mindlessly at the contents within.

"Waiting for something wonderful to appear?" I finally say, teasing her with her own line.

Suddenly Mom squeals. "You won't freaking believe this!" she cries. I leap to the entryway and peer down curiously. She wheels around bearing an enormous, proud grin, then reveals a frosty green can from behind her back.

"I found one last beer!" she exclaims ecstatically.

"Ha! Then let's start celebrating!" I cheer.

Language Lessons in the Lost Valley

Alone for the first time in ages, with no crew or schedule to keep, I let the mystique of my first stop in the South Pacific soak in. Before catching her plane back to California, Mom continued her sailing adventure—hitching a ride on another cruising sailboat 500 nautical miles toward Tahiti with some new friends. I smile every time I think of her while I'm wandering among ancient ruins, gawking at local art and handsome volcanic peaks, and bodysurfing with local kids. The fifteen Polynesian islands now known as the Marquesas are known to their native inhabitants as the Land of People—Henua Kenana in the northern dialect and Fenua Enata in the south. It's one of five archipelagos in the eastern Pacific to have been colonized by the French in the 1800s.

On top of their striking physical beauty, the islanders carry a commanding presence. Muscular, tattooed men paddle outriggers through mind-melting sunsets. Golden-skinned women shuck coconuts and bathe golden-skinned babies in their front yards. Adolescent girls stroll to the market wearing seed jewelry and floral crowns, their waist-length black hair swaying and catching the sunlight. Teen boys race horses bareback down dirt roads, hoping to be noticed, while pigs and goats forage freely nearby. Lively groups of kids climb trees, kick soccer balls, and splash in the waves. Elderly relatives relax nearby. No one hurries. Fish dries on community drying racks. Weathered stone tiki carvings squat and stare. Windows framed by woven bamboo walls are dressed with colorful floral-print curtains waving lazily in the breeze. Island music wafts from within.

I'm mesmerized by these islanders, still living largely from the rich land and abundant sea, but I can't communicate with them. My Spanish was flowing after a year and half in Central America, but even with the audio CD lessons, my French is hopeless. The English-French dictionary does me no good, since letters have a totally different pronunciation in French. To my ear, the native tongue sounds much easier, plus it seems more respectful to speak to the Marquesans in their own language. So I start learning basic words, to the delight of those I ask.

I sail into a magnificent mountain-rimmed bay, to hole up and wait for the ferocious late July trades to settle down before hopping to the next island. I paddle to the beach on my longboard instead of launching the dinghy. Barefoot and blissful, I mosey through the valley among scattered abandoned homes and loaded fruit trees. Jumping down from a guava branch, I collect my yellow-skinned loot in my shirt, and collapse in the shade to bite into the sweet pink flesh. M-m-m-m-mmm! Chewing slowly to savor the edible treasure, I watch a rainbow fan and fade between the rushing clouds overhead.

Oops, I just ate a worm! I spit out the squirming bite and throw the offending guava into the trees as an older woman appears from behind the nearby home. I leap to my feet in respect and embarrassment. Her unrestrained chuckle assures me she's not angry. She motions me to follow, so I stuff the other guavas in my bag and catch up. Her worn pareo flows about her ankles with each rhythmic stride. She leads me to her home, and motions for me to sit down at a gorgeous, hand-carved wooden table in the front yard. She disappears inside, then soon returns with a Marquesan-English dictionary and a tray of fruits, which she loads into my bag. I surmise that she wants to prevent me from being caught "stealing" again. We sit at the shaded table, passing and pointing at the book to learn about each other.

"*To'u inoa o Felicity*," she says pointing to herself. "*Eaha to oe inoa?*" (My name is Felicity. What's your name?)

"Liz," I tell her, "or, Elizabeth."

"*Elitapeta!*" she exclaims. It must be the local pronunciation. We continue asking questions, and with the use of the dictionary, I learn that she is seventy years old, although she looks much younger, and was born here in the valley as one of eleven children, all delivered at home by her father. She's floored to find out that I'm alone on my sailboat. She calls me her *Kaiu keapu menike oko* (strong little American captain), squeezes me in her soft arms, and ushers me toward an empty bedroom. I explain that it's important for me to sleep on the boat in the strong winds, so Felicity and her husband, Ceryl, send me home with a plate of food and an invitation to visit again soon.

"*Oio'i!*" (Tomorrow!) she calls as I wander back toward the beach.

"*Oio'i, Mama'u Felicity!*" (Tomorrow, grandmother Felicity!) I call back.

The next afternoon, Felicity sits patiently across from me as I repeat the Marquesan word for hello. "*K-a-o-h-a*," I say slowly. She looks at me from behind thin-rimmed glasses with a smile so loving it's like being wrapped in warm velvet. "*Meita'i*" (Good), she confirms with a nod. I repeat it and then move down the list of words I'm hoping she will teach me.

Over the next couple weeks, my language skills improve, and Felicity and Ceryl fatten me up on wild pig, homegrown roots, fresh coconut milk, shellfish, and more. I also install mast steps up to the first spreader on *Swell*, watch a lunar eclipse between the racing cumulus clouds, enjoy mystical hikes to the waterfalls and float back down the river, and surf the windswell peaks breaking at the river mouth. The winds are finally settling; it's time to move on.

Felicity and I hug one last time. She wipes tears from her eyes as she wraps the silk scarf I gave her around her neck and makes a pretentious face, pretending to be fashionable. I know she doesn't need it, or care about material things, but I want her to remember me and know how much her kindness has meant to me. She and Ceryl walk me to the shoreline.

"*A ti'ohi, Elitapeta,*" she says. "*A oho te i'i.*" (Be careful. Be strong.)

"*Mo'i e ha'a pe'a pe'a, Mama'u Felicity. Vai'ei nui!*" (Don't worry, Grandma Felicity. Thank you very much!)

I look back and wave a few more times as I knee-paddle my longboard toward *Swell*, wearing a backpack stuffed with parting gifts of fruit.

Messages from Above

Arriving in a rather exposed little bay on a new island a couple of weeks later, I set both fore and aft anchors before swimming ashore to walk through the small hillside village. I'm admiring the tall trees that cover the road, when a handsome local guy out in his front yard repairing his canoe says hello.

"*Kaoha nui!*" he says with a smile. His muscles are wrapped in gorgeous Marquesan tattoos and thick dark hair falls around his face.

"*Kaoha!*" I return.

"My name Hiva," he says, "Where you from?"

Before I can answer, a mango falls from the tree above, splattering the earth between us. I leap backwards. He recoils too, then hurries over to wipe the bits of mango from my shins with a rag. He offers to show me around later in the day. He's charming, and I certainly have no other plans—nor have I heard much from Gaspar—so I nod in agreement and continue wandering down the road.

That afternoon Hiva arrives at *Swell* in his newly repaired canoe. He invites me to climb on the back and he paddles us toward the shore. We explore the east side of the bay, leaping across the smooth, dark reef and boulders to peer in caves and tide pools. Hiva wrangles eels out of their holes and cracks open urchins to show me how to suck the tongue-like meat out of them. When we leap in the sea to cool off, he points to fist-sized live cowries and a fluorescent purple starfish clinging to the dark rocks. Next, he wants to show me where the royal family once lived. We wander back into the valley, where he cuts a path through overgrown ruins with his machete. We pick starfruit and oranges along a steep trail to the peak, where we break out of the foliage for a beautiful view of *Swell* in the quiet bay. Mysterious rock spires tower behind us; clouds whip around their tall, domed peaks. When he leans in and caresses my hair, I pull away gently.

"*Hoa?*" (Friends?) I say. He nods in understanding. I figure we should wrap it up for today.

The next morning around 7 am I see his canoe approaching. "You come?" he asks politely. How can I resist his bright smile, golden skin, and broad shoulders? And, why should I?

I gather a few items and climb down to perch again, backwards, on the canoe's rear. He strokes south, out around the next headland. I'm enchanted by the silent, rhythmic advance of the slender canoe until we land on a white sand beach lining a sharply ascending valley. A pack of wild horses looks up from their drink at a nearby freshwater stream trickling into the sea. Hiva heads off to harvest avocados up the valley; I stay put on the empty beach, happy as a sand crab.

Back at the village later, he invites me to come for lunch at his parents' home. After meeting his mother, father, and nephews, I follow him to an open-air garage, where he bows his head to say a prayer, then picks up a shotgun. I must look startled because he puts down the gun and starts making animal noises and lowering his upper body as if head-butting. *Oh, okay, I think we're going goat hunting.* I have mixed feelings of dread and excitement as we tiptoe through the wild acres of his family's land. An hour later, he fires at an adolescent black billy goat. It's a perfect shot; the goat instantly falls dead. He then strips the bark off a branch, and uses it to tie the back legs of the goat to a tree branch. He guts and beheads it, then lets the blood drain. The black fur gleams in the bright midafternoon sun as the carcass spins slowly. My emotions spin too—from sympathy, to disgust, to appreciation and admiration. When the blood stops dripping, Hiva stuffs what's left in his backpack and we walk back to the family home on the cliff overlooking the bay. *Goat for lunch, no big deal.*

At home Hiva skins the goat, while his mother heats a large pot of water and shucks a pile of brown coconuts. Three structures and several large trees surround a grassy yard area. An open-air kitchen lies opposite a tin-roofed house, and there's a hangout area with palm frond thatching for shade in between. I play tag with the two nephews until Hiva's mother yells something that must mean the food is ready. She removes the boiled goat meat from the pot and drizzles it in fresh coconut milk. When she's finished, the boys and I take the pressed coconut gratings to the chickens behind the house, then we all sit around an outside table under the shade of a gnarled old mango tree for a feast. Breadfruit pounded and mixed with coconut milk into *kaaku*, watercress soup, and manioc root accompany the goat. Ripe mangos and sweet, mutant-sized grapefruits are stacked on the table for dessert. I stuff myself, enjoying every bite of the delicious fresh food, since I find limited motivation to cook alone, mostly eating from cans and packages.

I slowly chew each bite of goat with new respect. Meat in Southern California grocery stores never had a face, family, or fur.

Over the meal, Hiva's father, who speaks good English, explains how their people were decimated by diseases brought by European sailors during colonial times. The small population that survived has endured, but is in desperate need of genetic variation in their offspring. "This is a good reason that you should stay in the bay and marry my son," he says with a smile.

Suddenly a mango falls from the tree above, landing square in the middle of the table, bursting open to expose its pulp and sweet golden juice. Hiva quickly says something to his father in Marquesan, who then turns to me and says, "This is a very impressive sign! Hiva says a mango fell between both of you on the first day you met, and now this!"

The table goes silent; everyone looks at me. The nephews tug at me from both sides. I blush awkwardly and fidget in my seat. *If there were a decent wave to surf nearby, I would totally consider it!*

Shooting Star Wishes

I'm both nervous and excited about being alone at sea for my first significant ocean passage of five hundred miles to the remote atolls scattered to the south. As Hiva's island shrinks into the distance, the sea welcomes me graciously—small cumulus puffs drift west through blue skies with twelve to fifteen knots of wind flowing over my stern quarter.

I had raised the anchors at first light. With Hiva's heart clearly growing fonder by the minute, it was time to move on. I've got a schedule to keep, with two friends and then a group of filmmakers joining me soon. I wrote Hiva a letter and gave it to another sailor in the bay to deliver. I hope he'll be able to understand why I must go.

There is hardly any swell and the boat is well-balanced on a broad reach, so I decide to give the wind vane another try. The vane starts steering and doesn't stop; the wing and gears and rudder are all moving in tandem, keeping us steadily on course. I celebrate with guavas and SAO, the local version of saltines. I'm thrilled that the Moniter wind vane is no longer just a fancy piece of stainless steel on the stern. I fine-tune the line that allows me to adjust our course from the head of the cockpit and give my new crew a name: Monita—little monkey, like my Dad used to call me. He always said monkeys like me make great crew.

I buzz about making my floating home more functional. First, I saw down a piece of bamboo and lash it to the steering arch to make a holder for a rigging knife. Then I reinforce the lashings on the fishing reel strapped to the aft stanchion. Next, I screw down a drink holder beside the helm, and after studying my knot book, I fashion a hanging rope sling for my little blue vase. I slip one of the gardenias that Hiva gave me into it.

I keep myself so busy that I hardly even think about being alone, but sailing solo has a few noticeable benefits. There's only one place in the cockpit that's always shady and dry—and today, it's all mine. I feel a bit more relaxed, too, knowing that if I screw up, my own life is the only one at stake. Oftentimes, I wish I had four hands: Alone, the boat jobs take a little longer and can be more complicated, but with ample patience and persistence there's usually a way. When hoisting the outboard from the dinghy onto *Swell*'s stern bracket before a passage, I have to use my hands to heave on the davit line, while both my feet and teeth brace stabilizing ropes to keep the outboard from swinging around wildly as it rises.

The wind dies on the second day and I don't turn on the engine even though I'm moving at only about two knots. Monita steers slowly through the brilliant fluorescent-blue sea. After some chores, I lay back, munch crackers, and watch the clouds. This solitude and speed are delightful—a time and space of pure communion with the sea. Something I've long been thirsty for feels quenched, as if finally getting a moment alone with a long-time crush. This peace, this freedom … it's utterly satiating … intense … delicious! I can't name or pinpoint it, but I'm sure it's what keeps sailors returning to the sea. I soak it up, grateful for everything and everyone that led me to this moment.

This feeling must be the reason Barry never tired of being at sea. When I emailed to tell him that I wanted to try sailing solo, he was a bit surprised; I had been dead set against it before leaving. "It's just something I feel the need to do," I'd written to him.

"Then you must. I know you can do it. Prepare well, my girl, and remember to wear your harness," he replied.

Although Barry had made local solo trips, he preferred sharing his mad love for being on the ocean. Over his forty-some years of sailing, he took innumerable guests out on his sailboats—friends, family, colleagues, students, and perfect strangers—on day trips, weekly afternoon races, sunset sails, weekend cruises, and hundreds of longer voyages along the California coast and to the Channel Islands. He even auctioned off trips aboard his boats to raise money for Jean's tireless charity work, likely as a good excuse to go sailing. I know that he hoped to give all of his crew a taste of this wild, wonderful open-ocean feeling.

For four more carefree days, the sparkles of sunlight on my beloved sea are the only jewels I could ever want. Not too fast, not too slow. Nothing broken, nothing scary, nothing but the enjoyable side of sailing. I listen to music, write poems, do hand laundry, and nibble on fruits. And each night, *Swell* and I parallel the glowing stripe of the Milky Way overhead. Stargazing long hours from my cockpit bed, I think about the Cloud Goddess and send shooting star wishes to my family and friends; I don't need anything else at the moment.

Then, as darkness falls on my fifth and final evening at sea, the wind abruptly switches 180 degrees. I spend the whole night tacking precariously between three unlit atolls, awaiting daylight to decide on my destination. Meanwhile, a nasty cold takes up residence in my sinuses. I check my position at least a hundred times, paranoid about getting too close to the long stretches of submerged reefs that helped earn this chain of atolls its nickname, The Dangerous Archipelago. Just before dawn I wipe my nose on my sleeve, and roll my eyes at the twelve-mile figure eight I sailed overnight.

The sun's first rays light up a flat green patch of palms on an atoll up ahead. It was once an ancient volcanic island that now, over millions of years, has sunk back into the sea. Only the circular rim of the coral reef that once surrounded the island continues to grow toward the sea surface. Such ring-shaped atolls shelter an interior lagoon that can make for a protected anchorage if you can find a navigable entrance through the reef. I check the chart; finding no way in, we continue south.

Zzzzzzzzzzzzzz! The fishing reel sings and I fight in my first fish of the passage—a beautiful female mahi mahi. I see her mate trailing her and feel sad to take her. I must do this to eat. I reach out to gaff her, but she makes a final thrashing leap and shakes herself free. I'm actually relieved.

An hour later the line runs out again, harder this time, and ten minutes later, I haul aboard a gorgeous bigeye tuna. Something about being alone makes me feel more like an equal to this fish—both of us just trying to survive on this wild, open sea.

I look into its wide black eye and almost throw it back, but instead, kneeling by its side, with my left hand gently resting on its opalescent flank, I say, "Thank you, beauty, for your life."

With a swift jab of my knife to its brain, I watch its neon-purple stripes fade and retractable dorsal fin go limp.

An hour later I find myself in a nervous fluster, approaching my first atoll pass. My *Charlie's Charts* guidebook explains, "A pass is a break in the circular coral atoll that, if deep enough, allows entrance into the calmer waters inside the atoll's interior lagoon."

The book also describes this particular pass as "difficult, with only a forty-five-foot wide channel and currents reaching velocities of six knots or more." I'm supposed to enter the pass "on slack low tide with overhead sun." I have neither. To further complicate the situation, a line of black thunderheads tailgates me toward the entrance. Should I stay another night at sea? I'm exhausted. Another full night of vigilance in these dangerous waters seems unwise, but what if *Swell* is swept onto the reef? Dad and I had tried to secure insurance for *Swell* but couldn't find a company to accept a twenty-seven-year-old solo female captain, so regular maintenance and prudent choices are my best insurance.

I approach the pass cautiously, but when the ocean floor leaps up to eighty feet and I spot a small patch of sand, I toss my anchor and hope for the best. It's going to be a long night. The northwest wind has died, but it left a sloppy bump on the sea and *Swell* rolls and bucks unpredictably. If the wind comes up from the west as it did the night before, I will quickly be in a dangerous position against the lee shore. I anxiously shuffle around on deck, furling the mainsail, coiling ropes. A flock of children on the beach wave and holler while three humpbacks surface not a hundred yards away, but I'm too nervous about my anchor arrangement to appreciate the marvelous welcome.

A small fishing boat comes out of the pass headed for sea. I wave the fisherman over, dart below, and return with a bag of tuna steaks from my catch that morning. I have much more than I can eat and this weather is no good for drying it. The enormous Puamotu man flashes a toothless smile, accepts the bag, and asks me in French why I'm anchored outside the pass. The audio lessons are paying off, because I understand enough to attempt a reply.

"*Peur. Ja'i peur!*" (I'm scared!) I explain.

He laughs and signals for me to follow him through the pass. Thankfully the anchor comes up without a snag, and I line up closely behind him. The outbound currents churn and yank *Swell*'s bow to port, then starboard. I leap like a frightened cat when a small standing wave crashes over the stern, spilling across the cockpit. The engine is at full throttle, but we're barely making a single knot of headway. The fisherman patiently remains just ahead of *Swell*, looking back now and then to make sure I'm advancing. I smile through my clenched jaw and stiff spine, as *Swell* fights her way inside.

As we near the lagoon, the force of the current slackens. The fisherman leads me between two bus-sized coral heads awash at the lagoon's surface, and toward a calm spot out of the current, with an ideal depth for anchoring. I thank him profusely as he waves and speeds away. Dropping the anchor, I thank God, the Universe, the Cloud Goddess, Poseidon, my angels … and whoever else might have helped this all work out so smoothly.

With survival temporarily off the checklist, I look around in awe. Palms sway over a small row of simple homes lining a white-sand beach, and the sea is as clear as a pool of Evian.

Clementine's Island Tour

The next morning, as I tie the dinghy up to the quay of the tiny town, I'm greeted by a curious flock of kids. They squeak with delight at the chalk and jump-ropes I pull from my backpack, and I join three elderly ladies on a nearby bench to watch the children jump and draw on the cement landing area. The distinguished Puamotu dames are wearing handmade hats, each uniquely decorated, and they repeatedly ask me a question that I can't understand.

"*Où est ton mari?*" (Where's your husband?)

I pull out my pocket dictionary. One of the women flips through and points. I read, "*Mari* (n, m), husband." I laugh and finger through the English side of the dictionary to find "Alone (adj/adv), *seul, seule, tout seul.*"

"*Je suis seule*" (I am on my own), I tell them.

They squeal and pet me and squeeze my hands. Shaking their heads and holding their cheeks, they point to *Swell* and then back to me and talk quickly among themselves.

Before long, I set off to check out the tiny seaside village. I don't make it far before a great round woman on an adult-sized tricycle approaches. I'm a bit intimidated at first, but as she gets closer, a wide smile spreads across her lovely Polynesian features. She stops and introduces herself as Clementine.

She motions repeatedly toward the large, low basket on the back of her bike, but I have no clue what she's trying to tell me.

"*Içi!*" she says. "*Monte!*" (Here! Get on!)

I dig into my backpack for my dictionary again. She points to me and then to the basket, again and again. A little girl comes over and climbs into the basket, and holds onto Clementine's shoulders to help her explain. They both point to me. The old ladies on the bench holler, "*Allez! Allez! Monte!*" (Go! Go! Get on!)

I hesitantly climb into the basket and take hold of Clementine's shoulders. I don't know what the plan is, but off we go as she presses casually on the pedals, hardly seeming to notice my weight. She points out the Catholic church, the elementary school, and the post office. As the dirt road veers left, my spontaneous tour guide waves to people tending their yards. The brightly colored homes are each uniquely decorated with shells and flowers and coconuts. Clementine swerves among kids playing marbles on the dirt roads, and two young girls soon join the tour on their bikes. Next, we pass the store, the town generator, and the Mormon and Protestant churches. It only takes us half an hour to ride through all the streets of the village.

Then we pedal out to a coconut grove where Clementine's *mari* is working. He's the fisherman who had guided me into the pass! He opens us some fresh young coconuts to drink. As we sit under the swaying palms sipping nature's most perfect refreshment, there's nowhere I'd rather be. I'm in total disbelief at the kindness they've shown me. *I cannot wait to write Barry about this!*

A Perfect Misconception

Our jaws fall simultaneously as Ryan, Taylor, and I watch left-handers reeling down the reef with no one out. We spend all morning in the waves, soaking up the surf miracle and high-fiving the friendly locals who paddle out too. Ryan and Taylor get some brilliant rides. I, on the other hand, am having a hell of a hard time.

My fun-loving surf buddies from back home arrived a few days ago on a backyard-built plywood speedboat they had hired at the nearest island with an airport. They hauled an impressive array of edible goodies and fun surprises from the Land of Plenty, too. I was both thrilled and impressed they'd figured out a way to find me out here in the middle of nowhere. But I should have known, these two are always game for an adventure. The surf even turned on to welcome them.

"Perfect waves," I mutter bitterly after bubbling up through the white-wash with another bleeding scratch. I had thought that surfing picturesque waves like these would be easy. I was so wrong! These fast, shallow reef waves leave no place to be but inside the tube.

Tube riding has always been elusive in my surf arsenal. It was easy to dodge the frightening vortexes in the softer waves of California. This is a whole new wave world to me and, after a morning of scuffles with the reef, I'm gravely discouraged and covered in scrapes. Despite the pleasantly warm sea temperature, this is no place for a bikini—I already ripped the butt out of my favorite surf shorts. I continue babbling negatively to myself as the surge sucks me back out through the partly exposed fingers of reef. There is just no way around it—at my skill level of backside tube riding, I am going to hit the reef. Rather than call it a day when I obviously can't find my rhythm, I stubbornly force a few more waves.

Sensing my frustration, Taylor talks me through the process. He's a regular-footer too. "Okay, Lizzy, you gotta take off behind the peak, and just lean into the face when it starts to pitch in front of you. Use your right hand on your rail for stability."

Easier said than done, I conclude, after a few more trips over the falls. After traveling over 9,000 sea miles in search of waves like these, I'm disgusted that I can't even properly ride them!

Another clean line rises and shifts in front of us, putting me in the perfect spot. The massive local guy with a mohawk nods at me, signaling me to go. "It's yours, Lizzy. You've got this one," Ryan encourages.

I have only a second to judge the takeoff. A little in, or out? Deeper or more on the shoulder? I turn, put my head down, and stroke hard to get under the lip. The wave and I stand up in sync, and my feet glue to the top of my board. I stick my left arm in the face and watch the clear sheet of water launch out. But as the lip comes down, I realize I've aimed too low. It nails me on the head. The wave grabs me—we go up together, out together, and down together. The reef catches my bare back while the wave drags me shoreward. When I sputter to the top, I see that my hands and feet are now bleeding too. Ryan signals to be sure I'm okay. I give him thumbs-up, but fight back tears. Not from the pain, but because I'm trying so hard and failing so terribly.

Back aboard *Swell* later, I'm still grouchy. Ryan scrubs my back wound with iodine, while Taylor pleads, "Lizzy, you can't expect to be able to ride waves like this your first time. It took me years to figure out backside barrels."

I refuse to give up. The next day, with the salt water stinging in my wounds, I finally lock into a tube and come out unscathed. The boys cheer and we celebrate that evening with a bonfire and music on the beach, even though my battles with tube riding are far from over.

Dreams and Debts

After an epic few weeks of surf exploration, stuck anchors, dumb jokes, and wily sharks, Ryan and Taylor head off on a cargo ship for their next surfing quest. For a sweet, solo week before the film crew arrives, I dissolve happily into the sparse archipelago of palms, coral, lagoon, and sky. Just gazing at this remote ocean wilderness soothes me. I surf a dying swell with local kids on old beat-up boards in the morning. When the tide changes, I drift with the current into the pass, flying over schools of fish and the colorful coral seafloor with my ankle tied to the dinghy's bowline. The locals here also welcome me wholly, inviting me for meals and even offering me black pearls and handmade crafts. Their richness is not in having, but in giving.

A lovely light breeze blows over the atoll, but Gaspar, who has resurfaced via email, warns me to pay close attention to wind shifts that could expose my anchorage. Aboard *Swell*, my first attempt at baking bread produces something more anchorlike than edible, but I marvel at how the simple act of kneading the dough is satisfying. I dance to Ryan's playlist and pluck at the guitar Kemi gave me back in Panamá. It feels so good to slow down.

In the afternoons, the long bare strips of coral and white sand call. I wander the fingers of exposed reef to study the crabs, fish, and corals. The sea air is decadently fresh. Eels slither completely out of the water and wiggle over the dry reef to the next coral pool. Reef sharks swim right into the shallows, their fins cutting silently along the surface. The reef is so alive I can almost feel it breathing. My mind was blown to learn from the locals that an island not that far from here was used to test nuclear weapons by the French until the mid-'90s. *How could anyone bomb this?*

Surrounded by nature's magic, I wonder about the ways of the West, and why we live like we do back home. Most of my friends are grinding their lives away behind a desk or register, paying off student loans, rent, or mortgages. Most don't enjoy what they do, but everyone needs an income and the corporate ladder promises credentials and material security. Still, what is security with no freedom? Money with no time? Work without passion?

Of course, not everyone would want this sailing life, either, but I wish it were easier for people to pursue their own dreams and desires. I write to Barry about it in my next letter: "How can people learn their strengths, and explore their passions and potential?" I type. "My situation is an anomaly, but I recognize what most people back home are facing and it pains me. The current system devalues our dreams, unless they produce financial gains. Most feel obligated to take the road that keeps them sheltered and fed, and then drown the yearning of their souls with alcohol, drugs, and pills. It hurts to think about our true desires when they seem too inaccessible. They become accustomed to a demure work life with no time to really question it until retirement. But by then their bodies are worn out and minds accustomed to certainty and structure. Too many dreams are going hauntingly unfulfilled."

"You and your generation must shape the world you want to live in," Barry replies. "It takes courage and creativity to think outside of society's box, but most of the changes I've seen in my eighty-three years have happened because of people who persisted toward a dream or a belief about what is 'right.' The Environmental Studies Program is a good example. When the oil platform blew up off the Santa Barbara coast in January of 1969, crude oil spilled into the channel and covered beaches. Students complained that their education was not equipping them for this kind of problem. I met with a group of 21 faculty to discuss the possibility of promoting some form of environmental education at UCSB. By the fall of 1970, the ES program had been started. Our first graduating class had only 12 students, but today there are more than 5,000 alumni. Each graduate becomes an active part of our society's environmental awakening. Just look at you. Keep going, dear. People will take notice. Maybe a few more dreams will be chased because of you."

His reply makes me feel a little better; I hadn't thought about it like this. Still, despite Barry's encouragement and how backwards the system seems, I have to face the fact that my savings are running low. Plus, if I am to get across the Pacific this season like all the other cruisers, I need to get moving. But the film crew arrives tomorrow, plus my brother is getting married in a few weeks—my father has proposed to fly me home from Tahiti on a frequent flyer ticket. Following the filming rendezvous, I must find a safe place to leave *Swell*.

10,909
Nautical Miles Traveled

Wind
in
My Hair

Change of Course

My three weeks in San Diego passed in a flash. It was wonderful to be home for James's wedding, but between errands, visits with friends, and shopping lists, I was a human pinball. I'm exhausted, lying here restless in my bunk in the predawn hours, trying to decide what to do next. *Swell* gently pulls against her docklines at the marina in Tahiti, as if she's ready to get back out to sea.

With cyclone season approaching, I feel the pressure to leave right away if I'm going to make it to New Zealand—the safest, most common place cruisers choose to spend the South Pacific storm season. It would be about 3,000 nautical miles of sailing with only a couple quick stops. Although I'd love to stick around, cyclones do hit French Polynesia and my current visa is only for one month. I'm also worried that the community I'm building through my blog and magazine articles will lose interest if I don't keep moving to ever-new destinations. I hesitate to jeopardize the trickle of income they provide. Despite my fatigue, heading west seems like the best option.

While I lie there mulling over the necessary voyage preparation to leave for New Zealand, it occurs to me that I am shaping my trip around assumptions of what I think my supporters back home want me to do. They don't know how busy I constantly am to keep up with the endless maintenance, passage prep, checking the weather, emails, crew scheduling, social invites from other cruisers, and writing updates, on top of daily chores and feeding myself.

What do I want to do? I suddenly ask myself, staring up at the light blue ceiling where the dawn light illuminates the photo of my family and a sticker of Mother Mary above my bunk. My mind flashes to that leisurely week in the outer islands after Ryan and Taylor had left.

I want to slow down.

I want the freedom to move at a more natural pace. I want time to reflect and work on myself. I want more nature and solitude. I want to live by the moon. No one is requiring me to hurry across the Pacific in one season; I've been putting that pressure on myself because it's what all the other cruisers I've met are doing. *What about going north?*

A surge of excitement flushes through me. I throw back my sheet, leap from my bunk, and pull down the roll of charts from the bungeed stack above the nav station. While back in San Diego, I'd come across the *National Geographic Magazine* I'd saved since my youth, containing an article about Robin Lee Graham's sailing adventure aboard *Dove*. I scan the chart, and there it is—the little string of islands in the Republic of Kiribati he had visited—1,500 miles to the north, and out of the cyclone danger zone. It's almost perpendicular to the trades from here, so if I choose a good weather window, I should be able to make it back and explore more of this area after cyclone season.

A young sailor from a neighboring boat has a car and agrees to help me run errands to provision for the trip north.

"There's nothing but palm trees up there," he warns. "I'd get more rice."

His words excite me even more. I pile the cart high with cans and dry goods, and I even spring for a bike, knowing I'll have time to explore during the five months of cyclone season. The next day he helps me change my engine's water pump impeller and tighten the spring on my shaft packing system. I buzz through my checklist with adventure on my mind—I take on fuel, top off my water tanks, look over my ropes and rig, and head to downtown Papeete to check out of the country with customs and immigration.

And then, on my last evening tied to the dock, I receive an email from the Spaniard. "I already tired of Central America. Is too many tourists and water very polluted. *Te echo de menos mucho* (I miss you dearly) *y el Pacifico* too.

I'm coming back for find you. I arrive in Marquesas in one month. *Es possible* for you leave *Swell* in a marina in Tahiti and fly up to meet me? We can enjoy Marquesas together, then sail down to pick up *Swellito*. *Te quiero*, Gaspy."

I blink. I blink again. I reread it. I stare in disbelief at the words in front of me. I shoot up from the table and dance around the cabin. My true love is heading my way!

Feels Like Freedom

I sail *Swell* out of the harbor the next morning with no hurry, no guests on the way, and a variety of nearby destinations to choose from. I wrote the Spaniard right back with my plan to head north for cyclone season, and explained that I didn't have the money to fly up to meet him and pay the dock fees for *Swell*. "How about we meet in the middle?" I proposed. He agreed that in five weeks' time, we'd meet at a small island in between Tahiti and the Marquesas, and then take on the passage to Kiribati with our boats side by side.

I have plenty of time to make my way to where we'll rendezvous. It feels foreign not to have a course already plotted as I slip out of the pass, but I tell myself that this is exactly the luxury I've desired. Instead of letting a schedule or obligation plot my course, I will let the wind, weather, and swell direction choose my next ports of call.

As I move off the island and scrutinize the angle of the wind, a spotted ray leaps repeatedly from the sea off my port bow, precisely in the direction that seems to be the best heading. I take this as an affirmation, and *Swell* lurches in acceleration as I push out the boom and ease the jib into the plump trim of a broad reach. I set the steering vane, turn up the volume on my new French audio lessons, and lie back like a kid in a lazy river to enjoy where the elements take me.

Over the weeks to come, I find a rhythm with the swells and wind. When I find an anchorage near a wave, the wind happens to drop off. And as the swell dwindles, the wind fills in and carries me onward. Is it just lucky timing, or the result of tuning into the rhythms of nature? In either case, with all the conflicting and uncontrollable factors in sailing to surf, each opportunity to ride waves must be seized!

When the anchor is down, I keep things simple: I paddle to the breaks instead of launching my dinghy, eat minimally, and spend mornings playing in the waves. I return to *Swell* for a midday hiatus, sunscreen-caked and red-eyed. Pulling a ripe avocado from the cooler, I slice it in half, drizzle it with hot sauce, then splay across the cabin floor where the breeze from the forward hatch cools my sunburnt body, savoring each spoonful.

After napping or writing, I often paddle back out for an evening session, then use candles and headlamps when I return to *Swell* so I don't have to run the generator to charge the batteries. I sleep early, and wake up before the sun to see if there's surf again. Despite my burning shoulders, anything but full attention to the waves feels sacrilegious. Such is life dedicated to a sport as ephemeral as surfing!

When the forecast predicts a drop in the trades, I decide to take advantage of it to move more easily east. At sea again, the wind in my hair feels like freedom. Between sail adjustments, I sing and dance topless in the sunshine. Is it okay to be this happy all by myself?

I hadn't always been so excited to be alone. In fact, I used to be terrified of it. Before my voyage, I would panic at the thought of spending a Saturday night by myself. I had abundant friends, boyfriends, and overlapping schedules—always making more plans than I could keep. I think I was avoiding being alone—maybe so I wouldn't have to face the parts of myself I didn't like?

Luckily, most things are scarier when you're thinking about them than when you're actually doing them, and my fears about being alone proved unfounded. Now that I've had some extended stretches of solitude aboard *Swell*, it's a relief to know that I actually enjoy my own company.

Since my choices affect only me, I'm learning more about what I like, what I want, and how I thrive. I don't have to explain myself. The days ebb and flow with the rhythms of my body and the environment around me. I move between tasks and basic human needs in a spontaneous, instinctual manner. The simplicity of it delights me. I can pee right off the leeward side, take a bite out of the block of cheese for dinner, or devise an extravagant new recipe that only I will suffer through if it's a failure. I can be totally immersed in a project and then drop down suddenly for a ten-minute siesta. In fact, I find myself indulging in intermittent catnaps, as if I'm catching up on years of missed sleep. When the faintest hint of fatigue tugs at me, I curl up and shut my eyes—sometimes in the cockpit or on the cabin floor with a damp towel or a week's-worn T-shirt as a pillow.

Out here, there is no one to compare myself with—there's not even a full-length mirror to critique my appearance. I let my hair go wild. I laugh out loud, and break into dance without a second thought. I can fester in my filth or spend half an hour massaging shampoo into my scalp. I wear any odd ensemble from the clothing bin—or nothing at all. Some granny panties that Mom gave me have become my go-to sailing uniform. I can scream, cry, and sing all in one breath with no one to judge me. I want everyone to feel this deep liberation.

Being alone allows me to tune in to signs, nuances, and feelings. I refocus on *buena manifestación*, being present, rooting out my negative thoughts, more flowing, and less forcing. I change my mind and my destination as often as I want. If that little voice inside me—the one I have always been so good at ignoring—says, "Don't go today," departure plans are pushed back without another thought. I begin to seek a relationship with that voice, those intuitive moments, and I notice positive outcomes each time I go within, listen, and act from my gut. There must be something to this.

Without anyone to remind me of my humanness, I float in the clouds, dissolve into the wind-ripples, and dance with the glittering moonbeams illuminating the dark sea crests. I'm free to fall through the sky with the shooting stars and raindrops. I let go of limits I've placed on myself for the sake of how other people might judge me, and try to recognize my own self-judgments too. I feel ready to be me, whatever the consequences.

"Maybe I'm losing it," I say to the circling frigate bird, "but I don't care. This feels so right!"

Pēni Te Fare

Daydreaming, I follow my furry new friend on a morning walk along the edge of the reef. Rocky, a sweet, lanky local dog, yips and wags his tail, madly bounding after fish in the tide pools while I pick shells, cartwheel, gaze at sea life, suck on urchins, and admire knotted driftwood along the mix of beach and reef. When the midmorning sun grows too strong, we head back across the islet toward the bush where I stashed my longboard early this morning. I sidestep a pile of coconut husks as we come around the front of a home, and then nearly trip over the foot of a wooden ladder that blends into the sand below.

"Whoa!" I exclaim as I catch my balance. I look up to see the hulking figure of an old white-haired Polynesian man teetering at the top of a rickety handmade ladder, spackling spatula in hand. He's filling the cracks between the new plywood sheets on his lagoon-front dwelling. His great round belly up there looks about as steady as a bowling ball balancing on a toothpick.

"*'Iaorana!*" The Tahitian greeting sails from his mouth.

"*'Iaorana!*" I reply.

Despite the obvious strength that remains in the man's body, the great mass of his chest leaning way out while he works with both of his hands concerns me. I cringe as each gust of wind makes his tuft of white hair lean farther and farther over, threatening to upset his fine balance. To make matters worse, I notice he has only six toes between his two feet.

To my great relief, he comes down, and introduces himself as Tautu. He walks over to a faucet for a drink of water, and offers me a glass.

I'm parched from the morning's excursion, so I gladly accept and follow him into the overhanging shade of his house. After a bit of verbal floundering, I understand that he is getting ready to paint the house—*pēni te* in Tahitian. He has spent all of his seventy-some years living on the island, the last ten alone. His wife had passed fifteen years ago, and his only son had moved away to find work.

I spontaneously offer to help. I never want to see him on that ladder again! A great smile spreads across his face. We finish up the spackling, and make a plan to meet at 7:30 am tomorrow to start painting.

I wake the next morning to clear skies and paddle my longboard ashore. First, Tautu and I roll two empty fuel drums over and set them on end, then place two long two-by-six-inch boards atop them for scaffolding. I work on the upper walls, while he covers the lower. Despite the towering language barrier between us, his calm, wise presence reminds me of being with Barry. The thick white paint goes on sticky by midmorning, and we work our way around the house, following the shade. Rocky chases crabs nearby.

Around 11 am, Tautu lumbers down to a platform in the lagoon shallows where his neighbor leaves him a daily supply of fish. He cleans and scales five or six small reef fish, then walks back behind the house, where a large iron spike protrudes from the ground. He thrusts a brown coconut onto the metal spike, tearing off the dried husk circularly until only the hard, round inner shell remains. He then taps around its circumference with the dull side of a large kitchen knife, and the nut magically falls open into two perfect halves. Next, he pulls out a wooden board with a metal grater attached and places it on the step of his house. Sitting down on the wooden end, he scrapes both halves rhythmically until all the coconut meat is grated into the bowl between his feet.

I watch curiously, continuing to roll the walls with white paint, carefully covering up small patches Tautu had missed. Soon after, he calls out something that I take to mean, "Lunch is ready!"

Following him into the house, I wash my hands while he sets an overflowing pot of white rice on the table in the kitchen next to a glass bowl of carefully sliced raw fish and onions. He then fills a square of white tea cloth with a couple handfuls of the freshly grated coconut meat, and squeezes it out over the fish. The thick white milk dribbles down his hands and into the bowl. With a few squeezes of lime, lunch is served.

Sitting at the table across from Tautu, I think back to my many lunches with Barry, and days spent helping around his house—hauling firewood, taking the trash bins in and out, or climbing up to fix something difficult to reach. Young and old need each other. I want to live in a world where there is time to help others, where the elderly are not put away in nursing homes. Barry was in good spirits when I called a couple weeks ago. He'd been out sailing aboard a friend's boat, and even took an icy dip in the sea, one of his favorite pastimes. My plan to go north excited him; his encouragement continues to be unfailing.

Three days later, the final touches to the second coat of paint make the house gleam like an overly whitened smile. As he does every evening, Tautu sends me home with more fish than I can eat for dinner. I tie them together and place them on the nose of my longboard. A curious pack of small black-tip reef sharks follows me home. I drop them a fish or two once I'm safely onboard.

Rotten Reunion

I haven't heard from the Spaniard in a month, and I'm beginning to worry that something happened to him. I'm here where we'd planned to meet, but there isn't another boat in sight. Nearly every day, I connect to the Sailmail station via the radio and download my emails. Before this stretch of silence, he was emailing constantly. Then all at once, no news?

Finally one stormy morning, his name pops up in my inbox. I open and read, "Lissy, I am arriving in four or five days more." Yay! But wait, there's more … "I need to tell you that I invite Elena to meet me since you couldn't come and we are sailing together for three weeks—is the girl from Easter Island I told you about when we meet in Galápagos. I hope you not be angry. We both get ciguatera very bad and very sick most of the time. She return home by plane yesterday. I decide to pass another time with her to be sure when I come to see you. *Hasta pronto. Te quiero.* Gaspy."

My heart hits the cabin sole. How could he? Why didn't he tell me sooner? The wind howls through the rig and driving rain beats down on the decks. I'm suddenly terribly lonely. How could he leave me wondering for weeks, while he's been off on a romantic sail with someone else? For the next few days I mourn the future I'd been anticipating together. Being alone no longer feels peaceful. I mope around *Swell*, swinging between sadness and anger.

I must make a choice. I can leave quickly, or stay here and face him. I don't feel good about seeing him in my fragile emotional state. I'm hurt and jealous, and I know I won't be able to let it go right away. This is no way to start our dream life. My gut screams "Run!" But my stupid heart wants so badly to feel his love once more. I slowly prep the boat for departure, but all the negative emotion has left me weak. I'm cautious because I know that in order to go to sea, I have to be at my best.

Two more suns set before I see his yellow-striped hull entering the pass. When he drops his anchor near *Swell*, I head over to greet him and wince through an awkward hug. He looks thin and bitter. He brings up the ciguatera poisoning and I look at him without much sympathy.

Contaminated fish karma, I think smugly.

I wait for an apology. I wait for a shower of affection, or an affirmation that Elena isn't the girl of his dreams. That he loves me more and everything is going to be just like it was.

Instead he blames the situation on me. "*Oye*, you should be come up to meet me," he says. "You is just *celosa* (jealous). Is not so big deal."

Upwind Education

The next morning the trade winds pick up hard from the southeast. Wind waves build steadily across miles of fetch in the lagoon, quickly making our anchorage unsafe. Gaspar proposes that we sail to another island to the northeast and spend the holidays with his friends who own a pearl farm there. Part of me still wants to salvage what we'd shared in the Galápagos, plus the passage will be all upwind—something I would never attempt by myself. Maybe I should take this chance to learn from him about sailing against the wind? The few attempts I've made—like the propane-less passage with McKenzie—proved extremely difficult. Learning how to sail *Swell* proficiently upwind would open up a whole new array of destinations.

There isn't much time to think, as the wind waves in the lagoon grow steadily. I agree to his plan and ready *Swell* for passage. I'm not sold on his skills as a lover, but I do trust his sailing knowledge. Gaspar talks me through our strategy. "We going to tack *mucho*. Is better if the wind direction change. Don't hold *Swellito* too close to *el viento* (the wind). Give her enough room to dance. Make sure your sails always tight and flat. I stay close by. *No te olvidas* (don't forget), Lissy, we are not hurry!" he says.

I nervously double-lash the dinghy on deck and stow everything more thoroughly than usual in anticipation of the upwind slog. I've learned time and again that *Swell*—with her long boom and big mainsail—can be easily overpowered. I'll have to stay on my toes to keep my sail plan balanced between being shortened but in control, and overpowered but making headway. If everything goes as planned, it will be three days and two nights of upwind sailing.

We raise our anchors at the same time, but my chain sticks on some coral below. Gaspar had scolded me for not diving the anchor every day to be sure it didn't get wrapped on the coral, but I hadn't listened.

Octobasse heads out the pass, Gaspar not realizing my predicament. I desperately try to motor in different directions to see if the chain will come free. When that doesn't work, I dig out my mask and snorkel. I will need some slack in the chain in order to untangle it from the coral, so I drive the boat forward into the wind. When *Swell* is as far to windward as possible, I dash to the bow and dive in, pulling myself down the chain. I must reach the place it's stuck, thirty feet below, before the boat blows back and puts tension on it again. To my dismay, I see that the chain has wound itself around a large coral head. I manage to unravel one wrap before the slack tightens. Then I shoot for the surface, haul myself up over *Swell*'s rail, and hop behind the helm to motor her forward again. On my second attempt, I remove one more wrap. As I surface, I see *Octobasse* has moved farther out the pass. I haul myself back on board and drive *Swell* forward a third time.

My nervousness about the upwind passage is making everything more difficult. I cough out a few sobs while slipping the shifter into forward again, then sprint to the bow for another descent. I swim down, but I'm already short of breath. I fight the chain out of the last few snags and twists, slicing my hands on the sharp coral in the process, but one final link has entered a slit in the coral hardly big enough for it to pass through.

My lungs scream for air, so I get ready to lunge for the surface. Just before I push off, though, something comes into view from behind my head. My body freezes as a silhouetted pack of reef sharks swims over, paying me no mind. Once they've passed, I flee to the surface, sucking air heavily and seeing stars. When I've caught my breath, I pull myself aboard and lie flat on the deck to rest. From where my cheek presses against the rough nonskid deck, I catch a glimpse of *Octobasse* coming back into the pass.

"About time," I mumble.

Irritated and prideful, I hype myself up for one last go. I don't need his help. I repeatedly breathe deeply to saturate my lungs. This time I know exactly what I have to do. I motor *Swell* forward a fourth time, pull the shifter back into neutral, and leap over the side in one motion, kicking straight for the bottom. I grab the chain on either side of the small opening and work it back and forth with all my strength into the perfect position so that when the tension catches, it will yank the chain free. I watch the slack steadily disappear, and then, Pop! The stuck link bursts out of the small opening. I kick to the surface once more. By this time, *Octobasse* is circling.

"*¿Que pasa?*" (What happened?) the Spaniard yells over the wind.

"I got it!" I call back—proud, bitter, and light-headed.

I haul the anchor into its cradle and lash it to the nearby cleat. "Hell of a start," I say to myself.

The first challenge is in my wake, but each gust of wind that roars across my ears foretells the coming sea trials. I breathe through the fear and remind myself to move slowly and focus only on the next objective. First, I have to navigate *Swell* out of the tricky pass without hitting the reef. I steer her into the narrow passage and watch the bottom jump to frighteningly shallow depths, but *Swell* slides cleanly over. When the current spits us out into deep water, I turn the bow into the wind, raise the mainsail to the third reef, roll out a little headsail, and fall in behind *Octobasse*.

Our first day out goes better than expected. My growing confidence is reflected by the increasing amount of sail I raise. We tack every five to six hours, which Gaspar explains will keep us centered in relation to our destination in case the wind shifts. But as night falls, the wind and seas increase. *Swell* bucks and bashes, and every fifth wave washes across the foredeck and leaks into the hatches. The cloud cover and new moon make for an extra dark night. I squint into the blackness, hoping to see approaching squalls before they hit us.

Items begin to work themselves loose in the cabin, and it soon looks as if I'm hosting a nautical yard sale. Wood joints and chainplates moan, and as much as I want to deny it—I'm seasick. I lean into the leeward corner of the spray dodger and shut my eyes for a moment. What am I doing out here? I'm scared, I feel like shit, and I'm wrecking my precious floating home. I hate this. But I'm committed now. Gaspar and I speak every few hours over the radio, and I spill my concerns about feeling weak against the heavy gusts and bully seas.

"We're fighting so hard and I feel seasick. And the squalls are on top of me before I can see them."

"*Cálmate*, my little rider. Try to relax. We making good progress. Everything harder in the night. I know is uncomfortable, *pero* try to remember that *Swellito* is made for this!" he encourages.

Relax? Impossible! I stare at the radar through the night to track the incessant squalls. The cuts from the coral on my hands sting as I pull lines and raise and lower sail to accommodate the varying winds. It's already cyclone season, meaning more squalls and atmospheric volatility.

The next morning, I lift my head from the soggy cockpit cushion in a fog of nausea and fatigue, to see a dark cloudline bearing down upon us. I dash to the mast to reef the main and I make it back to the cockpit just before the massive squall slams us with fury. I'm almost in tears as *Swell* heels over on her rail, even with the tiny amount of sail left up. When the second gust hits, Monita, the wind vane, loses control of the steering, so I leap to the wheel. We lean over and increase speed, but to my surprise, we're not overpowered, and *Swell* cuts cleanly through the water.

As the curtain of rain envelops us, a ray of golden morning light sneaks in through a gap in the clouds, illuminating a fluffy white layer of droplets on the sea surface being blown around madly. The rain pelts the ocean with such force that each raindrop shatters into a million scattering fragments. The warm golden sunbeam lights up every flying bead of water—I've never seen anything like it.

I stand breathless at the wheel, hypnotized by this ferociously beautiful face of the sea. As *Swell* plows through the magical scene, my fear transforms into gratitude. I'm soaked to the bone and my thighs burn from leaning into the sharp heel of the boat, but a rush of vitality surges through me. I vow to cease my mental protests and embrace the opportunity to expand my seafaring knowledge. No matter what becomes of the Spaniard and me, I'm pushing past my comfort zone toward new knowledge, and beholding this marvelous expression of nature is already a precious reward.

My outlook may be improved, but the second day and night hold much of the same: frequent sail changes, squall dodging, wetness, and nausea. By the third morning, there's only thirty more miles to go, but each one is a fight. We make headway only by constantly tacking according to minor shifts in the wind direction. By 11 am I have gone only eight miles. Fatigued by the constant maneuvering, I see a break in the squalls and go below to nurse my cuts and have a short rest.

I'm not sure how much time has passed when an abrupt pitch to starboard and a surge of speed awaken me. I launch out of my berth, but it's too late. The sea rises over the starboard rail as the gust pins us over. I release the jib sheet in a panic. The relentless flapping of the sail from the fierce winds tears three long horizontal rips in the headsail before I manage to haul it in.

I stare up at the tails of the shredded sail that wave frantically like little white surrender flags. I want to surrender too. I moan aloud at the thought of spending another soggy, sleepless night at sea. "Bullshit!" I holler at the wind.

But I don't have time for a tantrum. Each second that passes without making headway lessens my chances of arrival before dark. I duck below and wrestle out my spare headsail, then haul it up to the foredeck, install the Solent stay, and clip each of the the sail's hanks onto the cable.

By the time it catches the wind, I've lost an hour of daylight. And when I look at our speed with the little jib set, my heart sinks: three and a half knots. I add the power of the engine and stay at the wheel full-time, steering and tacking strategically with each squall to use the stronger winds to gain speed.

As the sun checks out, we've still got a few miles to go. *Swell* and *Octobasse* criss-cross through yet another menacing squall as we finally approach the pass. Without much light, it will be a nerve-wracking entry through the unfamiliar slit in the reef, but Gaspar has been here before, and I trust he can guide us in. I drop the little jib, then fall in line behind him, but he suddenly makes a drastic course change. I hear his Spanish accent break in over the radio.

"*Swellito*, I have a problem *con mi motor* (with my motor). Go ahead without me. The current *es demasiado fuerte* (is too strong) to enter by sail."

The outgoing tide is pulling water out of the pass at more than four knots, so without auxiliary power from his motor, Gaspar will have to wait for slack tide. That leaves me to traverse the pass and navigate to the closest protected anchorage alone in the coming darkness.

Love Stinks

"Lissy! Li-i-i-i-i-ssy! *¡Llevántate!*" (Get up!) I hear Gaspar's voice outside the next morning and open my eyes, but I don't want to move.

Both boats are safely at anchor behind the submerged spit of reef at the south end of the lagoon. All senses on high, I managed to run the pass, dodge pearl lines and coral heads, and make it to the barely discernable anchorage with only a glow on the western horizon to guide me. The bedraggled *Octobasse* showed up five hours later.

I crawl out of the cabin to see the Spaniard swimming beside *Swell*.

"You are one tough little rider," he says. "You impress me on this passage."

"*Gracias*, but my sail, it's badly ripped."

"You like sewing?" he asks with a wink. I shrug my shoulders.

"*¿Desayuno?*" (Breakfast?) I ask.

The weather gets worse before it gets better; gusts and squalls violently whip through the anchorage. I catch up on sleep, talk long hours with Gaspar, and use a Sharpie to mark the exact points of *Swell*'s leaks so I can try to fix them when the weather clears. One final raging gale blows over the atoll at more than forty knots, and then ... stillness.

I'm happy to see the sun the following morning; it's time to do some exploring. Gaspar and I freedive, wander through the village, share meals, and hang out with Josh and the wonderful crew at the pearl farm. We both try to rekindle the feeling we'd shared in Galápagos, especially with Christmas only a few days away, but my distrust and sensitivity continue to get in the way. I wish he would just apologize and try to see things my way. When he talks about the other girl, it plays on my insecurities, as do his criticisms of my character. Photos of beautiful women from magazines are pasted all over his walls, as well as pictures of him with his old girlfriends. One evening while I knead pizza dough, I ask about them.

"What's with all the photos of women?"

"I like them. *Están hermosas.* (They are beautiful.) Who cares, Lissy?

Is just photos. You are real," he replies. "Don't you think you're beautiful too?" I don't know how to answer. His question shines a light directly on a sore spot.

"Not as beautiful as them," I muster. I hate him for knowing exactly how to expose my weaknesses. I try to remember what the lady in the clouds had told me, but I'm having a hard time.

Little by little, my inner voice becomes clearer about the relationship, and I know that I must move on alone. Gaspar can be a prick, but I'm just as difficult in my own ways. We're both too prideful to own up to our faults, so trying to ameliorate our weaknesses together will never work. I make the decision to sail north to Kiribati alone—1,195 nautical miles from where we are.

I intend to leave as soon as possible. I must repair the sail, fix some leaks, and buy some fruits and veggies. The townspeople promise that a supply boat will soon arrive with a shipment of produce, but day after day, no ship arrives. My longing for vegetables intensifies. I'm also out of cheese, a serious calamity for me! A quarter-size abscess bursts open on my right arm. I wonder if it's from the stress or the lack of fresh food.

I need a place to spread out the sail to make the repair. Josh and my new friends at the pearl farm find me a dark little room to work in. I'm grateful to have it, even though it reeks of cat pee, and I spend three days hand-sewing the tears. Once I'm finished, the only thing I smell is freedom. Passage preparation begins. I've given up on fresh provisions, but then a stout little cargo ship comes charging over the horizon, and I stuff my canvas bags with the expensive, but prized vegetables.

Gaspar is more understanding than I expected about my decision to go on without him, and he agrees when I ask him to find a different location to wait out the rest of cyclone season. On our final morning together, he shows me the best way to pre-rig my storm jib, so that it will be ready to raise quickly, warning me to use it anytime the wind strengthens, since the patched headsail won't handle much excess strain. I thank him for the good times and all that he taught me. After a last breakfast together, I raise anchor and steer *Swell* out of the lagoon. *Octobasse* and the Spaniard morph into a yellowy blob behind my watery-eyed last glances.

New To-Dos and a Silver Lining

As *Swell* pushes out the pass into the open ocean, I feel reborn. I'm going on alone, because my heart knows it's better for me this way, even though it would have been safer to take on this enormous stretch of the remote Pacific in a caravan with the *Octobasse*. I'm abuzz from following my truth—the kind of empowering rush that follows a soul-serving decision, logical or not. If Shannon was right about God favoring the brave, I will have the powers that be on my side. I pull up the sails and settle into a smooth beam reach, then sit back to unwind and digest all that has happened since Gaspar and I reunited. Passages have become a relief in that way—a gap in time and space where I can process what has happened in my prior reality of being "somewhere." In the "nowhereness" of the sea, my mind can turn things over carefully and study them from every side.

Part of me is devastated that it didn't work out with the Spaniard, but I'll cherish the fun memories. He has certainly made me a better sailor, and pointed out a few places where *Swell* could be more functional at sea. In his company, I also found the confidence to freedive to sixty feet and climb fifty-foot coconut trees. My boat might be a little less shiny now, but Gaspar taught me to enjoy myself more and fret less about aesthetics.

But as our love had turned south it brought out the worst parts of me, and Gaspar had been quick to point them out. A great deal of inner work remains if I want to find a lasting love and sailing partner. And if self-love has to come first, I better get to work.

As *Swell* slides smoothly through the perpendicular seas, I pull out my diary and write at the top of a blank page: "Today I'm going to try to make some progress on myself, starting with these lists." First comes, "EVERYTHING I DISLIKE ABOUT MYSELF." I jot down eighteen items as they come to mind, including being greedy, jealous, hypercritical, and too reactive.

Writing them out feels like a first step in changing—like I'm formally acknowledging each issue and making a promise to myself. My next list is titled: "THINGS I WOULD LIKE TO FORGIVE MYSELF FOR." I include everything from being mean to my little sister, to lying to a few of my boyfriends, to lashing out at my parents, and sleeping with a couple guys I didn't really want to.

The final list reads: "WHO I WANT TO BE." It includes being generous, honest with myself and others, confident, more emotionally stable, positive, patient, easygoing, and nonjudgmental.

Everyone sees me as this confident sailor girl, but it's clear that no matter how much praise I receive for captaining *Swell*, no matter how far I sail, or how many magazines feature my photos, none of it adds up to me loving myself. Navigating to self-love is not as straightforward as plugging a waypoint into my GPS. I don't really know where I'm going, nor how to proceed. I just know I have to get there.

In contrast to my tumultuous inner seas, the Pacific is nothing but lovely, shimmering blue in every direction. I have yet to see any traffic besides clouds and birds. Monita and the northeast wind hold *Swell* on a steady beam reach directly toward our island destination. For the first three days we average 140 miles per day. I mark our position on my big paper chart of the Pacific every morning and evening. Slowly but surely, the penciled X's move north. I devour books, write poems, catch up on emails, nurse my abscess, snack on saltines, and gaze out at the ocean for long spells—as if she holds all the answers.

To me, the sea is more she than he, with her frequent mood swings, exquisite curves, ability to make you stare, and obvious sensitivity to the moon. Our relationship goes beyond romance. She's always there—providing play, companionship, perspective, nourishment, and emotional relief with her liquid embrace. There are times I can't understand her, but I can't always understand myself either. It's okay. Loving her gives me so much more than fearing her.

On my fourth day at sea, a front line of dark clouds stalks *Swell*, bringing persistent rain and increased wind. Overnight, I reduce sail to three reefs in the main and a sliver of headsail. The waves have grown taller and closer together on our beam, shoving us around and often crumbling sideways across the deck or into the cockpit. I can either be wet and salty outside or dry but suffocating inside the sealed cabin. I hate admitting it, but I'm seasick again. A persistent feeling of nausea and sleepiness fogs over me with the onset of the rough seas. By now I'm resigned to the fact that sailing is often suffering, but I like that the discomfort and unpredictability put me in touch with something primal, real, human. The less privileged majority of humanity confronts these realities daily. I hate being nauseous, tired, wet, filthy, hungry, and uncertain, but at the same time, I like exploring my thresholds and strengthening mind over matter.

Around 5 pm I come up for air and stare at an approaching squall. I lack the enthusiasm to further reef the sails, thanks to my seasickness. I slip on my raincoat and brace for the onslaught, figuring we'll just ride it out. As the storm closes in, the wind shifts ten degrees, knocking us off course. Monita, after steering reliably for five days, loses control, sending us into sail-flapping irons—the worst possible state for the weakened headsail. I hurry to release the jib sheet and pull the roller furling line with all my might to roll up the sail. When I raise my eyes from the winch on my last heave, I see an enormous new tear parallel to my recent repairs.

My knees go weak at the shock of my new reality. Tears merge with the rain and salt spray already on my face, but it's pointless to cry. I crawl to the bow in my harness and wedge myself into a seated position between the dinghy and the lifelines to figure out how to get the ripped sail down and the storm jib in place before dark. I must do it carefully and with full presence. Failure to execute this properly could prove disastrous.

After talking myself through a strategy, I crawl back to the cockpit, start the engine, turn *Swell* downwind, and engage the autopilot to steer.

Next I raise the storm jib on the Solent stay to further reduce the amount of wind hitting the headsail. It will have to be pulled completely out to its maximum size before I can release the halyard and haul the whole sail down the furler track. Motoring at full speed with the wind, I hope to reduce the apparent wind speed in order to get the sail down without causing more damage.

It works! I tackle the headsail as it lowers smoothly atop the overturned dinghy, squish it together, roll it aft, and shove it down the main hatch. It lands on the cabin floor in a soggy mountain of canvas.

Once the storm jib is set and Monita is steering again, the pride of my accomplishment soon fades into dread. I stare down into the cabin and want to vomit at the thought of repairing the sail while we're bouncing around like this, plus it stinks! The odor of ripe cat urine now joins the already stuffy cabin. I grumble and tramp over my soggy new roommate that evening, while intermittent squalls pound us. The next morning a new groundswell from the north adds to the intense rolling from being undercanvassed in the beam seas. But rolling or not, with five hundred miles to the nearest island in any direction, the sail repair must commence.

First I rummage to find the head of the sail and haul it all the way up into the forepeak. Then I pull the clew and tack back toward the galley. The sail covers the entire cabin. In an awkward position, somewhere between sitting and lying atop it, I stick my last ten inches of Dacron sail tape across the worst section of the damage, and reinforce it with hand stitching, then patch the rest of the rip by stitching sail material to both sides of the tear. *Swell* bobs along. Her unsteady motion combined with the tedious work and stinging odor make me hurry topside for fresh air between rounds of sewing.

I write in the log at 12:45 am that night: "Nearly finished sewing, no thanks to this indecisive weather! That last wicked little squall lasted half an hour! I released the mainsheet all the way out, but nooooooo, that wasn't enough. It made me take off my last pair of dry underwear to go up on deck and reef the main to the third reef in the chilly rain. Wet again. Is it too late to make macaroni and cheese? Of course not."

In the morning, I decide to reinforce the entire length of the fragile luff with double strips of duct tape. Some hand stitching every few feet should help hold the tape in place. I pray the sail will make it through the last 500 miles. I haven't seen another boat on the entire passage.

The wind drops enough, after two and a half full days of sewing, to raise "Ol' Faithful" back into place. She's soon full of wind once more and her new silver lining gives her a look of armored confidence. I find two flying fish on deck; their deaths will not be in vain. After opening the hatches to air out the cabin, I set about cooking my first real meal in days to celebrate the second anniversary of my voyage. While I'm washing potatoes and frying the fish, a wave hits our side and shoots a few gallons of sea perfectly down the middle hatch, drenching my bunk and bedding. Ocean 1. Captain 0.

I sit in the cockpit at sunset with the music turned up, savoring my meal and musing about the past year. A high-pitched squeak interrupts my thoughts. Pilot whales! Their hulking black bodies surface astern, trying to squeeze a bit of a glide out of *Swell*'s small wake. I sit on the aft deck with my dinner and watch them surf, slightly jealous, but elated by their thrilling company. They roll on their sides and look up at me curiously before heading west again. I wish the pod well, my eyes following them toward the unbroken horizon.

The sea air is heavy and rich as I fill my lungs and sway back and forth in my forty-foot rocking chair, looking out at my vast offshore backyard. A fleet of what appears to be a small type of shearwater floats amongst the wind waves just ahead of *Swell*'s trajectory. Upon being displaced, they chatter, and loop through the sky. I apologize for the disruption. Their miniature, feathered bodies seem so fragile to be so far out at sea, but I should know by now that there is more to blue-water survival than size and might.

12,834
Nautical Miles Traveled

Precious Teachers

I-Matangs and an Unwanted Surprise

There it is! A low hunk of land lists just above sea level like an almost-submerged birthday cake with scattered palm-tree candles. After crossing the equator on our seventh night, *Swell* slips into the lee of the southernmost island of the Republic of Kiribati archipelago around 8 am. The sea instantly flattens. I celebrate with a badly needed shower, hauling a bucket of sea over the rail and then dousing myself.

I made it! Without anyone's help! I'm free again and excited for a new start in a new land. The coconut palms wave at me enthusiastically in the breeze. I wave back, euphoric at the tranquility after eight days of constant rolling. As the atoll takes shape, I absorb the earthy smells, new birds, the surface currents and shoreline contours. Details glow when the mind is untainted by familiarity. The atoll's strip of white beach runs into a rocky, fragmented reef that drops quickly into deep water, allowing me to get close enough to observe the short bunches of shrubs, crabs dashing across the sand, and lime-green seaweed covering the shallows. Wait, what are those odd green-colored clouds floating above the island?

That afternoon, I drop anchor near a large pier, and a salty expat character in his fifties races over from another boat.

"Hey. How you doing? I'm Chuck. Welcome! I know how it is to arrive after a long voyage. I brought you dinner. You're a surfer? Get some sleep and come by tomorrow. I can fill you in on the place." He passes me a plate of hot food and smiles as if he has great, wonderful secrets.

"Thank you, Chuck!" I call as he speeds away.

The next day, Chuck gives me the general lay of the land before I head off to find the immigration office. On my way, I run into Chris, a solo sailor from one of the other three boats in the bay. He's headed to the market on his scooter and offers me a ride, so I gladly climb on the back.

With the first moments of landfall heightening my senses, I can hardly believe I'm on a motorbike whizzing down a one-lane road lined with stunning palms and vibrant village life. Colorful laundry hangs outside scattered palm-thatched homes near piles of coconut husks and kids playing. Whiffs of smoke rising from outdoor kitchens tickle my nostrils. The bright, blue sky blurs with greens and yellows from the overhead palm fronds moving by at twenty-five miles per hour. I can't contain my smile. A surge of inspiration tingles through me. I must put my personal to-do lists into action, and work to eliminate behaviors that aren't serving me anymore. Every new arrival is the chance to create myself anew.

The next morning my inner bottom lip is sunburnt and blistered from smiling so much on the motorbike. I can't smile at all now, but even so, I'm warmly welcomed into the small group of foreigners spending the cyclone season in the low-latitude safety of the equatorial island. We are the I-Matangs, a Kiribati word that means "people from another world."

There's Chuck, of course, the sparkling-eyed perma-grom who fled his Southern California Jehovah's Witness upbringing to chase surf all over the Pacific. He's spent most of his adult life in the islands of Kiribati, and recently bought a sailboat to start a local charter business.

Chris, the handsome late-forties Canadian UN consultant and single-hander who took me to the market, was diverted north to avoid a tropical storm on a late-season passage from Tahiti to Samoa aboard his boat, *Elise*. While underway, he collided with something in the night—possibly half-submerged debris, or maybe even a whale. Luckily, a flimsy quarter-inch layer of fiberglass remained intact across the four-foot gouge, and he didn't have to resort to his life raft. He carefully made his way to the closest island, which was here. He's now got to figure out a way to fix the damage with the island's highly limited resources.

Melanie and Cedric are a cheerful cruising couple in their early forties aboard *Island Breeze*, a chubby little steel sloop with rust bleeding from her joints. After determining that time and freedom are the greatest riches, they had given up land life and material possessions to sail away into a life of simplicity. Melanie, a practicing Tibetan Buddhist, was raised in Texas. Cedric is French and is the essence of living in the present.

Henry is a jolly, retired American marine biologist who lives in the village. A former professor at UCSB—before my time there—he instantly takes a fatherly liking to me. He married a lovely local woman, Teretia, and their heart-melting, four-year-old daughter, Reaua, arrived shortly after as a surprise. Even at seventy years old, Henry's got endless energy—surfing, fishing, playing with Reaua, and running a small local restaurant.

It's easy not to think about Gaspar as I'm embraced by this wonderfully diverse and friendly group. We're all moored at an anchorage not far from Henry's place, behind a large pier the Japanese built in a trade for fishing rights to the incredibly rich surrounding seas. I-Kiribati men gather on the pier to fish, or drink, or fish and drink. A supply ship arrives from the capital city of Tarawa, listing heavily with a constant flow of water pumping from its bilges; the people and the pigs on deck look pleased to be getting off.

I spend my first few days in the bay rushing to get the boat cleaned up for the arrival of another filmer. I'm participating in this women's surf movie called *Dear & Yonder*, as part of my ongoing effort to attract sponsors and pay the bills. When I spent a couple of weeks with the directors some months earlier, the waves were uncooperative. So they're sending Dave to capture more surfing footage.

Dave arrives with not only two huge Pelican cases full of camera gear, but also a new headsail for *Swell*! My friend Richard from *Latitude 38* magazine had put the word out in the sailing community that I was in need of a sail, and Holly, who owns a Cal 40 in Long Beach, had found one sitting in her garage and offered it up for free. My sister picked it up in Los Angeles and delivered it to Dave at the airport before he flew out. If it weren't for them, I might have had to ask the locals to teach me how they make their sails from rice sacks!

Dave and I launch into two weeks of capturing life aboard *Swell*, avoiding close-ups of my blistered lip. His hardworking, go-with-the-flow spirit invites good timing and serendipity. We track down a few waves, but he also captures me fishing, diving, fixing the motor, harvesting seaweed, cooking, sailing, climbing coconut trees, playing with dolphins, hanging with local kids, and doing yoga.

A few mornings before Dave's flight will take him home to Hawai'i, a little yellow speck appears on the horizon. My heart drops. No, it can't be.

After finishing breakfast and discussing the day's plan, I pop my head out of the cabin just in time to see *Octobasse* approaching the anchorage.

"Seriously?" I yell to the wind.

"Lissy!" Gaspar calls, once in range. I swim over angrily, and he greets me with, "What happen to your face?"

"What are you doing here? We agreed you would sail somewhere else for cyclone season!?"

"*Oye*. Then you don't want *el dibujo de* (the drawing for) Valentine's Day I make for you?" he asks sarcastically, waving a paper with colorful hearts.

"Uggggggghhhh!" I groan and swim away.

Buddha on the Bus

I can't believe it. I just can't believe it! Why is he here? Gaspar has completely dishonored our agreement and even wants to try our relationship again! Did he hear anything I had said? A rainbow of emotions, running the spectrum from love to hate, resurfaces like a bad case of acid reflux.

When Dave flies home I continue to try to keep my distance, but the Spaniard quickly charms my I-Matang friends, and whether it's a potluck dinner or a sunset beer, he is in attendance. Since I don't want to get back together, he finds a way to antagonize me in front of everyone. I begin to isolate myself in order to avoid him, but it's next to impossible in this tiny, secluded place.

"Hey, Lizzy," I hear Chuck outside *Swell* one morning. I pop out on deck. "The north swell is up; let's go check out some spots on the other side of the bay this afternoon!"

I prep my board and can't wait to go explore the new breaks with Chuck, until he comes back to pick me up and Gaspar's in the boat. As soon as I climb aboard, Gaspar says, "What a shame. No chance of catching a fish now that there's a woman on board."

I'm instantly irritated, but I wait until we're in the lineup to get even. He's a beginner surfer and I snicker as he goes over the falls in his reef booties, then I shred by and spray him on the next wave.

In the days to come I search for something positive in the situation, a way to use some *buena manifestación* magic, but I'm at a total loss. I just want him to disappear. I'm rushing to catch a bus to the store, when Gaspar paddles over on his pink kayak. "Lissy, *por favor*. Can I borrow your bike?"

I begrudgingly give him the key to my bike, which is locked ashore, and head off by dinghy to catch the bus. I climb aboard, find an empty row near the back, and glare bitterly out the window as Gaspar rides by—smiling and carefree—on *my* bike. A minute later, Melanie, my Tibetan Buddhist sailing neighbor, boards the bus and sits down beside me.

"Hi," I say with a sigh. This whole Gaspar situation is getting the best of me today.

"Are you okay?" Melanie asks.

"Yeah, I'm fine," I lie.

"Well if you'd like to talk about something, I'm happy to listen," she says sweetly.

She's a radiant woman with bold red hair, high full cheekbones, and smiling eyes behind thick-rimmed glasses. Although I don't know her very well, she makes me feel safe. But I don't need to bore her with my dramatic love saga.

We both quietly survey the chaos in the bus. Islanders of all ages pile on, and when no seats remain, the aisle fills with standing passengers. Mothers pass their babies to someone with a seat as the bus begins to roll. At the main road, the bus goes right instead of left, away from the store. With the language barrier and mob of passengers, there's nothing to do but go along for the ride. We head into the next town and pick up some elderly women at the health center, then drop them off again a few miles farther down the road. After making a U-turn, we then stop to pick up some coolers from a short, animated man. Finally, we start off in the right direction, but soon turn off for another detour down a rutted dirt road. Ten minutes of bouncing later, we load up a family of seven and their two pigs. Arriving at the store seems less and less probable.

Meanwhile, my insides are eating me up. When the bus takes yet another detour, I gush my story to Melanie. She listens intently without interrupting, and after I've spilled everything, she takes a deep breath.

"That's hard," she says sincerely. And she shares a simple message: "You know, my guru explains that we must turn our poison into medicine. Buddhists believe that difficult people and situations in our lives are our most precious teachers. They give us the greatest opportunities to practice our virtues."

"Really?" I reply with tears in my eyes.

"Yes, by doing this, we can turn our adversities into opportunities to grow. It is the work of a lifetime, but applying this teaching always helps change my perspective."

Her words are a beam of light piercing the darkness in my mind. The negative cloud begins to lift as I finally see a positive use for my irritating and inescapable situation. Melanie shares more about her own journey, expanding on these principles. Between her humble presence and the intriguing information, I don't mind that the bus is stopped again, waiting for more passengers.

I thank her as we finally pull up at the store more than an hour later. I step off the bus feeling like a different person. I have a new mission.

Gaspar has finished his shopping and he greets me with an ice cream in his hand. "What takes you so long?" he asks while licking his melting bar. "*¡Que día hermoso para pasear en bicicleta!*" (What a beautiful day for a bike ride!)

His arrogant glee would have irritated me earlier that morning, but now I am armed with my new secret weapon.

Practice my virtues. Practice my virtues. I repeat in my head. "*Sí*, what a beautiful day!"

He looks at me sideways, scrunching his brow, expecting a frown or a harsh reply. I walk past him, smiling, in my invisible new armor. Either I am going to be miserable for all of cyclone season, wishing he would go away, or accept my unwanted reality and step up to the bat.

I can't believe how quickly the situation turns around. I feel renewed and empowered. I challenge myself to remain calm in the face of what previously provoked anger or sadness. Now that I have a way to use the situation as a personal challenge, I turn it into a game.

I spend more time with Melanie. She teaches me some meditation techniques and gives me a poster that interprets a well-known Buddhist text—*Eight Verses for Training the Mind*—to hang in my cabin. Among the verses are avowals to never think of oneself as better than others; avoid all negative emotions; offer victory to jealous people when they treat you badly; cherish difficult people as precious treasure; and avoid worldly concerns like gain-loss, pleasure-pain, praise-blame, fame-dishonor.

So, difficult people and situations are actually *the path* to personal growth. This notion makes the elusive goal within reach. If challenges are the tool for liberation, then all I have to do is use the experiences that life provides to keep refining myself and becoming more like that enlightened person on my list of WHO I WANT TO BE. *This makes sense!*

Nuclear Bombs and the Reset Button

While enjoying my new perspective and waiting for a shipment of propane to arrive, I put some miles on my bike—riding between the scattered villages named for the original World War II stations. Men wrap their lower half in bright cloth *lavalavas*, and women wear handmade *tibuta* shirts and skirts. The stilted *kiakias* (homes) are built mostly from parts of coconut palms. Communication is a challenge, but the I-Kiribati are both welcoming and creative. The employees at the town hall even make me a makeshift desk one afternoon so I can use their Internet connection.

Although the peoples of Kiribati speak Gilbertese and differ in culture from those I'd encountered in French Polynesia, they share some grievous historical similarities. Alongside colonization (mostly by the British in Kiribati), evangelical missionaries did extensive work in the Pacific Islands starting in the 1800s. Seven churches line the main road within the span of five miles, serving a population of about 2,000. The missionaries forced Western beliefs and customs upon the indigenous populations and forbade singing and dancing for a long, dark period. This interrupted the passage of the native peoples' oral history. Their relationship to nature changed too: Reverent and long-standing resource management practices, like fishing limits, gradually disappeared. They now appear stuck between the two culturally conflicting worlds, and most families and villages are divided by the small discrepancies in the various forms of Christianity.

And although the nuclear testing here was much less extensive than the horrors the French inflicted on the Polynesian islands—exploding around 180 nuclear bombs in the Tuamotu Archipelago between 1966 and 1996—both the United Kingdom and the United States unleashed nuclear weapons on this island, Kiritimati, in the late fifties and early sixties. It was also used as a strategic base for the Allies during World War II.

Nuclear fallout from the uncontained explosions spread across the Pacific, and continues to be linked to health problems. I was spooked by the green clouds that linger daily above the island, thinking they had something to do with radiation residuals, but Henry quickly assured me that they are caused by a reflection off the turquoise color of the atoll's enormous, shallow lagoon. "We can't see the leftover radiation," he said, "but it's here." A UK official is currently here managing ongoing nuclear "cleanup," but after seeing him toss plastic trash right out his car window, I lost faith in his efforts.

One sunny afternoon after filling my water jugs ashore, I trudge back toward *Swell*, using my bike as a dolly to push the ten-gallon load back toward the pier. I hear a cacophony of sounds coming from below a low, broad-leafed tree and swerve right to find a small group of kids crowded into the shade, all heartily jamming on instruments made from trash.

A boy of about ten is drumming on an old, tin powdered-milk container with a broken fork and a small stick. Another plucks a string bass made from a plastic jug, a long stick, and fishing line. A tall skinny girl, maybe eleven, drags a small plastic soda bottle across an old piece of corrugated aluminum roofing. A smaller girl uses an empty beer can filled with pebbles as a shaker. The last member of the ragtag band, a tiny girl who can't be more than four, is sending bold huffs of air through an orange trombone-shaped flower, making it toot wildly. I clap madly when they finish. The beer can is passed to me as they start in again. Like everywhere I've sailed, children don't care about language differences or skin color; they're always excited to make friends.

All of the I-Matangs pitch in to help Chris get through his implausible hull repair. He manages to get the boat hoisted out of the water and delivered to a grove nearby. My contribution is mostly in the realm of moral support and hydration, arriving with some encouraging words in the afternoon, and climbing the surrounding coconut trees for "atoll Gatorade," as he calls it. From up in the tree I watch I-Kiribati men sing merrily as they collect sap from the flowering shoots of coconut palms; they'll ferment it and turn it into toddy, the local alcoholic beverage.

Gaspar continues to make an effort to rekindle our romance, and although it's flattering, I resist. Until one evening after a little party at Henry's bar, I see the silhouette of Gaspar's hair under a tree beside the road. Feeling confident with my new knowledge, I stop and sit down next to him without saying a word. I don't move away when he puts his arm around me. We lean back into the sand together, and stare up at the stars. My new outlook makes me think being closer with him again will be okay. It could be part of practicing my virtues and learning to control my emotions.

"You know, Lissy, maybe I understand you *mejor ahora* (better now). Maybe we can at least be *amiguetes* (friends)," he offers.

"Maybe," I tease, appreciating his effort and openness. We ride double on my bike back toward the anchorage, him pedaling and me on the handlebars.

"Lissy!" I hear outside *Swell* the next morning. "*¿Quieres nadar conmigo?*" (Want to swim with me?) I don my fins and we swim off to explore the nearby coast. Although he's awkward in the surf, he has a dancer's grace underwater—calm and confident as he kicks down to the seafloor to point out an octopus or conch. We marvel at multicolored sponges, gaze at swirling packs of baitfish, and dodge wily barracudas. A fart slips out when I'm fifteen feet down and the bubbles float up toward the surface; Gaspar's mask explodes with laughter. On the next dive down, he reaches out to me and we kick on together, hand in hand.

The morning swim turns into pancakes. Pancakes turn into a siesta. The siesta into sweet love—but this time with the notion that nothing is forever. We don't need to own each other, nor do we owe each other anything besides honesty. With fewer expectations, we start over.

Don't Ponder Others

After an overnight passage, *Swell* and *Octobasse* ghost along, side by side, in light following winds at dawn. The next island, one hundred and fifty miles north, welcomes us around midmorning with a slack tide at the pass, a pod of leaping dolphins, and local men criss-crossing the turquoise waters in one-man sailing canoes, out for their morning catch.

I navigate *Swell* through the pass and into a little bay, then circle around looking for the best place to anchor. The water is a silty turquoise, making it difficult to judge its depth. As I'm preparing to drop the hook, a blue dinghy comes charging over from a sailboat tied to the sunken barge with a slender middle-aged woman driving. She introduces herself as Loreen and before I can get a word in, she launches into informing me that she and her husband have been here for over a year, telling me what the island's like, and advising me on who I should and shouldn't talk to. *Swell* is drifting into shallow waters before she's even taken a breath.

"Thank you, Loreen. Now I need to get anchored," I say.

She races off toward *Octobasse* and I hear her repeat her spiel to Gaspar. I'm relieved when my anchor sets, so I can go rest; my stomach is still in knots from a bout of food poisoning the night before. I wake to the sound of violent splashing an hour later. Baitfish? A shark? I scurry topside to see Loreen in a pink, full-body rashguard and matching swimcap doing a grossly exaggerated butterfly stroke beside my boat. I duck down, pretending not to see her, and quickly retreat to napping.

When I launch the dinghy the following day, Gaspar and I head off to check in with the officials and explore the main village. The island has no running water, no phones, no Internet, no airport, no toilets, no doctors, and certainly no Target or West Marine. There is a modest cement government building, a post office, a basketball court, and some shaded benches and tables belonging to the cruise liner that stops in for a few hours once a month. There's also a dark, musty little "store" with one row of shelves offering sugar, soy sauce, some scary-looking cans of beef, weevil-filled bags of rice and flour, and Australian beer. Supply ships pass even less frequently here. I'm not complaining. This is why I wanted to come here. To simplify. Get away from it all. Work on myself. Find some peace.

I sit outside the immigration office staring down at my scarred and callused feet while Gaspar completes his paperwork. Finally, a towering, barefoot man calls me inside and I hand over my passport and boat documents. He eyes me suspiciously.

"Not same boat? Only you?" he questions, furrowing his tall, tanned brow.

"Yes, sir," I reply respectfully.

He retorts with an exaggerated exhale. I look back at him blankly and shrug my shoulders. His brow relaxes and his full lips part into a giddy, half-moon grin. He prattles off something in Gilbertese to the two men sitting cross-legged on a table behind him. They both turn and stare.

"*Mauri*," I offer. Gilbertese for "hello."

"You the first girl come alone on yacht," he explains. I accept the honor with a nod, pleased to provide them with a new perspective of a woman. Here, a female captain is about as common as a dog flying a plane back home.

After we're done, Gaspar and I wander around the village, admiring the thatch-roofed homes, communal seaweed and fish-drying systems, and handcrafted canoes that line the lagoon. By chance, we meet another Spaniard. He runs the generator that provides electricity to the government buildings and a few homes and is married to a jovial Kiribati woman. They invite us to a barbeque that evening. After our tour, we help them prepare food and sip their homemade coconut toddy. By the time night falls, a dozen local friends have gathered around playing music and chatting merrily.

And then Loreen and her husband appear. Loreen, wearing a shockingly short skirt, snaps at me for not having come to see her yet. I start to explain that we've been taking it easy because of the food poisoning.

Before I can finish my sentence, she cuts me off and starts pummeling me with questions about how I got my boat and where I have sailed. When I begin to answer, she looks away uninterested. I escape as soon as possible, and watch her attach herself to Gaspar, rubbing her body on his and throwing her head back with laughter. For the rest of the evening I hang out with the kids, slinking to the other side of the room every time Loreen nears. Gaspar sees through her quickly, but his social cunning is better than mine. He knows it's better to keep the dangerous ones close.

After we've eaten, Gaspar and I walk out to the village basketball court to shoot some hoops in the moonlight. We start a game of one-on-one, but halfway through, Loreen appears. She runs around the court trying desperately to block the ball, all the while asking us inappropriate questions and insisting we come to her boat for dinner the following night.

Without Melanie's influence, I would have quickly made it clear that I wasn't looking to be friends, maybe even let an elbow fly at her irritating mouth. I refrain, though, wondering how this clearly difficult person fits into my path to enlightenment.

The next evening, I drag my feet getting ready for dinner. I am dreading an evening in a confined space with that woman. Gaspar convinces me to consider it entertainment, and so off we dinghy to the *South Wind*. Loreen comes out of the boat in a shirt that she's wearing as a dress. A necklace of enormous pointy urchin spines hangs around her neck. She cracks a witchy smile through excessive compound, eyeliner, and mascara. Dinner is leftover quiche and octopus salad.

As a conversation about sailing ping-pongs between Gaspar and Richard, Loreen's husband, she somehow always finds something negative to interject about her "evil sister" or the exorbitant slip fees in Hawaii … The Kiribati people are ignorant and have terrible hygiene … The weather here is unbearably hot … It's impossible to get any decent food … Richard is pleasant, though, and even offers me one of the Kiribati fishing hats he was given.

As the evening winds down, questions start to come our way. How long have we been together? Where had we met? What are our plans? I let Gaspar do the talking. He pulls me onto his lap, elaborating about how wonderful I am and how we've found true love and decided to sail on together.

"We both want to have *niños* (kids)," he carries on, exaggerating. Loreen grows visibly displeased. I'm fairly certain she hoped we'd join them in some sort of sexual group escapade.

I begin yawning profusely and thank them for the meal. Clearly disappointed, she offers tea or more wine, but we repeat our thanks and stand up to leave. As we say goodbye she dives toward Gaspar to kiss him on the lips and he turns his head just in time.

After that, I decide to politely steer clear of Loreen. If she's a spiritual teacher, I'm not ready for that class. But the more I avoid her, the more she forces her way near. While Gaspar and I are on a drift dive in the pass, she shows up hunting for octopus. We wave courteously and swim the other way, eventually drifting up onto a strip of sand to bask in the sun. Not more than five minutes pass, and here she comes with an octopus on her spear, beating it madly on the rocks nearby. She continues her daily butterfly swims alongside *Swell*, crashes our potluck dinner with some newly arrived cruisers, and always tries to head off any sort of exploratory mission that Gaspar and I set off on.

Finally, I'm fed up. Maybe I'm taking the wrong approach? Maybe, instead, I should just go talk to her? Gaspar tries to discourage me.

"She's *loca* (crazy), Lissy. *Nada* (nothing) you can do," he says. But Melanie's wisdom has already helped me so much. I'm convinced it can help her, too. So I dinghy over to the *South Wind* one quiet afternoon.

"Hello," I call. "Anyone here?"

"Yes, hello," I hear Loreen say. "Come in."

I step aboard and push through the screen with a sinking feeling. I reach the bottom step and she comes around the corner stark naked. I realize my mistake too late. I want to turn and run. She looks as bitter and shriveled as a rancid Slim Jim. I pity her, but she scares me a little too.

"Hi, Loreen. I just wanted to see if we could talk. But if you're busy, I can come back another time," I stutter, backing out the stairs and staring up at the ceiling.

"No, no. It's fine. Have a seat." She ushers me toward a seat and sits down across from me—still totally nude. Sweat beads form on my forehead and upper lip.

"It's just … well … I feel like there's an odd tension between us. We are both going to be here for a while longer, so I was hoping we could clear it up."

"Oh re-e-e-e-ally, what do you mean?" she says in an exaggerated drawl.

I mention her passive-aggressive comments, the way she acts toward Gaspar, when she pulled up her skirt on the basketball court, and how it feels like she shows up wherever we are.

"What are you talking about? I haven't done anything wrong. How could you accuse me …" Her volume climbs to a yell.

"Sorry, no, I didn't mean that you had done anything wrong, it just seems like … hmmm … well … I don't know … Is there something troubling you?"

She bursts into tears and between sobs launches into stories from her youth, her bare chest heaving. It turns out that she has been depressed for years and was hoping I would be her friend.

"Please," I break in. "Let me just share some wisdom that a friend recently told me."

I explain Melanie's ideas as best I can, and how she might try to apply them. But Loreen continues, as if she didn't hear any of it.

"Everybody goes through hard things," I say. "But we have to find a way to get past them. If we can see our hardships as what got us to where we are now, it's easier to accept them as part of our journey. You're somewhere pretty good now, right? I mean, people only dream about doing this kind of exotic sailing, and Richard is such a nice man."

"How can you tell me to be happy?" she says. "You're completely free and a rich guy gave you a boat. You can do whatever you want."

"Well, that's not exactly the case, Loreen. And I'm not saying I'm good at being happy either. That's probably why I recognize it in you. I just thought I'd share what's helped me recently."

A couple of hours later I leave feeling confused and drained. No matter what ropes I tossed to her to help her climb out of her misery, she found a way to dismiss them. I guess Gaspar was right—not everyone is looking to end his or her suffering. And it's clear that I'm no guru yet. I must focus on myself.

That evening, I pick up the Pema Chödrön book that Melanie had given me. And as if the universe is sending me a message, I open to a list of Buddhist wisdoms; the first one on the page reads: "Don't ponder others."

13,004
Nautical Miles Traveled

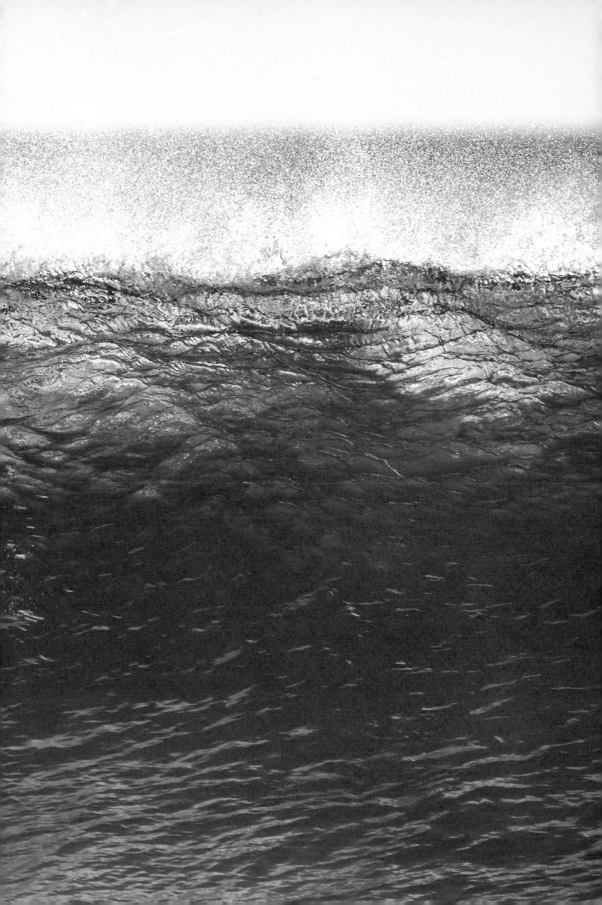

Autonomy
Afar

Pedaling Daydreams

The trade winds whisper across my ears as I push the bike pedals and swerve between mud puddles. Gaspar finally sailed away two weeks ago, so I've had time to explore and meet the locals. I don't know if I'll ever see him again, and I'm thankful we parted on good terms. I held tight to Melanie's wisdom, and stayed patient for the most part but came away convinced, yet again, that I prefer to be solo for now.

The road winds through a thick palm forest to a village farther north. Overhead, the tall trees nod and rustle, as if gossiping while I pass. Where their shadows stop, the equatorial sun is oppressive. I wipe the sweat from my brow, suck at the steamy air, and keep pedaling. When the road cuts closer to the lagoon, hues of milky turquoise stack up behind the arcing trunks of the palms that lean deeply over the lagoon's edge.

I've spent a lot of time marveling at the paradisaical scenery here, which contrasts with the harsh realities of life that I've encountered. Without foreign aid, easily cured illnesses go untreated. Kids suffer with horrible skin rashes and chronic diarrhea from the polluted drinking water. Their arms and legs are covered in scars from bug bites. Education is limited to elementary levels. Stories of birthing and infant deaths and amputations are frequent.

Being a woman here looks tough. Domestic violence and incest are normal. Women are men's possessions, useful for sex, sweeping, weaving, cooking, washing, sewing, hauling water, and raising children. They also collect the seaweed for drying, pandanus leaves for weaving, and coconut husks for cooking. They bathe fully clothed in the brackish groundwater because there is no privacy. Coconut fiber and rags are used for menstruation. Lice infestations are rampant. Items like elastic hair ties, tampons, shampoo and conditioner, washing machines, baby wipes, and strollers don't exist. Women gather in big circles under each village's open-air, tin-roofed meeting house, or *maneaba*, sewing together old tarps or rice bags to make sails, twisting coconut fibers into rope, making hand brooms, or weaving hats, bags, and sleeping mats from dried pandanus leaves.

Frankly, being a man doesn't look much easier. They make constant home repairs, go fishing in the blazing tropical sun, and dry copra—one of the few ways to earn money—by collecting mature brown coconuts in the forest, hauling them home by the dozens, splitting them open (with a hatchet if your family is lucky enough to own one), then laying the open halves out to dry in the sun. After three or four days of praying it doesn't rain, they dislodge the dried meat from the coconut shell and load it into sacks. Captains from the few passing ships then purchase the sacks by weight. With seafood as a dietary staple here, fishing is life. The men go trolling on their sailing canoes with one hand on the rudder, one hand on the line that trims the sail, with the nylon fishing line wrapped around their big toe. The canoes are anything but sturdy or stable, but they wrangle huge tuna and game fish. There are no VHF radios, no Coast Guard, no life rafts to get in if the canoe cracks or they are blown too far offshore.

But despite the perpetual discomfort, back-breaking work, and constant uncertainty, the I-Kiribati generally seem lighthearted. They exude a live-for-the-day feeling that makes life seem less serious. Heck, why make a big deal, when a fever could kill you tomorrow!

No matter how long it takes for the supply boat to show up, the I-Kiribati will endure. They eat everything that moves: fish, sharks, turtles, dogs, seabirds—and they know how to laugh. The best jokers are revered, and rightly so: Laughing makes hunger, pain, monotony, or sadness a little easier to bear.

I grow thirsty, pull off the road, and wander through the coconut grove with my eyes cast skyward. My fingers begin to tingle with excitement when I spot a choice young bunch of green coconuts. The climb takes absolute concentration. I grip around the back of the trunk and walk my bare feet up the front. At the top, I collapse into a tight hug of the trunk, then twist two coconuts from the bunch and drop them gingerly. My knee-length shorts allow me to slide straight down. After opening the coconuts with a knife, I suck down the sweet liquid and hop back on my bike.

Kiakias freckle the roadside as I approach a village. The glare off the roof of the *maneaba* is blinding as I pull over into its shade. Independence Day festivities are only a month away and every islander is busy. The women sit, lean, or lie among heaps of loose plant fibers. They are making elaborate, double-layered grass skirts for dancing. My friend Taurenga sets a plate of dried bananas in front of me as I join the circle.

"*Ko rabwa*" (Thank you), I reply with an appreciative nod. The women tease and bicker over whose son will sail away as my husband. I only understand what Taurenga can translate. Their laughter is delightfully unchecked—flooding the *maneaba* with boisterous cackles and belly laughs. I stand up with one of the finished skirts, tie it around my waist, and try to mimic their dancing. They hoot with hilarity.

"You no I-Matang, you I-Kiribati woman!" one woman cries, rising to her feet to dance too. I feel safe and happy here with them. Their inner beauty and confidence radiate so strongly that missing teeth or body shape or hairs on a chin are meaningless. "Beauty" itself takes a new shape in my mind from being near them. An hour passes and I pull out some DVDs and a mix of medical supplies to leave with them. As far as it feels from modern civilization, the people here love watching movies. Families gather around a communal TV at the *maneaba*. I wave goodbye to everyone and carry on. It's after 3 pm, and the kids will already be in the water.

Near a grassy trail, I stash my bike in the bushes and wander out to the beach. Squinting into the afternoon sun, I'm happy to see small swell-lines marching into the bay.

"Leees! Leees!" little Nato shouts, running toward me with a frantic smile. At least ten little boys leap and frolic in the waves that wedge up at the end of a half-submerged jetty. The boys run out over the cracked cement blocks of the WWII remnant, and hurl themselves off the end into an approaching wave face. They ride flat wooden planks or old bodyboard cadavers all the way to shore. Half of them are naked. The other half wear hand-sewn shorts, often ripped or too big. They trade off with the plywood or foam, because there aren't enough for everyone. I join the loop, run out the jetty wall, and leap into a wedging right, bodysurfing it in. Washing up, they laugh and scream and pat me. I take a few more and then sit with the pack of girls gathered by the bushes to watch. I wish they would come put their feet in the sea, but it's taboo for females here. Even though I despise this disparity, I don't feel it's my place to challenge their customs. In fact, I know there is much to learn from them. My eyes well up when I watch Nato pass his square of plywood off to the youngest boy, who has been waiting patiently for a turn. They hug each other in excitement before the little dude skips wildly out the jetty.

Lucky Hearts

"Is she going to vomit?" asks Teaboka, the youngest of the three fishermen, in Gilbertese. As we motor away from *Swell* in the twelve-foot tinny, Teuta, Nato's father, translates his question with a cracked-tooth grin. It's obvious Teaboka isn't thrilled about adding my company to their weekly Saturday fishing expedition. I'm not so sure either. We're headed offshore in this easily sinkable aluminum boat with an outboard motor that looks like it's past its prime.

"Does he know I sailed here?" I reply.

"It because Kiribati people believe women bring bad luck on the sea," he answers. I roll my eyes. I think it's more likely that women aboard cause competition for the men and thus, complication. Teuta laughs as the boat bounces toward the rocky shore in the drizzling rain. We land on the beach, and Beeto and Teuta search for the roundest coral stones lining the water's edge. I take note of the desired specs and hunt too. Teaboka takes off toward a cluster of bushes, returning with a stack of large round leaves and a hatful of hermit crabs. When our empty rice bag is nearly filled with stones, we pile aboard and head out the pass.

It feels good to be in open waters after almost six weeks at anchor, although I'm not fully awake. The squalls and pummeling rain had kept me up through the night. I'd tossed and turned, regretting my request to go fishing the night before at dinner with Nato's family. The weather is still stormy, and Kiribati fishermen are regularly lost at sea. What if the engine dies?

Beeto yanks a hermit crab out of its shell, then lashes its live, writhing body to the hook using a piece of dried grass, and tosses it over. We troll for flying fish without a bite for nearly an hour; I'm sure I've brought along the woman's curse.

Eventually, we manage to catch three flying fish. Each man hooks one to his trolling rig and we speed out to sea with them in tow. After another hour, the atoll is just a smudge on the gray horizon. The sky spits rain, and the sea churns with the mix of swells from all the squalls. Sitting with my back to the wind, the cold rain steadily pelts my rain jacket, interrupted by warmer dousings of seawater sporadically coming over the rail.

"We outside, but you still in the house!" Beeto says. Everyone bursts out laughing, comparing their useless ripped slickers to my head-to-ankle rain gear.

We soon catch a large wahoo, but the squalls and seas seem to be worsening. A failed engine would send us drifting toward the Gilbert or Marshall Island groups, 2,500 miles downwind. I praise myself for stashing a handheld GPS and VHF radio at the bottom of my dry bag.

As we fight our way back toward the island, we spot a lone man in an outrigger. His slender paddle is not enough against the vicious thirty-knot gusts. Using the thick monofilament tuna handline, we tie the outrigger to the back of the tinny and tow him into the headwinds. Shortly after, we spot another man in need of help, and soon we're plowing slowly landward with both canoes in tow, looking like three body segments of a water-walking insect.

"I drift out to sea once," Teuta recalls. "I float for three days." My eyes widen. He grins and nonchalantly tells the tale of being blown offshore on a similarly windy day, and then being randomly spotted by a passing US Coast Guard plane that dropped him a life raft and gave his coordinates to a nearby ship. *No one could be that lucky twice!*

When I turn to check our progress, I'm relieved to see the island is now at a swimmable distance. We drop off the two fishermen and they each give Teuta a fish in gratitude.

Our next pursuit is tuna. We motor up to where we can see the reef rising from deep water. Teaboka drops an old drum brake for an anchor, and the tinny drifts back over the abysmal depths. Teuta opens a couple of coconuts for drinks and snacks. I pull out a bag of peanuts. The men are cautious at first, but finally dip into the bag and are immediately taken by the foreign delicacy. After puffing a pandanus-leaf cigarette and munching on more peanuts, raw wahoo, and coconut meat, the men's thoughts turn back to fishing.

I look on as they rig their tackle. First, they cut meat from the wahoo into small pieces—if the one knife aboard is being used, the others simply bite chunks right off the fish's body—and pile them in the center of one of the round leaves. Then they skewer a piece of fish with a large hook and put it inside the same leaf, folding the leaf edges up all around it. Next, they select a stone, and wrap the thick monofilament from the hook around both the folded leaf and the stone, turning it into a compact package. With a hoot for luck, it's dropped over the rail and, as it sinks to around 300 feet, the fisherman gives a swift jerk on the line to open the leaf package, sending the stone to the seafloor and scattering the extra bits of bait to serve as chum.

Teaboka hooks the first tuna. The men work together in smooth unison pulling it to the surface, heaving it aboard, and killing the fish with three swift blows from a hand-carved club. I'm impressed at the size of the golden striped beauty, but to them it seems only a trifle.

I'm not quite ready to gnaw on the half-chewed, sun-warmed wahoo, so while the knife is free I slice some bait and try my hand at crafting one of the rock-and-leaf rigs. When I've finished, Beeto lets me use his handline. I wrap my creation in the thick monofilament and drop it over the side with my best version of the fish yelp. Not a minute goes by before it feels like I've snagged a sinking car. The monofilament wheels off the handline in hot stings across my bare hands. Luckily, I manage to keep the spool in the boat.

Once the beast tires a bit, I begin hauling it up from the deep. After ten minutes my arms burn, and I pass it off to Beeto. By the time the fish breaches the surface, all four of us have taken a turn heaving on the line. When the "big mama," as they call it, comes over the rail she's only slightly smaller than I am. Soon all three lines are back at 300 feet.

An hour passes with little action. Teuta hooks something, but it gets off. I curl into a blissful catnap on the bow until Beeto nudges me gently. "Leeess, Leeess. You try again," he says.

I lug myself vertical and take hold of his line. Before I've fully re-gained alertness, there's dead weight on the end of it, and another wild belaying of the monofilament. I pass off the handline and soon another big mama comes over the rail. It makes me sad to see the big beauties killed, but their meat, along with coconuts, is the main food source for the islanders.

When the men seem pleased with our catch, we head back. On the way, Teuta lops off the head of one of the great fish, reaches into its body, and pulls out the round red heart. Beeto and Teaboka grab at the lungs and other organs, gobbling them on the spot, but Teuta passes the heart to me with an air of honor. I've heard the fishermen's legend about eating the heart of the tuna and, after such a day of bonding, I can't let them down. I reach out and take the still warm heart in my hand and sink my teeth into it. The mildly nauseating moment is well worth the grand smiles of my proud new fishing buddies.

The following Saturday, I hear a knock on the hull in the early dawn hours.

"Haloooooo? Leeeeeeesss?" I leap out of bed and come out of the cabin to see Teuta, Beeto, and Teaboka smiling and hanging onto *Swell*'s rail from the tinny.

"They want you to come fish with us again," Teuta announces. "They think you very lucky."

Soul-o Sessions

When the first south swells show up in mid-April, a beautiful wave breaks at the pass. From my cockpit, I sit and watch the mesmerizing lefts spin through, unridden. It's every surfer's dream to have a perfect wave all to him or herself on a tropical island. I wait for the slack tide, then motor over with my board in the dinghy.

I dive down and rig a small mooring in the channel, as the currents are strong and I don't want my dinghy to be swept away. The scene is surreal as I paddle solo up the reef with flawless lines pouring in. I take a moment to observe, and then drop in on a shoulder to warm up. I hoot for myself as I drop in a little deeper each time and carve down the line. It's nice not to be forced to sit deeper than my skills allow or to have to wait for the scrap waves the crowd doesn't want. I can mess around and throw up a radical turn without worrying about wasting the wave if I fall.

Between waves, I think about how crazy it is that I actually made it into this moment. Peppered among the exhausting nights, lifting and hauling, ripped sails, clogged carburetors, perennial scrubbing of algae, persistent nausea, and unrelenting dampness are the moments like this for which my soul has yearned. As difficult as this voyage can be, there is something valuable in the process. Appreciation deepens for a prize earned through hardship. And every action along the way becomes sacred.

In the coming weeks, I grow more and more enamored with the solo sessions. But the risk of injury looms large in my mind. The consequences here are unthinkable. It's not safe to push my limits alone with zero access to medical care and no one around. So I take my time choosing waves. No other surfers are coming out, and no one is watching. I don't have to charge or "shred." I force less and just enjoy myself—changing up my stance, throwing my arms and smiling at the sky, or squatting low and leaning back into the face for another view. With ego removed, surfing is an entirely different experience.

I love to turn around and watch the waves breaking behind me. The pitch and curves of the lips are hypnotizing. Upon collision with the sea below, the wave explodes into bubbling foam. The turquoise sea rushes and blurs under my feet as I speed backward along the wave faces.

During these sessions, I surf for the feeling of freedom and unity, for the way the soft salt water caresses my skin and the sun warms my back, and to gaze at the ever-evolving clouds and majestic arcs of the wings of seabirds circling and diving around me. Each push of wave energy is a gift from the sea, from the wind, from the sun, from the whole miracle of our spinning planet and mysterious universe. Riding these waves feels more like worship than sport.

I feel both gratitude and guilt, watching men sail back and forth in their canoes, fishing for dinner for their families. Play seems so luxurious in a land where people spend all day just trying to eat. As the sun sinks, the sea blushes pink. Flying fish soar through the lineup, with tunas as big as golden retrievers bursting from the sea behind them in astounding, open-mouthed leaps. A tuna sandwich will never be the same.

Evasive Stillness

Chuck shows up for a week with some professional surfers on his charter boat, and it's fun to have some surfing company for a change. But between surfs, I have few excuses not to spend more time going within. There is so much I still need to work on. About twelve seconds after I sit down to try Melanie's meditation techniques, I'm restless, terribly uncomfortable, and my mind is clouded with ten pressing things I need to do.

I decide to read about meditation instead of actually sitting. I have a variety of books aboard that describe it, making it sound fairly simple, but when I attempt to sit still again, the same feelings of dread and discomfort quickly become intolerable. "Clear your mind," one book says. "Stop thinking." But how? My mind is a conveyor belt of endless thoughts with no off button. But even within the laughably short times I try, I am able to grasp the idea that my thoughts are not me. There is some great and powerful stillness below them.

I want freedom from the tyranny of my ceaseless mind and wild emotions. It's a matter of doing the work, persevering. I see that becoming a better me is going to take discipline. One book describes a condition of ataraxia: a lucid state of robust tranquility characterized by ongoing freedom from stress and worry. *I want that!*

For now, stillness of mind comes to me more easily through movement: surfing, working, and yoga. Although I've taken yoga classes sporadically over the years, I've never been disciplined about keeping a regular practice. I did it more to stretch than find inner calm. But now I have the time, and it's so much less painful than meditation.

A few afternoons a week, I dinghy over and tie off to the far side of the sunken barge, away from Loreen's usual haunts. An encounter with her would eliminate any hope for finding mental tranquility. I climb up on the old wheelhouse and roll out my mat across the rusted iron roof. Stepping onto the mat is like having a meeting with my higher self, the person I want to be. I stand in mountain pose and start breathing and moving in sync.

As April moves into May, I find rhythm to my yoga sessions, seeking the balance between strain and poise, grace and strength, effort and flow, too much and too little. Balancing breath and movement, I feel profound presence and connection with my body, the planet, and beyond. With the trades at my back and the sunset a dynamic tableau to the west, I am grateful to be a part, however insignificant, of all of this. I wish for more clarity, more awakening, a better grasp of universal truths. As the horizon glows orange behind the thick row of silhouetted palms, I am dedicated to moving closer to the untouchable, the Light, and a better me.

Farewell Frenzy

Cyclone season is well over. It's time to start prepping *Swell* for the voyage back to French Polynesia. But the longer I stay somewhere, the longer it takes to leave—more algae to scrub, more things to put away, and more goodbyes. And I must deal with my stowaways: A hardy family of cockroaches joined me at the marina in Tahiti and has taken up residence aboard. I've poured boric acid into nooks and corners and sealed off any accessible food sources, but they have only strengthened in numbers. As the battle to reclaim *Swell* persists, I've learned that Tahitian cockroaches are as strong and tough as Tahitian men, although the sight of their bronze bodies weakens my knees for entirely different reasons.

Luckily, some new cruisers in the bay have a trick. Larry and Trinda roll boric acid and evaporated milk together into irresistible cockroach candy that they distribute throughout their boat. I have both ingredients, so I pull everything out of the storage lockers, mix up the deadly treats, and toss them into *Swell*'s deepest corners, hoping to end the roaches' sailing vacation.

I then stow everything back in its place to some Jimmy Buffett tunes, then look over the engine. The alternator belt needs changing, as do the fuel filters. Transmission, coolant, and V-drive fluids need topping off. I solder an unruly starter wire. The next day I patch a few small rips in the mainsail and reverse the lines on the wind vane so Monita has fresh friction points. The headstay seems oddly loose, so I tighten it as much as possible at the fitting on the bottom. After adding extra pages into my logbook binder, I assess what's left of my food stores—rice, flour, a pumpkin, and some picked-through cans of food remain. My stores of propane and gasoline for the dinghy are nearly gone too. Everything must be rationed.

The next morning, I begin mowing the underwater lawn: Donning mask and fins, and armed with a scraper, I leap over the rail to clean *Swell*'s hull and anchor chain. As I finish the port side of the hull, friends Chris, Henry, and Reaua from the first island appear aboard *Elise*. Now it's even harder to concentrate on leaving.

I start goodbyes to local friends and, knowing I'll be where I can buy things soon, assemble a pile of items to give away. The isolation of this remote region intensifies my fears of scarcity, but I fight the instinct to cling to my possessions—especially because Gaspar frequently told me I was greedy. I pass on flashlights, dive gear, clothing, cushions, sunglasses, my retired headsail (which can be turned into smaller sails for the local canoes), knives, crayons, paper and pens for kids, two sets of foul-weather gear to Teuta, spare line, glues and resin, shoes and sandals, and a spare camera. I give my bike to a local family and they load me up with hand-woven pandanus hats and mats in gratitude. I know I must live up to the principles of generosity through which Barry, my father, and so many others have made living this dream possible. Contrary to logic, the giving actually makes me feel richer.

It takes another two weeks before I am finally ready to go. On one last drift dive at the pass I say goodbye to my undersea friends and urge the octopi to hide themselves well, as it's nearly Loreen's hunting hour. I have one last item to give away—the pumpkin. It's a precious commodity here; and with my seasickness I'm certain I won't cook it underway. I decide to give it to Loreen, despite not wanting to see her again.

"Every great teacher deserves a pumpkin," I joke with Chris. He thinks I've gone nuts.

I take a deep breath and head over to her boat. She is outside hanging laundry.

"Hi, Loreen. I'm leaving tomorrow. I know you'll be here for a while longer, so I wanted to give you guys this pumpkin and say goodbye." She accepts it gratefully, voice cracking.

And then she continues, "You're leaving? But first, there's something important Richard needs to tell you. It's something Gaspar said before he left, but I can't tell you. Only Richard can."

What is she talking about? She calls to Richard, but he's busy drilling a piece of teak in the wheelhouse of the barge and can't hear her. I'm itching to get going. "Why don't you just tell me, Loreen?"

"Well, it's just that … remember the day that the cruise ship came in?"

"Yes," I reply. Her face lights up.

"Well, we crossed Gaspar on the dock that day and he told us that he was 'going to look for hot chicks.'" Her face becomes eerily pleased.

I remember the day she is talking about. Gaspar had come back smirking, saying that he'd given Loreen something to gossip about.

My thoughts race. That is the important thing she wanted to tell me? She's still desperately looking for a way to hurt me!? As far as she knows, Gaspar and I are still a couple. I fall silent and my hands begin to sweat. She reaches over and rubs my back as if trying to console me.

A surge of anger crawls up my spine. My vision blurs. I want to knock her bitchy, wrinkled ass right into the water. I want to scream and tell her she's pathetic, conniving, and cheap, and that she is pushing the local octopus population to extinction. A few years prior I would have, but I use every bit of self-control I can muster—not because I want to be a good person, but because I know she's looking for drama. She is hoping to upset me. I take a deep breath and slip away from her bony fingers. Melanie's words echo through my mind, "Turn your poison into medicine." I turn to face her.

"Oh Loreen, that's really no big deal. Please don't worry about it anymore," I say. "Enjoy the pumpkin and good luck with yourself."

As I push off in the dinghy, I see Richard is waving. "Bye, Richard!" I call. "Thanks again for the hat!"

The Paddler's Song

Chris and I sail out of the pass simultaneously. He is headed southwest for Samoa, and my course for French Polynesia is almost directly south. We plan to talk on the SSB radio every day at noon to check in and exchange positions. A few hours later *Elise*'s sail is only a fleck of white on the western horizon. The weather is glorious. I sigh with relief. After the flurry of departure and my exasperating "teachers," this caliber of solitude and tranquility seems more precious than ever. The wind presses into *Swell*'s sails like a kiss from a long-lost lover, gently persuading us south.

I'm not breaking any speed records, but four to five knots feels just right. The sea and sky demand so little, and I'm grateful to catch up on some rest. I take advantage of the calm seas to splice a new snubber for the bow anchor and replace the power wire to the refrigerator. It's enough work to merit a dance party once the tools are put away. I turn up the stereo and head out into the cockpit to dance in my underwear. Arms fly and hips bop in wild, unchecked movements. I don't feel alone. The sea's surface sways, the sunlight's glitter leaps, and the surrounding clouds rise up in a standing ovation. I dance on, shaking my head to feel the wind in my hair.

That evening, as the heat of the day subsides, I lie on a cockpit cushion and reflect on what became of the cyclone season. It wasn't exactly the peaceful time I had envisioned, but I certainly feel that I made progress on my personal lists and learned a great deal, especially from the rugged and genuine people of Kiribati. The experience with them has left me pondering my idealized perception of individuality and autonomy.

It takes great strength of both body and mind to survive on those islands. No one gets by without the help of family and community. The collective good naturally takes priority over personal desires. Unlike in the developed world, they have to figure out how to get along, help each other, and forgive.

I recall the rhythmic melody of a paddler's song as he stroked his outrigger past *Swell* one afternoon, straight into three-foot wind chop. I heard the tenacious spirit of human survival in his steady, recurring refrain. He stroked on, never hesitating as waves splashed him and the wind and sea pressed against his canoe. I wrote to Barry about him: "With the shift from subsistence living to a cash economy well underway, will the paddler's grandchildren know that song? Will the skills and wit of a people tuned-in so intimately to their surroundings wane when modernity arrives? What will the I-Kiribati eat when the foreign fleets overfish these waters—imported Cheetos and hot dogs? And, most sobering of all, what if they are displaced altogether due to climate change and rising sea levels?"

The questions riddled me while I watched a cargo ship deliver two hundred orders of personal DVD players. Lying awake some nights, I bemoaned the loss of the old ways, then rolled over in my comfy bunk and thought, *Why shouldn't these people enjoy the comforts and thrills of modern life?* While I would never wish to deny anyone access to modern healthcare, comforts, education, and choices, I cringe to think of the cultural and environmental degradation that come hand in hand with westernization.

Barry agreed that the situation is distressing, and went on to reply, "I find it incredible that humankind has become globalized to this degree, and even more so, powerful enough to fiddle with the Earth's climate systems! Indigenous wisdom on living in harmony with the Earth will become more and more imperative as humanity seeks to restore the planet's climate balance. No place will go unaffected if the temperatures rise as predicted. What a terrible irony that peoples of the Pacific, who contribute so insignificantly to this problem, may be some of the worst afflicted." For more than twenty years Barry worked on his PhD thesis about the risks and hazards of oil production and transportation in the Santa Barbara

Channel. He was always pondering nondestructive alternatives to fossil fuels that could meet society's energy needs.

I sigh as my own "energy needs" pull me from my deep reflection. I go below to fish around for something to eat.

For Heaven's Sake

Our easy gliding ends abruptly the fourth morning out. I lift my head at dawn to see the sky bruised and swollen with bulbous clouds. I stay horizontal and pick up reading *Moby-Dick* where I left off yesterday, but not long after, *Swell* is swallowed into dreary grays. Indecisive winds swirl around us like mini tornados. I can almost feel the atmosphere lifting as we enter the doldrums again, properly called the Intertropical Convergence Zone (ITCZ). The mood turns downright gloomy, as if the air is sad to be going up instead of continuing its long oversea journey.

Sails in, sails out, up, down, rain, no rain, motor on, motor off, no wind, wind. "Okay, I get it, the joyride has officially ended," I call out to the peaks of the confused waves.

They continue to scurry in every direction as if there's been a bomb scare. *Swell* and I waltz onward with the help of the engine until the ITCZ finally spits us out on the other side around 10:30 pm into fifteen knots of east-southeast winds and clear skies.

I set the sails, plot our position, write in the logbook, and wipe down the cockpit cushion. I lie back, grateful to see the spacious galaxy above. I pull my headphones over my ears and find the Starry Night playlist on my iPod. Beethoven's *Moonlight Sonata* is still my favorite. I relax and dissolve into the exquisite notes and the multitude of twinkling lights from billions of light-years away. The same questions that the night sky usually evokes come to mind, but instead of feeling small and alone as I once did when I looked up, I feel expansive, powerful, and happy to be a part of it all. A warm tear rolls down my cheek. A surge of gratitude pulses through me for whatever force is at work helping me along this marvelous journey.

Without thinking, I find that my hand reaches down and I begin to touch myself—slowly at first, with my eyes to the sky. No sense of guilt or secrecy surfaces in me as it sometimes does. The act feels reverent and sacred, as if I'm honoring the heavens, and making love to the entire universe. The cool wind caresses my bare skin and twirls my hair. Beethoven's mystical notes transport me. *I'm in love with this beautiful mystery.*

And then I am suddenly flying through the stars, planets, and seas all at once—boundless, ecstatic, satiated, as the line temporarily blurs between I and That. An evening of divine pleasure fit for a goddess. No man necessary.

The Belly of Hell

Swell lurches with a gust. I leap from my bunk for the third time that night to clip my safety harness to the jackline and crawl forward to pull down more sail. As I emerge from the shelter of the spray dodger, blasts of wind and sea strip me of exhaustion. My hands grip and release in rote, rhythmic placements, while my bare toes spread and press into the worn, wet grip of the deck. I wedge myself into my usual sail reefing position below the boom. Tangled clumps of hair batter my face and block my already shadowy view of the line that needs tightening. It doesn't matter; I don't really need to see it. *Swell*'s aluminum and nylon limbs are now extensions of my own. I close my eyes and lean into each crank of the winch.

Sail shortened, *Swell*'s wild gallop eases into a smoother lope. I scan the horizon for lights, and make sure nothing on the deck has come loose. After a reverent gaze to my constellation friends, I duck back behind the dodger, dry myself off with a salty T-shirt, then go below to plot our position on the chart. Leaning back into the damp pile of sheets and pillows that line my sea berth, I look up at my family smiling down at me from the pictures on the ceiling.

I sink into light sleep until I hear, *Crack!*

I scramble back on deck in a fluster. Among the silhouettes of dangling lines and blocks, I see that the pin on the boom vang has severed, freeing the mainsail to smack and swing with the bucking motion of the swells. I make a provisional fix, then try to rest a bit more.

At dawn, the wind rips out of the east through piercingly clear skies. There is a manic, electric feeling in the air.

I take a morning drenching from the seas coming over the deck as I work through a better fix for the vang. We bash through the growing seas that day, and I'm frustrated as our heading slips west of our course with the shortened sails and westbound push of the seas.

"*Elise*, *Elise*, this is *Swell*, do you copy?" I hail Chris over the radio for our noon discourse.

"Hey *Swell*, I'm here. How you doing, girl?"

"I'm okay, but the wind came up hard overnight. We're hanging on, about five to ten degrees off course."

"Yeah, I downloaded the weather this morning and saw a strong pressure gradient forming over you."

"Hmmm … It's strong all right. How are you? What's your position?"

"I'm about two days out of Samoa and the wind has finally turned in my favor. Hang in there, Captain, I'll be keeping an eye on that system for you."

After we sign off, I download the weather files and to my horror, I see a massive low-pressure system building to the south of me. It looks like it will blow hard from the direction I'm trying to go over the next few days.

The skies remain eerily clear until dusk. The winds then falter, and a thick forest of towering thunderheads sprout up all around us. With no moon, I can only make out varying shades of blackness. I don my headband to keep the hair out of my eyes and prepare for what appears to be a jungle of thunderstorms.

I skirt just ahead of the first squall, then sit back under the starboard side of the dodger for a moment.

"Wait, what's that?" I say aloud.

The blackness is deepening off our port quarter. A mutant thunderhead erupts skyward—bloating and mushrooming and coming right toward us. I alter course to starboard and run up on deck to take more sail down. All at once the air becomes oddly still and hot. There is little chance of escape, but I turn on the engine and push the throttle forward, revving into high rpms in hopes of outrunning it. A bolt of lightning angrily stabs into the sea behind us, momentarily illuminating the face of the massive cloud beast.

I'm short of breath and wide-eyed as it barrels toward us. There's nothing more I can do. The sails flog and *Swell* bobs in the slack air. I clutch the mainsheet nervously. I want to close my eyes and disappear. I want to be anywhere but here. I mumble unintelligible prayers, suddenly pious and sorry for every bad thing I've ever done. But this only causes more dread as it brings to mind the preacher from *Moby-Dick* as he recounted the biblical story of Jonah: "... black sky and raging sea ... Terrors upon terrors run shouting through his soul ... Woe to him who seeks to pour oil on the waters when God has brewed them into a gale!"

In another instant the monster blindsides us with the swiftest, fiercest paw of wind I have ever felt. The boom smacks tight against its tackle and *Swell* is instantly pushed onto her starboard side. I frantically release the mainsheet, but soon the gust relinquishes us. A terrifying bolt of lightning shreds through the darkness much too close, accompanied by a booming, almighty crack of thunder. My nerves snap.

"Da-a-a-a-addy!" I cry out desperately into the night. He can't hear me. No one hears me. I am horribly and painfully alone.

Crack! The next bolt rips right over us, and again the deafening sound of the sky tearing open.

This is it, I think. *We're going to be struck.* My body trembles with fright and adrenaline as I brace for the hit. I taste blood. I sit up and try to gather myself. I must have bitten my tongue when the first violent gust hit us.

Rain begins to fall. It's more like a sky of water. It drowns out the sound of the rumbling engine. I remain perched on the wooden seat in the companionway, doing my best not to touch anything metal. The seconds seem like hours as I wonder about my fate, until finally the bolts of lightning move westward, raging on across the sea.

I hang my head and cry, burying my face in my clammy hands. I cry for my fear, my powerlessness, my aloneness, and the fact that the night has only just begun. *Dear God, if you can hear me, please transport me under the crisp, dry covers of a big queen-sized bed in a quiet room overlooking a flowery meadow.* A drop of water lands on the back of my neck and creeps down my spine, reminding me how far I am from that vision.

I squint out over the bow, tears still flowing down my cheeks. A small patch of stars ahead hints of hope, but lightning flashes a few miles off and dread returns in my chest.

The thunderheads keep me busy all night, but I manage to avoid being struck. At 5:30 am the eastern horizon is a chalky gray. I'm still perched on the companionway seat, exhaustion weighing on me between lingering pulses of adrenaline. Like fleeing vampires, the squalls vanish with the arrival of daylight. I retire from battle into my sea berth, desperate for rest.

Barely half an hour passes before strengthening winds yank me from my prone position to reduce sail again. I try to rest through the day, but the worsening conditions keep me busy. By evening the seas have doubled; we're in an all-out gale. There's no way to maintain our course as the wind has swung farther south. I try three reefs in the main plus the storm jib, hoping to point higher into the wind, but *Swell*'s collisions with the steep seas feel awfully violent. Thankfully, Monita maintains the steering, but I still don't get any sleep again that night—bracing, heaving, and wincing. Waves swat us here and there; *Swell* shudders and flexes. By 4 am it's too much. I crawl out on deck in the deafening winds and douse the main entirely, but without the drive a bit of mainsail provides, we're blown father and farther west. Each mile lost to leeward will have to be sailed double, to windward, later.

Heave-to, I think, as the storm tactic comes to mind. I remember my Santa Barbara rigger, Marty, walking me through the procedure. *Turn the wheel to windward, making the bow come across the wind as if you're going to tack, but instead of releasing the sheet, backwind the jib and leave it where it is. Then turn the wheel hard back over to leeward. The back-winded jib pushes the bow one way, as the rudder steers the other.* I give it a try. To my disbelief, our hectic advance turns into a calm and steady lifting and falling over the chaotic seas. *Swell*'s western drift decreases enormously. I collapse into my berth at dawn and manage to sleep for a few precious hours.

"*Swell, Swell ... Elise* here. You there, Lizzy?" I crawl out of my bunk at noon when I hear Chris's faint call over the radio.

"I'm ... here," I muster.

"I made it to Samoa this morning!" he says.

"Great, Chris ... so ... glad ... you made it ... safely." My words come out slow and fragmented. It feels like my brain and my tongue have become disconnected from nearly three days without sleep. Bit by bit I explain my situation. I tell him that my radio modem got wet, so I can't receive weather info or emails. He takes down my position and says he'll look at the weather forecast and call back in a couple of hours.

Later, he reports back: "Okay, Liz, you're in the middle of a huge, nasty front. But sometime tonight the wind should turn east and decrease slightly. When it does, you will have about eighteen hours to get as far southeast as you can. After that, it will shift back to the southeast and get very strong again. You'll have to go hard during that window of time if you want to make French Polynesia."

My heart sinks. I feel like giving up.

"You can do this, okay? I'm going to talk you through it," he encourages.

After signing off, I clean up the explosion in the cabin and heat some soup, eating for the first time in thirty hours. After surveying the still-raging gale outside, I lie back down and try for a bit more rest, praising the heave-to storm tactic that has allowed for this miraculous "time-out." I sleep hard for a couple more hours, then awaken suddenly, scrambling up on deck to check the wind direction.

Sure enough, it has calmed a bit and already shifted slightly to the east. I rush to reset the sails and get back on course. The big, sloppy leftover seas slow our progress, but we're able to hold almost a direct course for the westernmost islands in French Polynesia through the night. Chris feeds me weather information and confidence twice the next day. On the following morning, June 8, 2008, I relay him my position.

"You're almost there, Liz! Keep going! It looks like Bora Bora is going to be your best bet for landfall. If you make it, I'm going to put you up in a hotel when you get there," he says. The thought of this much-too-generous offer helps me escape from the hellish world I am currently trapped in.

"Really?" I ask.

"Really."

I drive *Swell* hard through that day with the remaining east winds, but the gale has blown me over sixty miles west. Chris is clear that I must try to make landfall by the following day; the gale to follow looks fierce.

"I hate you, ocean. I hate you, lightning. I hate being wet. I hate sailing!" I scream.

I don't shut my eyes once that night. Adrenaline has completely taken over. My body aches, the sores on my rear from the constant wetness have chafed open, and my hands are worn raw from the constant sail adjustments, but in spite of the pain, I tend religiously to *Swell*'s trim to keep our speed up and our bearing as direct as possible. *Don't give up the ship*, I hear Barry's voice in my mind. If I can stay focused, landfall might be possible by dark the following day.

The next morning I'm fairly optimistic, with thirty-nine and a half miles left to go at daybreak. I tack between a few squalls, and gain a fair bit of headway by 8 am. A small island appears from behind a squall not far to my east, but the guidebooks proclaim its south-facing pass is "dangerous and not to be attempted in heavy seas." Bora Bora is next—now just thirty-seven miles away. I must make it before dark!

I try different sail layouts to see what will allow me to sail closest to the wind, since it's blowing hard directly from my destination. The storm jib and triple-reefed main are not enough: I'm making less than three knots, at about thirty-five degrees off the wind. I try the headsail reefed down with similar results. I tack back and forth all morning, sometimes feeling like I'm going backwards. I turn on the engine and add the force of the motor but gain less than a knot and a few measly degrees. My spirits drop.

"Come on, are you serious? Throw me a friggin' bone!" I call to the sea. But there will be no bones, no breaks, no special exceptions. It's going to be a jaw-clenched scrap for those last thirty-some miles.

Two hours later a teeny speck of the island appears on the horizon ahead. Something in me grows fierce. I will do anything not to spend another night on this godforsaken ocean. Chris has already booked my hotel room, and the image of dry sheets, a hot shower, and fresh food provides intense motivation. I roll out the entire headsail and crank it as flat as my strength will allow. With a slight shift of the wind in our favor, our course is now just ten to fifteen degrees off the island! *Swell* is overpowered, but it's the only way I can make significant headway. The starboard rail is fully buried in the churning blue waters, but we plow upwind at over six knots.

The strongest gusts drive us on our side, then we round up a bit, and slam ferociously. The rig shudders so violently that I feel its vibration throughout my body. I grit my teeth at the helm and push on, praying nothing breaks. I notice the aluminum sleeve of the furler is bowing and flexing more than usual, though. The thru-hull on the galley sink is stuck open too, so on port tacks, water gushes up through its drain and cascades across the floor. The bilge pump runs to keep up with its constant flow.

By 2:30 pm I have fifteen miles to go. More than once I give up and reef the headsail in, but then my stubbornness takes over and I roll it back out. I'm too close not to make it. I drive *Swell* like a senseless madwoman—steering by hand, thighs tensed and braced, standing at the helm for hours and hours, indifferent to the blasts of sea, wind, and sun. I haven't eaten since the soup. The door to the forward cabin is jammed shut due to the wet, swollen wood, so I haven't been able to get a change of clothes. They are probably all wet anyway. All I can think is get there, get there, GET THERE!

The island's size increases painfully slowly. I do my best to ignore the swaying rig. About seven miles off, the seas finally begin to decrease. But it's after 6 pm; there is no way I'll make it into the lagoon before dark. My little chartplotter doesn't have enough detail to get me safely through the pass. I speak with Chris at 6:30 pm, forlorn and defeated.

"I didn't make it," I report. "I tried my hardest, but I just couldn't make it. I'm seven miles off and the wind is still howling on the nose."

"I know that pass well," he replies. "I'll give you the waypoints to get you in. It's wide and deep and there aren't too many obstacles once you're through it."

I cringe at the thought of a dicey entry in the dark, but I plug the points into my little GPS anyway. Around 9 pm, I hover near the pass, trying to decide what to do. Go in and risk hitting the reef in the dark? Or stay out and spend another miserable night on the sea? The silhouette of the island's towering crater mountain looms above. Beckoning lights shimmer around its base. But my vision blurs with fatigue and I decide I am safer staying outside for one more night.

While straightening up the cockpit, I hear some cruisers chatting on the VHF radio and decide to interrupt.

"Hello. This is the sailing vessel *Swell*. I'm approaching the Bora Bora pass and want to come through in the dark. Can anyone give me suggestions on the easiest place to anchor for the night once I'm inside?" A man's voice comes back.

"Is this Liz on *Swell*?"

"Yes, it is," I reply, taken aback.

"This is Steve on *Ironie*. We met in Panamá, remember?"

"Hi, Steve! Do you know if the lights on the channel markers are working? I've been at sea fifteen days, the last few very rough, I'm exhausted and just need to get my anchor down somewhere safe tonight."

"Okay. Yes, all the lights are functioning. When you pass the final green marker, turn to about eighty degrees and you will see a big fishing boat all lit up. Head toward that boat for about a mile. It's deep water. The anchorage is just before it to the east. There is an open mooring available next to us. Call when you get closer and we'll flash a spotlight to guide you in," he says.

"Thank you! I will see you soon, so long as I stay off the reef."

A squall rips over me a mile from the pass. I impatiently wait for it to clear, and then drop the remaining sails and motor for the green and red lights marking the entrance. Focusing hard in my shattered state, I maneuver through the three sets of lights with a last adrenaline surge. Once inside, the lagoon opens up and welcomes me into its calm embrace. I spot the fishing boat to the south. On my approach, Steve and his crew flash a spotlight and come over to help me tie up. A minute later *Swell* and I are secured to a blessed little orange buoy. I hug and thank them. My oceanic nightmare is over!

The Sea Waif and the Honeymooners

Utterly exhausted, I hardly sleep that night, maybe from all the leftover adrenaline. I get up early and launch into a cleaning frenzy—thrilled, but still in disbelief that I'm actually here. After prying open the jammed forward cabin door, I haul soggy cushions and piles of stinky, soaking-wet laundry up into the sun.

When I hear Chris's voice, I race to the radio. He's relieved to learn that I made it, and relays directions to the hotel. I drop off the mooring and motor around to the north side of the lagoon. The wind is howling, but *Swell* and I are no longer at its mercy. Tourists gawk from their hotel water shuttles, probably because we look like a float in a parade with the colorful bedding and wet clothes flapping off the lifelines and boom. I simultaneously rejoice and cringe at being back in the more developed world.

Five miles later, I spot a hotel with thatched bungalows stretching out over the turquoise lagoon, like Chris described. I drop the anchor, toss the dinghy over the side, shove my most presentable clothing into a backpack, and row toward the resort. Failing to locate an entrance, I find myself in a maze of pilings underneath the private bungalows and pop out into the roped-off "Swimming Only" area. My entrance is neither discreet nor glamorous, but check-in time has passed and damn if I'll waste even a moment of the luxury to come!

I beach the dinghy on a perfectly raked white-sand beach between lounge chairs and jog toward the lobby in my filthy cut-off jeans and bare feet—I had given every last pair of my shoes away before leaving Kiribati. My matted, greasy hair is hidden under an oversized hat, but there is no concealing the odor that is wafting off my unwashed body. The receptionist behind the desk cocks her head and stares at me curiously. She searches on the computer, but finally shakes her head and says, "I'm sorry, Miss Clark, there is no reservation under your name."

"There must be," I insist. "This is Le Meridien, right?"

"This is the Intercontinental Bora Bora, Mademoiselle."

I apologize, turn, and lope out of the lobby, dodging a chicly dressed Italian couple and hurdling over the bushes to cut the distance back to my dinghy. Apparently, Le Meridien is the next resort to the east. When I finally arrive, I'm ushered kindly into the resort by a Monsieur Pierre, who hands me a cocktail dressed up with a pineapple wedge. He does an impressive job of ignoring my castaway appearance on our tour of the hotel.

"Can you hold this a moment?" I ask Pierre, spotting the gift shop. I hand him my drink and rush over to find a pair of rubber sandals that fit, then pass the saleswoman my credit card.

Pierre steps in. "I assured Mr. McGeough that we would not accept any money from you. Charge this to Room 221, please, Charlotte." I look at them in shock. I slip on my new turquoise sandals, and Pierre leads me to my private beachside bungalow. He opens the heavy wooden door. My knees almost buckle as I step into my glorious, sparkling-clean haven.

As the door closes behind me, Pierre says, "Mr. McGeough arranged for you to have a massage. You can call the spa to book it whenever you'd like. Let us know if there's anything you need, Miss Clark."

The door closes and I find myself enveloped in comforting silence. The cool air is laced with the scent of flowers. Soft light filters through the veil of white curtains onto a wide, pillow-lined canopy bed draped in lace. The polished wooden floors are soothing under my feet. A small table in the center of the room is topped with an exotic bouquet and a note. It says "Go crazy, champ. Order whatever your heart desires. So proud of you, Chris."

I drop my backpack and twirl on one leg, then skip toward the other side of the room to find a bathroom bigger than the whole cabin of *Swell*. Slate stone walls open into an expansive sink area, then I turn to find myself face to face with a pristine white, open-air bathtub—jets and all. I open the faucets immediately, peel off my stinky clothes, and toss them into the far corner of the room. I stare at my skinny body in the mirrored walls of the bathroom. My stomach churns. I've forgotten my hunger in all the excitement. I prance to the bedside to peruse the in-room dining menu. My mouth waters. I quickly dial room service.

"Yes, hello. Can I please make an order for room 221? I will have the strawberry waffles with whipped cream, please. Two scrambled eggs, a large orange juice, a side order of fruit salad and cottage cheese and avocado. Oh, and a decaf coffee please."

I hang up and climb into my hot bath, dumbfounded by the drastic change in my reality. I lie back in the blessed waters, sinking my head below the surface to let the peaceful sound of the still water hold me as if I've returned to the womb. Everything is okay. Hell, it's more than okay! I'm in a porcelain bathtub!

I wash my skin and hair with excessive amounts of soap, working a mountainous lather onto my scalp. I clean the stinging, open sores on my backside, then rub the washcloth between every toe, every curve of my ear, every inch of my bare skin, until the water looks a bit swampish.

I hear a knock on the door. "Room service!"

Slipping into one of the white terrycloth robes, I go to the door, and push the loaded cart out to my back porch. Flowering jasmine vines and sunshine greet me as I sit down eagerly with my feast. Just before my first bite, I pause, look at the food and my surroundings, suddenly breathless with gratitude. I blurt out, "Thank you, Chris! Thank you, God, and all my angels!"

With every bite, I'm riding a flavor roller coaster. I chew emphatically. I can almost feel my body soaking up the nourishment as my fork works circles around the tray, sipping coffee and juice periodically. When there isn't a scrap left, I lick the whipped cream off my utensils and slouch back in my chair to enjoy the most basic of life's delights—a full belly. I haven't stopped eating for a full minute when fatigue crashes on me like a wave.

Parting the draped lace on my princess bed, I leap in headfirst and greet my four new pillow friends, then slip between the crisp white sheets. Paradise. I lie there in astonishment at the feeling of dry bedding, stillness, and safety.

After a couple hours I get up. No luck reaching my family on Skype, so I decide to take myself out to dinner. I pull on a hand-me-down red dress a friend had given me, fluff my hair, smear Neosporin with Pain Relief on my lips as gloss, and walk out of my room in my new flip-flops as if the dining room is awaiting its guest of honor.

A young couple walks toward me on the bridge over the turtle pond and I smile as they approach, excited to say hello. But they both look away and walk quickly past me. I shrug it off and carry on. Another couple reaches the restaurant doors just before I do. The man pushes open the door for his companion but lets it swing closed right in my face. Perplexed, I push myself through.

A pudgy older Frenchman greets me after seating the couple. "Good evening, mademoiselle. Looking for someone?" he inquires.

"No, sir. It's just me. I'd like to eat dinner."

His face contorts in confusion and pity, but he picks up one lonely menu, and leads me through the rows of gum-swapping, heart-pounding, same-side-of-the-booth-sitting newlywed couples toward an empty table for two near the center of the room. The muffle of voices falls silent.

No one's eyes move. Something tells me I'm gravely out of place. A third wheel. A homewrecker. Smack in the middle of honeymooner's paradise. And in a red dress, to make matters worse!

As the Frenchman turns to pull the chair out for me, I spot salvation behind him. An empty cocktail lounge on a covered patio—open and airy, with a cozy raised booth.

"Excuse me, sir," I lean in and say, pointing, "would it be okay if I sit over there?"

With a calculating glance he pauses, "Usually we don't serve dinner in that section, but I think we could make an exception tonight."

Everyone, myself included, is relieved as he leads me out of the room. I hop into my booth and pore over the menu. I gaze at the couples from time to time as I wait for my food to arrive. I guess I envy them a little; I do wish I had someone to talk to after victory at sea and more than two weeks alone. I feel a volcano of words inside me, desperate to erupt.

"I'm fine," I tell my chicken Caesar salad. "I just miss my family and friends."

Just then I notice a gray tabby kitten peering at me from under the table. I toss him a scrap of chicken. He gobbles it down, then hurries back to safety below a nearby chair. We share my meal and when he finally brushes up on my leg, I'm sure he is a little angel sent to keep me company.

14,659
Nautical Miles Traveled

The Boatyard

I Believe in Angels

Rust chips fly as anchor chain spews out of *Swell*'s chain locker into the bay in front of the Bora Bora Yacht Club. My hotel holiday is over. Looking more closely, I find that some of the links have only an eighth of an inch of steel remaining, so when a cruising boat nearby vacates a mooring, I haul the compromised chain back up and tie off to the mooring ball instead. I will have to pull all 300 feet of chain onto the deck, cut out the rusted links, then splice whatever is usable onto my length of nylon rode. But first, I must go ashore and check in with the yacht club.

The young, friendly owners of the club greet me at the dock. Jessica is from California and Teiva is Tahitian and speaks perfect English. Upon learning I've arrived from Kiribati alone, they take extra care to make me feel welcome. Jessica invites me to ride with her to the market. As I'm loading my dinghy with the grocery purchases, she and Teiva insist I return for dinner with them that evening.

Between meals at the yacht club in the coming days, I face the daunting task of putting *Swell* back together after the passage. At least the laundry is clean: Just before checkout, I'd gathered the heap of dirty washing aboard *Swell*, and stomped it clean in the hotel bathtub. If not for Jess and Teiva's kindness and those blessed days Chris had provided at Le Meridien, I might have packed a backpack and surfboard and given up this whole sailing gig.

Once the anchoring gear is dialed, it's time to figure out why the headstay is so loose. I dig out the bosun's chair and pull myself up the mast with the clever four-to-one pulley system that rigger Marty devised back in California. The one-way pulley ticks as I heave myself higher and higher above the bay. At the top, I peer over the furler sleeve to find a chilling sight. Most of the individual wires of the headstay cable are broken. I count them: Only six of the nineteen wires are still intact, holding up the mast and furling headsail! It looks as if the protective plastic sleeve at the top of the furler had worn through and the aluminum beneath it was rubbing directly on the cable.

Visions of that final day at sea flash through my mind. It's a miracle that the whole mast hadn't come down while I was pushing *Swell* so hard. Slightly dazed, I lower myself slowly to the deck, again grateful to whichever angels had been watching over me. I will have to order a new cable and maybe even a new furler.

While I work out how to proceed, Jess and Teiva make it clear that I have an open invitation to share every meal with them. They need an extra hand behind the bar one evening, so I gladly help serve drinks and food for a party of 200 Spanish hairdressers. A few of them talk me into hosting a bay cruise aboard *Swell*, so the following afternoon I secure an extra halyard to the foredeck to take the weight off the severed cable, and pick up the fun-loving group of Spaniards at their hotel. After a fine sunset cruise, they load me up with donated cash and well wishes.

I lie in my bunk that evening, feeling glad I had listened to my heart and not rushed west to New Zealand all those months ago. Thanks to the generosity of the blog readers and supporters sending occasional donations, I'm staying financially afloat. And today, another charitable surprise arrived: After reading a mass email I sent out about my distressing headstay situation, a yacht captain I met in Kiribati wrote back offering to help me get a discount on a brand new furler and headstay. Yay!

But there's another pressing problem: *Swell* is taking on water. The pace of the leak has increased slowly over the five months since I first noticed water in the bilge, and it's now nearly six gallons a day. There's a tiny space below the transmission where I can shine a flashlight and see persistent wetness, but the engine's position blocks me from tracing the actual source of the leak. I checked the hull below the waterline when I first noticed the issue, and I found a crack along the base of a small skeg which a previous owner had thru-bolted onto the hull between the keel and the rudder (likely intended for better tracking downwind). Maybe the force of waves hitting the skeg broke the seals around the bolts that hold it to the hull? Maybe the seawater is seeping in around those bolts?

I can't sail on like this. *Swell* and I prep to leave Bora Bora for the nearest boatyard. Jess and Teiva wish me well and refuse to accept any payment for use of their mooring and the many meals.

On the Hard

Swell waits her turn in the boatyard marina tied to the dock alongside eight or ten other sailboats. We both feel like wild animals trapped in a corral after living free on the ocean for seven straight months. I pace about the cabin until the owner of the yard knocks sharply on the hull. "Weell be reedy for you at ten sirty," he says with a thick French accent.

"Are you sure? I can wait until tomorrow if today is too busy ..." I stammer from the foredeck, my body tensing in visceral denial of the impending changes to my life afloat.

"*Non, non! On est prêt pour toi aujourd'hui*" (No, no! We're ready for you today), he replies.

I look down at *Swell* and sigh; rust stains run over her bulwarks. As much as I'm dreading the haul out, my faithful little ship needs some love.

At half past ten, I turn over the engine, toss off her lines, and a hulking yard worker named Taputu climbs aboard, ready to fend off the neighboring boats. *Swell* reverses out of the slot and turns like a show horse as I crank the wheel to port. To compensate for the trades blowing perpendicular to the ramp, I over-steer slightly to windward toward the submerged cradle. She slides in, dead center.

"*Pas mal pour une fille!*" (Not bad for a girl!) Taputu says with a smile as we secure the lines.

Soon *Swell* is propped up with wooden blocks and metal stilts. A yard worker hands me the power washer to clean the algae from her hull. Its force shoves me backwards as I pull the trigger, but I hold tight and get to work.

Finished, dripping with sweat and spattered in algae, I stare up at the worn patches of paint around *Swell*'s waterline—I don't know where to begin. That evening I write out a list of everything that needs to be done: Besides fiberglassing over the skeg to stop the leak, I must remove and replace the cracked wooden base for the anchor bracket; fix the rotted-out galley sink, the saltwater foot-pump spigot, and the stuck drain thru-hull; replace the headstay and install the new roller furler; remove the bubbling old paint around the waterline; disassemble and grease the stuck throttle; rebuild the head pump; fix or replace the charge controller for the solar panels; refinish the cabin floor and fix the cracked middle floor board; glass-in the insulation for the fridge; seal the stanchion bases; clean and regrease the windlass; and sand and paint the hull with anti-fouling. I guess they don't call it "the hard" for nothing.

This toxic pimple in paradise seems the same as other boatyards. Dreams sail in from near and far, a bit worn, to be plucked from the sea and stacked in still, neat rows. Yachties hurry to surmount land-bound obligations, climbing and descending their steel ladders spattered in paint, hands battered, hair sweat-matted, and backs tired. Weeds push out from under smashed rudders, rusted chain, exhausted steel cables, and used marine batteries. Boat owners and yard workers alike sand, grind, paint, glass, solder, patch, and upgrade from dawn to dusk. Toxic paint dust, thinners, and fiberglass fragments contaminate the earth below the boats. Scattered about, hardened paintbrushes, wads of masking tape, stiff paint rollers, discarded zincs, yellowed latex gloves, and used sanding discs tell stories of boat love and labor.

Just getting set up to live and work in the yard is a job in itself. I run my shorepower cord to connect *Swell*'s batteries to the electricity in the yard, but something isn't right because I keep getting shocked when I touch the metal stanchions. Thankfully James, my electrician in Santa Barbara, convinced Barry and me that a 220-volt battery charger was a worthy investment, but I don't think about the fact that I can't use my 110-volt power tools with the yard's 220-volt power until I plug in my mini vacuum the next day. It growls fiercely, lurches out of my hands, and plummets to its death on the cabin sole. The yard's secretary is happy to rent me a transformer for an exorbitant price.

Being terrestrial makes everything harder. The mosquitoes bite day and night—I often wear long pants despite the average eighty-degree heat. My little fans are not enough to deter the critters at night, so I mummify myself with a sheet to hide from their incessant biting. My refrigeration unit is water-cooled, so I can't use it on land. There is one grimy bathroom and cold shower for all the boaters and workers. The secretary is the only person in the yard who speaks English and she seems to enjoy being cold and unhelpful.

Looking over the list again, I sigh. I'm gonna be here for a decade. I can't call Dad again. This is my dream and I have to figure it out on my own. The only reasonable thing to do first is go surfing.

Courting a Land Mammal

I begin to make friends at a nearby break. Word travels quickly that there's a new girl on the island, traveling alone on a sailboat, and soon various guys stop by, offering to show me around.

After a little over a week, I'm feeling a bit better about my situation. My suitors have come through with some of my basic necessities: Tehau loaned me a sander and a grinder, Alex dropped off a cooler, and Jean Paul showed up with a rusty old bike that's yearning to be reborn.

I awake Monday morning feeling motivated, gather my little bucket of supplies and a change of clothes, and head for the shower. I turn around to step from the deck onto the first rung of the steel ladder, miss it entirely, and grab for the stanchion—which gives me a powerful shock. I let out a howl and drop the bucket as I grab onto the ladder with my other hand. Dangling by one arm, I'm dazed and grateful not to be in a crumpled wad in the mud beside my shower supplies, ten feet down.

Just then the boatyard electrician passes below me on his way to the marina. "*Bonjour*," I say. "When you have some time today, I seem to have a little electrical problem."

He stares up at me suspiciously as if he doesn't understand English, then cracks a smile. "Very nice *acrobatique*," he chuckles. Later, he stops by and surmises that I need a different adaptor for proper grounding between my French and American extension cords. If only it could be as easy to put an adaptor between my English and all the French being spoken around me.

The work progresses agonizingly slowly. I dig into a reasonably straight-forward task, only to find another three jobs or a mystery lurking within. Everywhere I turn, I run up against roadblocks. When I don't have what I need for a project, tracking down supplies means learning their names in French, and hitching or biking to town to search for them on what generally turns into a full-day adventure. Sometimes I come up empty-handed, forced to order online and wait on the slow, uncertain mail system.

I miss having Barry near. And our lovely lunches. I can picture him in sharp nautical garb, listening attentively as I described each of the quickly multiplying problems during *Swell*'s refit. He always asked thoughtful questions and offered his advice, but being the devoted mentor that he was to hundreds of students, Barry left it up to me to choose how to proceed. After our meal, he'd order us two bowls of cappuccino ice cream and gaze out the window at the shiny channel waters; I knew he wished he could sail away too. We'd then discuss current affairs, environmental news, exotic destinations, or my love life. When I called him last week, he got a kick out of hearing about my current courting situation.

Dating on a small island is tricky, any way you slice it, especially since fixing *Swell* is my first priority. Since they're friends, my suitors always come alone, not wanting the other guys to know they are pursuing me. Randomly throughout the day, one will appear out of nowhere with a bag of mangos or a fresh baguette. I stop and explain whatever I'm doing. Once that guy leaves, I dive back into my project just in time for another to show up, and it starts all over again.

Finally, I ask one of them to help me remove the seized bolts that hold the cracked anchor cradle to the foredeck: I need one set of arms below and one set above deck. I hold the wrench on the deck bolts. My suitor groans, sweats, and curses squished inside the dirty little chain locker. That's the last I see of him.

Another one takes a whole weekend to help me drop out the rudder. It's a brutal two days of contortions, sweat, and miscommunication in a tiny workspace. I can't understand which tool he needs, and then when I finally do, the handle of the wrench is too long to fit in the space or the nut we need to remove is frozen with corrosion. The elastic on the headlamp he's using is worn out, so it keeps slipping down over his eyes. Once the rudder is out, we both decide we're better off just as friends. Gradually the suitors' numbers dwindle: nobody wants a girlfriend with a boat on the "hard."

Thankfully, Taputu, who helped me guide *Swell* into the haul-out cradle, has taken to me in a fatherly way. In my deepest moments of frustration I go to him. Mostly using sign language, he figures out how to help. Some mornings he even tosses a chocolate croissant up into my cockpit. As the midday heat burns, the noise stops for one short hour while the workers gather to eat in the shade of a dry-docked boat. Taputu insists I join them daily. I sit with my French-English dictionary, notebook and pen, picking words out of their conversations and vegetables out of my beef curry. The secretary isn't thrilled about my presence, but day after day I turn her poison into medicine, giving her only kindness. Clock strikes 1 pm, she pulls one last heavy drag on her cigarette, flicks the butt, and everyone gets back to work.

The Ever-Expanding Project List

Life with fewer boys around is simpler, but not easier. To avoid the twenty-minute bike ride to the store, I get by on black coffee and plain oatmeal, lunches from the food truck with the yard crew, and chopped cabbage salads for dinner mixed with whatever canned food I dig out of my stocks. I can deal with the boring food, but the mosquitoes are relentless, and materials and yard fees are quickly adding up.

I finally start grinding the paint off the skeg with the power tools, and end up with toxic bottom paint in my ears, mouth, and eyes, so I copy the yard workers' look, and wrap an old T-shirt around my face. My arms tire quickly, though, and my strokes come out swirling and random. Every now and then Taputu walks by, grabs the grinder, and passes over the skeg in flawless, methodical strokes to show me how I should do it. I take mental notes, but I'm not strong enough to do it quite like he does. My muscles burn while dragonflies inspect morning puddles.

Once I strip the skeg down to bare wood, the small gap between it and the hull is more visible, so the next step is to fiberglass over the skeg-to-hull joint to create a watertight seal. The only fiberglass repair I've done is on my surfboards; this is a whole new level. So I set the project aside to gather more information, and tackle a job that seems less complicated: removing the paint around the waterline.

There must be sixteen layers of old paint on the boat and it happens that the very deepest one is bubbling and cracking—so it's back to the unwieldy grinder, which constantly wants to jump out of my hands. If I don't stay focused, it eats quickly past the paint and into the hull itself.

After a couple weeks, I finish what feels like a heroic paint-stripping performance, but Sylvain, the local fiberglass specialist, gives me some bad news. Because I have made deformities in the hull with the grinder, I'll have to sand the whole area again to flatten out the worst of them, fill the deepest nicks with two-part epoxy spackle, and sand it level with the hull when it dries.

"And zen, you muss poot seex coats of epoxy resin to make eet wa-tair-proof," Sylvain says. "And you weell haff to sand lightly between eech one."

Over lunch one day, Taputu asks me when I'm going to glass over the skeg. I shrug my shoulders. Cesar, a guy who paints boats on the other side of the yard, has joined our lunch circle today and after some discussion, he volunteers to help.

"It'll only take a couple hours," he says. "Then maybe you can help me with a big paint job on a boat I've got coming up soon."

I learn volumes about large-scale glassing from Cesar, and the skeg gets glassed to the hull perfectly, but the work list just keeps getting longer. I discover the fiberglass at the back edge of the keel is cracked and rotting, there are several deep blisters in the hull, and the rudder is waterlogged. Sometimes after lunch, I squeeze in a few questions to the yard crew, and if I'm lucky, someone comes over to have a look.

Thierry, the mechanic, lays a hand on my prop one day while looking at the cracks in the back of the keel. The prop shaft wiggles. "Too much loose," he says, "you need a new bearing." Sigh.

To deal with this means pulling out the propeller shaft, which looks simple enough, but the bolts on the shaft are corroded. I douse them in penetrating oil for a few days, and then spend hours banging with a hammer to loosen them. Once I finally get the shaft out, Thierry and Taputu help me extract the cutlass bearing from the hull. But it turns out there are no replacement cutlass bearings in the right size on the island, so I have to order one and wait.

One day after lunch Sylvain pokes at a small depression in the hull that appears wet. "You muss be see what's underneath, looks not good …"

I grind it down to find an old thru-hull that had been shoddily sealed from the inside with caulking.

"I can't take it anymore!" I cry to the passing clouds as another grinding and glassing job goes on the list. I lie in the grimy cockpit; tears flow down my cheeks. "I've had enough of this yard and all the projects and the toxins and being dirty all the time and the gross food and bugs. And the kisses. I hate those disgusting morning kisses!"

I've tried to embrace the customary French greeting—kissing a person on both cheeks—but I've decided that there are times and places where this custom is not appropriate, boatyards being high on the list. By 8 am everyone is sweating, but each new day calls for more kisses. There is no way to avoid crossing paths with the many workers and boat owners in the yard each morning. The awkward two seconds of facial proximity feel like an intrusion into my personal space with the bonus souvenir of commingled sweat and saliva. And everyone thinks it's totally normal!

I've learned who to tolerate and who to avoid, slinking around the yard to evade the lonely, unshaven French singlehanders who clearly take advantage of the custom, but often they pop out of nowhere and come at me, with their chapped and saliva-coated lips perked before they even say bonjour.

The Boatyard School of Enlightenment

Most days, it feels as if I'll never get out of here. I can't give up, though, and the only way out is through. The sun comes up and goes down over the rows of masts. Boats come and go, but *Swell* remains. One, two, three, nearly four months now.

The day arrives to help Cesar with the paint job in exchange for his assistance with my skeg. We work into the evening hours and then sit on a couple of palm stumps near the water's edge as he recounts his own path to arriving here. He left his home in Brazil straight out of high school to camp his way down the coast. Later, he went to Nepal and trekked through the snowy highlands in jeans and a pair of Converse. After that he traveled through Europe eating out of trash cans and living on the streets, mostly for the experience.

"I'm struggling," I tell him. "The labor is so physically intense. I'm not eating or sleeping well, either. And I dread the cold showers with these chilly September trades."

He looks at me sprightly. "You know, for a while I was living in England working as a prep cook in a restaurant, seven days a week. The hours were grueling and some days I could hardly find the strength to get up. It was ice cold in our flat and we had no hot water. I'd fill the tub with freezing cold water straight from the frosted pipes and force myself to get in. At first I hated it, but little by little I realized that the cold water revitalized me. After a while, I looked forward to those cold baths."

Over the next few days, I work at embracing the cold showers. With a changed perspective, I actually begin to appreciate the invigorating properties of the cool water on my skin.

I buy a net to deter the mosquitos, but my bunk is so narrow that the netting clings to me and the little blood-suckers stick their noses right through into my bare skin. But if adversity is the way to enlightenment, then I guess I should be thanking these mini-vampires, and the secretary, the newly discovered blisters in the hull, the clogged carburetor in my outboard, the cold showers, mud, constant noise, and my broken head-lamp. Fighting them does nothing to change my situation; I've tried that. It makes everything worse.

Acceptance is all that can save me.

Each day brings another challenge—be it with my own morale or a difficult person or project—but with more acceptance comes humor, new energy, and small miracles. By and by I stop itching as my body grows immune to the mosquito bites. I feel myself toughening to the discomfort and labor, brushing off irritations, and finding moments of solace in the morning dew, the cool evening breeze, and the silence of night. Reading from a copy of the *Bhagavad Gita*, I understand that anything done with love can be an act of devotion, so I try to put heart into the jobs instead of dreading them. Maybe this is karmic entanglement from past-life choices? *Or maybe it's just boat life.*

Either way, I do my best to find opportunities to work on myself—spending evenings studying French and Tahitian, or replaying the day's interactions in my mind to see where I could have reacted with less emotion and more control, less sensitivity and more humor. I realize that my reactions to the secretary's lack of compassion might come from my own demanding nature. Maybe when a man belittles my competence, it strikes a soft spot because of my own insecurities. Sometimes I do okay; other times I fail miserably, but the gods unfailingly present exactly what I need to work on.

Every day I get a little closer to the end, but now it's not only about getting *Swell* out of here, it's about who I am becoming in pursuit of that goal. The work, both on my boat and on myself, is the means to the dream, so it's really all a labor of love. For the dream, I'm willing to push myself further, both mentally and physically, and that's what breaks us through our self-imposed limitations.

By becoming aware of my own internal struggles, I gain the ability to sense the individual challenges of people around me. I realize they are either going to look at their issues, or keep encountering them again and again in the universal struggle to find meaning, happiness, security, balance, love, and peace amongst the seas of life. I feel less alone when I see that everyone is dealing with similar stuff, and I feel a new softness toward all of them: the courageous yard workers, the street kids, the secretary, the weeds that push from below the used oil collection tank, the stray cats hunting for their next meal, even the creepy kissers. Suddenly I'm connected to all living things through our struggles.

First-World Problems

I take my dad up on his offer of a frequent flyer ticket home for the holidays. *Swell* isn't finished, but after five grueling months in the boatyard, I'm ready for some family hugs and first-world problems. I hop a plane with a small bag of Polynesian souvenirs, a hand-carved wooden cane for Barry, and the clothes on my back.

Shortly after my arrival, my sister, Kathleen, and I head off to the supermarket. Stunned by the variety of products available, I wander aimlessly through the aisles, just marveling. A businessman bellows into his bluetooth earpiece about a merger while he bags a handful of bean sprouts, then saunters over to the meat counter and uses an exasperated display of sign language to order his desired cut. Over in the dairy section, a thin middle-aged woman thrusts her cart frantically past a mother and her kids by a stand of fruit roll-ups, as if the containers of fat-free cottage cheese on the other side are running away. I stand in quiet awe until Kathleen nudges me a little.

"Helloooo?" she coos, flashing Mom's list across my view. "Can you go grab some green tea for Dad?"

"Yeah, sure," I reply, and wander off to find the tea section. I stand in front of the massive selection dumbfounded by all the colorful packages, prices, and varieties.

Does Dad like green tea with jasmine? Or a hint of mint? Or maybe green apple blossom? Green tea with lemon essence? Pomegranate proclivities?

Kathleen appears a moment later, rolls her eyes at me, and selects one off the shelf. We head back to the one-bedroom condo my parents have downsized into near our family sailboat in the heart of San Diego. It's great to be back—the hugs, hot showers, conveniences, and food varieties are divine—but living in a 550-square-foot space with my mom, my sister and her dog, and my father when he's in town, soon revives some of our less pleasant family dynamics. My sister and I fight over the car. Mom says I'm selfish. Dad drinks, Mom and Dad bicker, then they both drink excessively to try to forget about it. Dad flies away on business. I'm frustrated over their continued sorrow. Rita, my sister's dog, looks at us like we're all crazy.

City life feels suffocating and adds to my irritability. I find myself pointing fingers. Ugly parts of my character resurface. Applying my new wisdom here with my family proves to be the most challenging and probably the most important. Once in a while, I talk about Melanie's principles, or the Four Agreements, or positive thinking, but it's clear that if I don't embody the ethics, my words are useless. Truly changing myself will be the only real way to spur change in anyone else.

I drive up to Santa Barbara to take Barry sailing on *Freya*. His health is good and he's thrilled to be out on the water. Then I track down needed boat parts and meet with sponsors. The good news is that the folks at Patagonia, who have been helping a bit since the beginning of the voyage, loved my blogs from Kiribati and they've invited me to be an official surf ambassador for the brand. It won't be a ton of money, but it definitely helps.

Sweat, Blood, and More Work

Back in the yard, my California polish quickly wears off. By midday my first day back, there is grime under my fingernails and sweat in my eyes. It's the height of summer in the South Pacific, which means stifling temperatures and less wind. I feel like an ant under a magnifying glass. By the third day I have pierced my left thumb with a screwdriver and ground the skin off my wrist with 40-grit paper on the power sander. I'm already longing for a salad and a hug.

There are only a few more tasks to finish: install the roller furler, fill and fair the rudder, paint the waterline stripes, roll on bottom paint, and polish the hull. Sylvain helps with the roller furler, and when I'm ready to paint the anti-fouling, a sweet French girl from another boat offers a hand. By early afternoon, Bernadette and I have slathered *Swell* with two coats of thick blue bottom paint. It took seven months, but *Swell*'s blue skirt is finally back on!

The next morning, I use nearly everything left in my bank account to pay my yard bill, and *Swell* floats gracefully off the haul-out track. I maneuver her to the marina, then buy a case of beer for the yard workers. It's Friday; we dance and celebrate inside the garage with local music as the rain plinks and patters on the corrugated metal roof.

Freedom is so close, but right away the days blur together again into another project marathon. It turns out the headsail Holly gave me doesn't fit the new roller furler, so I take it to a local sailmaker to have it cut down. I run a new halyard to replace the one that broke on the crossing with Mom all those months ago, but the job turns out to be ridiculously complicated. I install the new wind generator Patagonia bought me, replace the solar charge controller, and remount the refrigerator cold plate since I had removed it to fiberglass the insulation into the cold box. After three more weeks of nonstop work, the amount of chaos accumulated inside *Swell* is mindboggling: wood and metal scraps; half-used glues and caulking tubes; bits of wires; dirty rags; random screws, washers, and nuts; cans of paint, varnish, thinners, resins, and fiberglass; cat food from feeding the stray cats; used-up sandpaper; and tools everywhere!

Finally, on a Sunday afternoon, the tools and materials are stowed, the newly refinished floors swept, water tanks filled, decks scrubbed, bosun's chair put away, and sails and sheets back in place. I quietly cast off *Swell*'s lines and disappear across the turquoise lagoon.

14,659
Nautical Miles Traveled

Tube
Trials

Eight Tahitian Dads

Afloat again, *Swell* and I rush to meet an Aussie filmer to finish up the footage needed for the *Dear & Yonder* surf film. After a jam-packed ten days spent tracking down waves together, I settle back into life on the sea: My lagoon swimming pool shimmers each morning; I enjoy open-air showers on the aft deck, the chilly air in my refrigerator, and sleeping under the stars without mosquitoes buzzing. The new wind generator boosts the amount of power to the batteries, so now I'm able to use the lights, fridge, stereo, and computer without hauling out the portable gasoline generator every evening. Plus, I have the freedom to sail again.

I decide to see parts of Tahiti I haven't yet explored. It's time to face the wave phenomenon at Teahupo'o. Professional surfers fly in from around the world to challenge themselves and hopefully ride through one of its enormous round tubes.

There is a swell on the way and after building my skills surfing reef passes, I'm ready to give it a shot. I've seen the photos, and part of me wants nothing to do with its menacing thick lip, ledgy takeoff, and shallow reef, but another part of me—that slightly insane part—knows I can't sail away without at least making an attempt.

I spot two masts in a small fishing marina, as I steer *Swell* into the calm waters of the Teahupo'o lagoon between the green and red markers. A man in a single outrigger canoe with a surfboard across the front guides me around the coral heads of the shallow entrance. I hop to the bow to tie on dock lines and throw out bumpers, then back to the wheel to spin *Swell* 180 degrees into the premier Teahupo'o parking spot.

Fishermen gathered near an ice house stare from across the marina. A crowd of young Tahitian girls gather at the end of the dock watching curiously. I wave and smile. They wave and smile. The fishermen raise their beers. The girls go back to playing. It's Saturday afternoon in the quiet little town at the end of the road. The opposite side of the marina hosts a colorful lineup of local fishing boats. I introduce myself to the girls, then hop on my bike and pedal over to make sure it's okay to park *Swell* here at the dock.

"*Iaorana!*" I offer, skidding to a halt with my bare feet as brakes. The salty-looking Tahitian fishermen of ranging ages are sitting on crates, car hoods, a cooler, and a rusty-wheeled dolly. "*O vau Liz.*" (I'm Liz.)

For a moment they're silent and I feel a wave of shyness coming over me.

"*Eha to oe huru?*" (How's it going?) a large, jolly one asks.

"*Maita'i,*" I reply. "*E oe?*" (Good, and you?)

Clearly amused by my effort to speak Tahitian, the white-haired veteran sitting on the cooler pulls out an icy Hinano for me and scoots over to offer a seat. I sip the icy refreshment and answer their questions. Where did I come from? How long will I be here? Need any ice? Or fish? Alone!? Then be careful on the street at night and lock up your boat, they warn. Come let them know if I have any problems. *'Aita pe'ape'a* (don't worry), the dock is free. I soon have eight new Tahitian dads watching out for me. I stay for a while and listen to the rugged group joke and tell fishing yarns.

"*Māuruuru! Anānahi!*" (Thank you! See you tomorrow!) I call to them when I pedal off to check out the rest of the neighborhood.

The thundering sound on the outer reefs makes it impossible to sleep that night. I toss and turn with visions of the punishing lip and jagged coral below. At dawn, after a bit of nervous puttering, I reluctantly pull out my 6'4" and load into the dinghy. I wave goodbye to my Tahitian dads as I head off across the lagoon, talking myself through a strategy.

I idle the dinghy in the channel, scoping out the sets and the dynamic of the crowd. The cloud cover gives the surf a gray, angry look, as wave faces suck up and heave into cavernous water cylinders. The sets look manageable, though. It's only a couple feet overhead at most. I spot a few familiar faces that I've seen at other breaks, so I tie up to the buoy in the channel and paddle for the lineup.

I sit wide for a while to get comfortable and observe. And then, "This one, Liz, go!" one of the guys calls.

I paddle hard and get under it, grab my rail, and lock into backside three-wheel drive, bracing myself for disaster—but to my surprise, I make the drop and launch out the end.

That wasn't so bad!

Soon my fears have diffused and I paddle confidently across the lineup during a lull to greet the others with the customary local handshake.

"Liz," calls another guy I know. "You have a *pa'a ihu ... caca nez*." He signals to me with a grin, putting a finger to his nose to demonstrate where my booger is.

I quickly wipe it away and burst into embarrassed laughter. None of the other guys I'd greeted had bothered to tell me. I learned then, and again, that Teahupo'o always keeps you humble.

Trust the King

Sunrise in the Teahupo'o marina two weeks later finds me in a downward dog pose, staring at the grass growing out from the cracks in the rotting wooden planks of the dock. I've made progress in the lineup, especially thanks to a local waterman who has helped me catch waves during my recent sessions. After yoga, I make a cup of tea and scan the reef. The swell is the biggest yet, and I can see Raimana's boat tied to the buoy near the wave with half a dozen smaller boats trailing behind like baby ducks.

I load up and head over, but I'm deterred by a funky morning bump and the thickest crowd I've seen yet, so I attach my dinghy to the row of boats and lay back under my pareo, thinking about my most memorable big-wave sessions in other places: the heavy wipeouts and long hold-downs, scratching for the horizon when a set appears, duck-diving through the face of the first wave with open eyes wondering what's behind it. And patiently searching for the right wave, because there's nothing like the sensation of skittering down a water mountain. I both love and fear big waves, but Teahupo'o is on a scale of its own.

The crowd has thinned and the conditions are glassing off. The sets look frightening, but Raimana's presence makes me feel safer. A handful of guys paddle back to their boats, so I decide to go out and try to catch at least one wave. The sun breaks through the clouds as I make it to the lineup with the five remaining surfers. I luck into a small wave to warm up, and turn to see Raimana dropping into a beauty on his stand-up paddleboard. He pulls into the gaping tube and flies out near me in the channel.

When we arrive back at the lineup, he calls me over and directs me to sit just deeper than him. "You ready? Relax, take deep breaths, it's okay."

I feel surprisingly calm already. Soon a set rises out of the deep blue. The line of water stacks on itself and someone paddles for it. When the second wave approaches Raimana calls out, "Heeeeeeeeeeep! Hold off, guys! This is you, Liz. Paddle, go, paddle hard! Toward the reef!" I dig my arms into the water, totally committed. I get in easily. Drop. Roar. And in another instant, I go launching out the now-familiar exit ramp.

"Good," he says as I paddle back out with an uncontainable smile. "Now come here again. Sit here. I'm gonna push you this time. A bigger one."

What have I gotten myself into?

"Let's move out and a little deeper. Yes … a little more … a little more … Okay, here."

I can't imagine how we are going to catch a wave sitting here, but I'm certainly not going to argue.

"Don't worry, babe, you'll get in early," he coos.

This is a rare moment with Raimana's attention, the small crowd, and the beautiful conditions. I have to embrace my chance.

I'm poised, every cell in my body tingling with anticipation. Finally, it comes … The sight of it takes my breath away. A beast of a set sucks the water off the reef and stands up before us.

"Okay, now, this one! Hey boys, hey, it's Liz. Okay, girl, turn around, paddle past me to the inside. The inside! Now go, go, go!"

There's no backing out, and no time for fear. I have to make this drop or the wipeout will be horrendous … I put my trust in Raimana, put my head down, and paddle like hell.

He follows closely behind me, and when the mass of water starts to pitch, I feel his hand press firmly against the flat of my foot. With a strong shove he launches me into the wave. I could never have caught it on my 6'4" without his push. I rise to my feet and go cascading down the slope of water, gripping my rail for dear life. I barely make the drop, then accelerate across the enormous blue wall. One false move could mean the worst wipeout of my life. The wave releases me and I skitter into the safety zone, giddy and grateful to have escaped without punishment. I wasn't quite in the tube, but the size, the rush, the vision, and encouragement … I'm hooked!

There's a Hole in the Bucket, Dear Liza

Between the excitement of surfing Teahupo'o and my crew of new friends here, I'm in denial—the time left on my visa is ticking down, and there is water in the bilge again. I keep coming up with reasons to explain why the automatic bilge pump is cycling from time to time: It's been raining? Maybe there is a leak in the sink foot pump? The toilet pump? The water tank? I finally shine my light back into the spot under the engine and see a dribble of water coming from the same area that had been leaking before. I want to cry and vomit and stomp my feet, but instead I sit down with a large bag of cookies and munch on them slowly until they're all gone.

The leak is indeed still leaking. I must have been so busy with the filmer and surfing, and so sure that it couldn't possibly be the same problem, that I didn't even acknowledge the occasional sound of the pump. I motor a few miles west and tie off to a mooring that belongs to a dynamic French couple with a lagoon-front home just across the way. I met Georges and Marika when I arrived in the area, and sure hope they meant it when they said to come back if ever I needed anything. I need a home base while I sort out what to do next. They welcome my return to their petite paradise by the sea, spilling over with fun, creativity, and aquatic toys.

Over dinner together, Georges recommends a knowledgeable boat guy, who comes out to have a look a few days later. Pulling off the doors to the engine in preparation for his arrival, I'm surprised to find the head of a nut lying in the engine pan. I shine my flashlight around and see that one of the port motor mounts is cracked again. I can't comprehend it since I'd replaced both mounts in Panamá City. But I unbolt them completely, and when the expert arrives we use a halyard to lift the engine up enough to have better access to the leaky area. He reaches back to touch the wet fiberglass; it squishes softly under his fingers.

"Osmosis," he says. "It looks bad. I'll write you a letter to give to the immigration officials. They should give you an extension to stay until your boat is fixed."

The thought of being back in the boatyard gives me chills. Not only does the idea of grinding fiberglass turn my stomach, I can't afford to haul out again. Part of me wished for a way to stay a little longer in Polynesia, but this is not how I had imagined it.

Luckily Georges and Marika know the owner of a machine shop and when the man comes over for dinner one evening, he agrees to solder my broken mount back together. In the meantime, I'm lucky to be broken down here: My hosts often throw barbecues and prepare decadent meals, help me improve my terrible French, and welcome me to use their Internet, do laundry, and hang out.

I help with dishes, lawn mowing, sweeping, laundry—anything to feel like I'm earning my keep. As surfers start pouring in for the World Championship Tour contest at Teahupo'o, I pitch in to help Marika cook, serve, and clean up meals for the surfers staying with them. In between, I get to surf, eat Marika's mouthwatering chocolate cake, watch the contest from the channel, spy on pro surfers during backyard workouts, and attend tailgate concerts by local friends under the full moon.

But the trials continue. A fifty-knot squall nearly heaves *Swell* onto the reef right in front of the house, a two-wave hold-down at Teahupo'o leaves me with a week's worth of drowning nightmares, a car jack explodes in my face while I'm trying to install the new motor mount, and *Swell*'s mooring comes unscrewed one day while I'm doing laundry ashore. Luckily Mick Fanning and Taylor Knox rush to save her with Georges' Jet Ski before she drifts onto the reef. Then, to top it all off: five hideous days with dengue fever. If challenges are the door to personal growth, I'm on the path to sainthood, but sweet Jesus, can't it just be easy every once in a while?

Ah Rats!

There's no way around it. Once I'm feeling better, I head back to the boatyard to address the leak. As soon as I haul *Swell*, I fly back to the States to sign a contract and get to work on a photo book, which I hope will raise some much-needed funds for the repair.

During my time back, I spread the word that *Swell*'s leak isn't fixed. My friend Richard of *Latitude 38* sailing magazine publishes a small blurb about my latest predicament, asking readers for donations to help with repairs. I'm overwhelmed by the response. In less than a month I receive almost $2,000 from perfect strangers, accompanied by supportive notes and gratitude for my blog. It encourages me to know that I am fixing *Swell* not only for me, but to keep others dreaming too. After a wonderful visit with Barry in Santa Barbara, he also decides to pitch in.

Back aboard *Swell*, the new wave of support makes the work seems less lonely. But then: Hmmm, what's all this? Someone's been nibbling on my handline, and who got into the cacao powder? What are all these little turds?

Apparently, there's another reason to feel less lonely. It looks like *Swell* gained some new occupants while I was away. I find little black rat poops everywhere. There is not a nook or cranny that hasn't been nibbled or pooped on. Everything must be hauled out of every locker, drawer, and cupboard, washed or scrubbed, and put back in place. I hitchhike into town to find some rat traps. Leptospirosis, a potentially fatal disease transmitted by rat urine, is not to be taken lightly. I have to be careful not to scratch my eye or pick my nose while cleaning out the mad mess.

Those first few nights, I lie under the stars on my pool mat in the cockpit, listening to the rat tinker around in *Swell*'s belly. I wake each morning to empty traps and new poop trails. That sneaky bastard keeps stealing the bait. Despite the rodent battle going on inside the cabin, I tell the secretary that I want to hire the fiberglass specialist, Sylvain, to help me figure out how to fix the leak. I still have no clue how the water is getting in, since from the outside of the hull, the fiberglass appears to be completely intact. She informs me that Sylvain is leaving on his own boat for an extended voyage, but that a new guy named Laurent will come around this afternoon to have a look.

A short wiry Frenchman in his fifties with a pointy face and Einstein hair shows up after lunch. I do my best to explain the problem and how we tried to fix it, but he hardly listens, then replies too fast for me to understand. But I do get it when he says he is busy for another month so it would be better to find someone else. And I owe him 5,500 francs for his hour of assessment.

For the next few days, I mope and mull over what to do. Meanwhile, that clever rat licks all the peanut butter off the trap and even finds his way into my prized bag of Trader Joe's trail mix that I'd hung in the middle of the cabin to keep out of his reach. My dislike for my new crewmate has turned into loathing. Both the rat and the leak are outsmarting me; I'm feeling like such a chump.

That evening around midnight I'm barely asleep when I hear, *Whap!* I leap up like an Amazon warrior, ready for battle. There he is, dead on the trap: The snap bar has squared him in the head. The cashew that I'd tied to the trap with thread worked. A mix of triumph, pity, and nausea churns in me. "Sorry little dude. We weren't meant to live together." The next morning, I send him out to sea on a plywood raft with a little prayer, clean the last of the poops, and put away that dreadful trap.

Around midday I'm outside under *Swell*, looking for the hose, when Sylvain stops by to say bonjour. I don't want to unload on him, but I explain that I still haven't figured out what to do.

"I propose you zis," he says. "I weel help you find zee source of zee leak, and afder Laurent can do zee reparacion."

"Really?" I feel my face light up like a Christmas tree.

"Take sat (h)ose, turn za pressure up, and bring eet over eer."

I pass him the pressurized hose, then he instructs me to go up into the cabin, pull off the engine cover, and look at the cursed spot under the engine.

"Okay!" he shouts. "Eere it come." He directs the high-pressure water into the propeller shaft tube below. Water shoots out from under the engine like a geyser.

"*Oui!* Yes! That's it!" I call. It hasn't been ten minutes and Sylvain has figured it out.

He smiles, and wasting no time, explains what to do next. "Zee leak is coming from somewhere inside zee shaft tube. Zee best way to start eez grind down zee area near zee cutlass bearing to see if zere is somesing unusual because zis eez the easiest place to access. If zee problem is not ere, it weel be a much, much bigger job," he warns.

I take a deep breath. "*Merci,* Sylvain. *Merci beaucoup,*" I say, bowing sincerely.

That afternoon I don my grinding gear and get to work. I touch the spinning disc to the hull where the prop shaft comes out, and grind it down until I hit the bronze tube underneath. Amazingly, as Sylvain suspected, there is a hole in it. It looks like it has been made intentionally, maybe to use a set screw to hold the cutlass bearing in place. I grind the other side down and find the same thing. I drag Sylvain over to have a look.

He explains that I have two options. Either I properly patch these two places with fiberglass and hope that takes care of it. Or I take out the whole tube and replace it, which means dropping out the rudder and removing the prop shaft again, lifting out the engine, and basically doing demolition on the entire aft keel area to remove the tube.

My mouth goes dry. "I'll try the easier option first. *Merci encore,* Sylvain." (Thanks again.)

And then … What's this? New rat poops? No … it can't be. They're everywhere again! It turns out my rat was plural! And just as I go to put the stairs back over the engine, I spot another surprise. The motor mounts! They're broken again after less than ten hours of use!?

Back to the Blue(s)

After I've ground, chiseled, sanded, heat-gunned, and cleaned the holes in the shaft tube as best as possible, Laurent helps me glass over them. Meanwhile five more rats are trapped! I slap a coat of bottom paint on the hull, the tractor rumbles, and Taputu and the other yard workers lower *Swell* back into the sea.

"*Maita'i?*" (All good?) Taputu calls, referring to the leak. I remove the stairs, shine my light, and see no evidence of moisture.

"*Maita'i!*" I confirm. We use ropes to guide *Swell* over to the dock since the boatyard mechanic is coming to troubleshoot and install the new motor mounts that afternoon.

The next morning, I open the floorboard that covers the bilge, and to my horror, I see six inches of water shimmering below. My mind goes numb. I slowly pull off the stairs and point the light on the infamous location of the leak, filled with dread. Sure enough, salt water trickles in—and it trickles from my tear ducts, too. How can it be? No! *Swell* is still leaking. I curl up under the fan to cry.

Whispers whirl through the boatyard about my news. People pat my back or tip a nod of quiet mourning. Plan B requires removing and replacing the entire four-foot-long bronze shaft tube that is fiberglassed directly into the structure of the hull. I can't bear the thought of hauling her right back out. Christmas is little more than a week away, and my brother is coming to visit.

That afternoon, the owner of the yard, who rarely converses with clients, stops me as I climb onto the dock. My eyes are swollen. I feel fragile and forlorn. He takes me by the shoulders. "Take a brrreak, make a tour of zee islands, forrrget about zis for a while. I'll clear your visa with immigration and you can beegeen again after zee New Year, *d'accord*? (okay?)"

"*Oui, merci*," I sniffle.

Big Bro and the Lost Chain

James appears at the airport with heaps of goodies—including a midsized jib—in a rolling bag so big, I hope the rest of the family will topple out when he opens it. He's beaming; I dive into his sincere blue eyes and hug him tightly.

Back aboard *Swell*, I apologize for the mess. I had just hosted a spontaneous guest over the previous weekend—Jesse, the submarine pilot from my time with McKenzie. When Jesse and I left the marina, the engine had made a terrible grinding noise. Turns out the mechanic had poorly aligned the engine after installing the new motor mounts. We had to sail back to the slip upwind and spend the rest of his visit working out the engine alignment. So much for Jesse's weekend getaway, but we discovered and fixed the reason for the repetitive broken motor mounts!

With *Swell*'s engine now dialed in, I'm relieved to put boat projects aside and ease into a carefree island tour with James. My brother—clever, capable, and a man of few words—maneuvers *Swell* toward the windward side, motoring inside the lagoon. I look down at the depth gauge: 125 feet. My mind flashes to my brand-new length of anchor chain that I had hurriedly loaded into the locker while preparing for James's visit. It's completely twisted. I should drop the anchor and let a bunch of chain out right here where it's deep, to let it untangle itself.

I wrench off the bolts that hold the chain cap to the windlass. With the cap on, I can't even get the chain to come out of the locker because it's so jumbled below. So I remove the cap, shove the anchor off its cradle, and proceed to release the chain slowly, using the clutch of the windlass. But without the cap, the chain begins to run out much too quickly. Before I can tighten the clutch wheel, the chain jumps off the windlass entirely and starts screaming straight out of the locker unchecked. My expensive new chain is paying out like a runaway locomotive.

"No!" I cry in despair. In my hurry to get *Swell* back in the water and ready for my brother's visit, I hadn't yet secured the other end of the chain to the boat!

"Let it go!" James yells back.

Together as kids, we had witnessed our friend lose a finger in an equivalent incident. I'm petrified to grab at my precious chain, and instead I fruitlessly try to slow it with the flat of my foot. In another breath, the end whips out, and all 300 feet of chain plus my beloved Bruce anchor disappear into the green depths. Silence falls over the scene.

I stand there stunned, then run to the GPS to mark our location so that, Poseidon willing, I can recover it. James hugs me. We circle a few times while I decide what to do next. As horrified as I am at the loss, my brother only has a short time to visit, and the chain isn't going anywhere.

"It's okay," I concede. "It's still going to be there next week. I'll rig up a piece of the old chain on a spare anchor."

James steers us south through the lagoon, while I put some anchoring gear together. At sundown, we make our way through a tight passage in the coral into a perfect patch of sandy shallows near a lovely islet. Thankfully I only have a doughnut-hole-sized blood blister pulsating on the bottom of my foot to remind me of my mistake. We cook up a feast and toast togetherness in the cockpit while the round eye of a true, blue moon peers over the islet's whispering palms. My big bro and I converse about life well into the night while moonbeams illuminate the shallows, leaping and twirling across their sandy underwater dance floor.

We share ten more days of glorious sailing adventures around the islands, ringing in 2010 as impromptu bartenders at Jessica and Teiva's restaurant in Bora Bora. James is still my rock—an exemplary human of the highest integrity, always willing to listen and give thoughtful advice, and endlessly explore the philosophies of life. Thinking back to the days I spent as a depressed heap on his couch, I'm so grateful he's my brother and so proud to show him how far I've come, both inside and out.

After James flies back to California, a mission is in order to recover my anchor and chain, so I sail back to the bay of the incident. I call a friend who is a scuba guide and explain my predicament. We load her gear aboard *Swell* the next day and head off to the waypoint I marked on the GPS. Heavy rains have turned the water dark green with silt, and Manuelle is not optimistic.

"Why don't we attach a dive weight to a long piece of rope and toss it over when I think we're near the spot? That way you can follow it down and have a reference point," I suggest, desperate for anything that will increase the chance of success.

"Good idea," she agrees. We tie some ropes together, and toss the weighted end over the side with the other end attached to a buoy, as I try to get *Swell* to hover just above the spot marked on the GPS. Manuelle preps her gear and hops in, while *Swell* drifts in neutral. My eyes are pinned nervously to her bubbles as she descends into the murky deep. It hasn't been five minutes when, to my surprise, her masked face pops above the surface.

"Unbelievable!" she sputters. "The weight landed a centimeter from the end of the chain! All I had to do was attach the rope and come back up."

Holy Days

With a bit more time before going back to the boatyard for Round Three, I catch wind that Jimmy Buffett is playing a secret concert on Bora Bora. I've got to make it back up there for the show. Dad raised us on his albums and I grew to adore Jimmy's poetic travel ballads and nautically inclined tunes. My family quotes his hundreds of songs like bible verses.

I'm near the front with Jessica and Teiva when Jimmy walks on stage at a local restaurant. There he is—the legend and lyricist—just fifteen feet away! He sings wholeheartedly with his familiar Southern twang, barefoot and smiling, just like at the last show I went to in California—minus the crowd of 130,000 crazy "parrotheads."

Jessica and I sing along from our table—we seem to be the only two among the fifty spectators who know the lyrics. When it comes time for his most famous song, "Cheeseburger in Paradise," Jimmy explains that his female backup singers couldn't make it and he needs some help from the audience. He looks right at Jess and me, then calls us up on stage. I don't miss a word. Jimmy is floored!

After the show, I wander to the front of the restaurant and peek into the private side room guarded by a very tall, stern-faced security guard.

"Hello, sir, I just want to make sure everything is okay with the band," I prattle away, hoping to talk to Jimmy.

"Yes, everything is just fine, thank ..."

"Let her in," Jimmy's familiar voice interrupts from behind him.

The group of five or six men falls silent as I step into the air-conditioned room.

"Well, come in, then. Here, have a seat," Jimmy says kindly as he scoots to one side of the couch. "Meet the band."

Slightly speechless yet pleasantly inebriated, I shake hands with everyone and reply to their questions about having sailed from California. I explain to Jimmy that his lyrics had helped shape my sailing dream and approach to life and I thank him for all the joy that his music has brought my family and me. He's flattered but humbly turns the conversation back to me.

I wake with a headache the next morning, but there's whitewater on the reef. The north swell is up and I can't resist. I spend all afternoon in the surf. Back on *Swell*, Jessica calls asking if I can help at the bar that night. Despite my fatigue, I pull on some clean clothes and go ashore. At the bar, I lean in to ask Jess how she's feeling after our big night. She rolls her eyes and continues to count change for the impatient customer beside me.

"Actually, it looks like we don't need you after all. It's not too busy. But order some food," she says.

"Okay, no worries," I reply, and turn around just in time to see Jimmy and his friends duck under the shaggy palm fronds of the bar's thatched roof. He takes off his jacket and walks over to where I'm standing.

"Oh hey, Liz." He smiles. "Hi Jess! Well, it looks like we came to the right place. Can we eat here?"

"Of course!" Jess replies.

"Are you busy, Liz?" Jimmy asks. "Why don't you join us for dinner?" Seriously! "I'd be honored!" I tell him.

"How was your day?" Jimmy asks after we're seated around a table.

"Not bad! I woke up with a headache, but I surfed this afternoon."

"Surf? Where?" he asks excitedly.

"Just out at the pass. It very rarely breaks, but today was pretty nice."

"Can you take me out there tomorrow?" he asks.

The next day at ten o'clock sharp, Jimmy circles *Swell* on his stand-up paddleboard. "Come aboard," I call. "I'm nearly ready."

I give him a tour, then we head off to check the waves aboard his plush charter catamaran.

"It's not the easiest wave," I explain as we head toward the break. "It's kind of shifty and there were long waits between sets yesterday, so it was easy to lose track of the takeoff zone."

He's determined to try. We paddle over, and right away a set rolls in and catches him inside. I cringe as his big stand-up paddleboard drags him toward the reef with another wave behind it.

Good god, I'm going to kill him! To my relief, he comes back out laughing, takes a few deep breaths, and paddles a bit farther outside.

"Try to look for the waves that come in more from the north," I suggest. "They stay open a bit." I've barely finished my sentence when a lovely head-high wave springs up from the north. Jimmy is perfectly positioned.

"Go for it!" I encourage. "This is the one!" He strokes without hesitation, catches it, and away he glides down the line, then comes back grinning and glowing from his ride.

"Thanks for that one, Lizzy!" he says, as we high-five in celebration.

Oli and the VIP Yard

My holiday ends abruptly when the weather forecast warns of an approaching cyclone. I sail directly back to the boatyard, hauling *Swell* out a week earlier than planned so as not to have to weather the storm in the water. The crew tows her to an overflow yard down the street. I joke with them, asking if this is the VIP yard, since there are only a few other boats. *Swell*'s decks must be stripped to make her as streamlined as possible in preparation for the powerful winds. The sails, solar panels, and wind generator must all come off.

Once *Swell* is bare and battened, my Italian girlfriend, Simona, who lives across the street, invites me to stay at her house during the storm. For three days it blows with a ferocity I've never felt. From the window, I can see *Swell*'s rig trembling from the winds.

Luckily, Cyclone Oli passes without too much damage. While walking back toward the VIP yard, something white flashes among a pile of washed-up debris. Looking closer, I see a bedraggled baby seabird. There isn't a tree or nesting area nearby; it must have been blown from its nest during the storm. I can't possibly leave it here all alone, so I scoop it up and bring it back to *Swell*.

Over the next week, I hitch to town to buy fresh fish for my little friend and use frozen water bottles from Simona's freezer to keep it cold. I suspect the bird is a male and call him Oli. At first, I have to force his sharp black beak open, but soon Oli is eating on his own. By the end of the week he's fluffed up and chirping when he's hungry. After seeing the photos I send, Barry identifies him as likely a blue or black noddy tern. Little Oli stays near me at all times, needing to be fed every half an hour. While I prepare *Swell* for Laurent to cut away the hull and remove the shaft tube, Oli keeps me company. He chirps endearingly as I drop out the rudder and remove the propeller shaft. He pecks at the pile of tools beside me while I unbolt the transmission from the engine. He naps in his cozy nest of rags while I dismantle the V-drive and disconnect all the hoses and wires that run through the area. Luckily, removing the transmission provides enough access to the repair area that I don't actually have to remove the main body of the engine. Oli is pleased whenever I finish a job and my attention returns to him.

He grows steadily, feathers thickening, and I cherish his companionship—the way he cocks his head when he looks at me, and snuggles up for a nap in the fold of my T-shirt. I'm the only one living aboard among a flock of fancy catamarans in the VIP yard. The one adjacent to *Swell* serves as a fantastic yoga platform with an ocean view. A hose in the corner of the yard becomes my new shower. There are plenty of mosquitoes around, but at least no creepy kissers!

The morning *Swell* is ready for the demolition to begin, the secretary confirms that Laurent will arrive shortly after 7:30 am. I start growing impatient at 8:30 am. No Laurent ... Another hour passes ... No Laurent. I find him in the workshop, glassing a damaged rudder.

"*Bonjour*, Laurent," I greet him.

"*Bonjour*," he replies.

"I don't mean to bother you," I say in French, "but I thought we were getting started today?"

"Ah, en fact, I have meeny small projects in zis moment. I prefer to feeneesh zee uzer jobs first. I weel be ready to start your prrroject in about two monz," he says and returns to working on the rudder.

Oh Moon, Won't You Buy Me a Mercedes Benz

I mope around the yard all week, fretting over how to proceed until I receive an unsolicited email from another Cal 40 owner who has dealt with the same problem. Fin heard about my leak through the *Latitude 38* article and took the time to write me about how he and his friend Doug had removed the bronze tube without cutting it out of the fiberglass.

"After removing the V-drive and prop shaft, Doug made up a slide hammer from a half-inch stainless rod approximately six feet long and threaded at each end. The rod was inserted into the old tube from the outside, and then a cap matching the tube diameter was screwed on to the inboard side. This cap is what ultimately pulled the tube out of the boat. Washers on the rod centered it inside the tube. The rod had a weighted slide on the outside end, which was used to hammer the tube out of the fiberglass."

I forage around the yard for scrap parts to build a slide hammer. A few days later, my *extracteur* is welded together, but the machine shop has made the cap from aluminum instead of steel. I know the aluminum will be too soft, but I agree to try it anyway.

I borrow a massive sledgehammer from the yard, since I hadn't found a weighted slide, and wind up for the swing. The hulking head of the hammer meets the welded plate like a bad gong and reverberates through my body. The tube doesn't budge. By the fifteenth hit I've broken through the welding on the plate. I go up to see what's happening inside and find the aluminum cap completely crumpled. I carry the broken parts to the other side of the boatyard while workers and yachties stare curiously.

"*Extracteur!*" I yell. I'm like a bad rash that won't go away.

I implore the welder to make me a cap from steel and reweld the plate onto the pipe. In the meantime, I grind off the recent fiberglass repair job all the way to the bronze tube. With the tube now exposed on both sides, I hammer at it to try to loosen its bond with the fiberglass. With no neighbors in the VIP yard, I'm free to pound on it anytime I please, which is often. When my beefed-up *extracteur* is ready to go, Taputu comes over to help. But within a few swings, the cap is sucked sideways into the tube. Fail.

Even worse, my baby bird is sick. Oli eats less and less, so I load him into in my bike basket and pedal off to find a veterinarian in town. He sells me a nutrient supplement and explains that very few young seabirds survive without their mother. I give Oli a dose of the supplement, but after an hour, he can hardly lift his wee head. It's too late. He takes his last breath as I hold him cupped in my hands. I burst into tears and stroke his still warm feathers.

The fragility of life seems cruel. My little friend is gone. *Swell* feels terribly empty—no more chirps, no more stinky fish feedings, and no more adorable fuzzy head popping up to say good morning. Instead, only progress-less projects in this boatyard purgatory.

To make matters worse, the filthy bathroom is so far away that I've been defecating in plastic bags. There's no end to the humbling around here.

On many days, I want to give up; Oli's departure stirs my deep abandoment issues, but I when I look around, I remember I'm not the only one who is feeling lonely and unheard. The same small island kids from the rough neighborhood nearby wander in the streets every day. Stray dogs meander through, hungry and forlorn. Playing with the kids and feeding the dogs makes me feel better. I also use a technique learned from a Pema Chödrön book. It's called tonglen: I sit and breathe in the pain and unwanted sufferings of myself and others, and breathe out feelings of relief, connection, and happiness for all beings. It's a simple idea, but doing this meditation helps me feel less alone.

In the afternoons, hordes of young Tahitians blare music, ride bikes, play, and hang out under the coconut trees outside the new chain-link fence surrounding the VIP yard. When it cools off enough, everyone comes together on the forty-yard stretch of asphalt outside the gate where the day's quarrels, crushes, and moods play out in a daily soccer match.

Teams fluctuate in number and skill—girls, boys, women, and men of all ages mix freely. No shoes, no jerseys, no referees, but street rules and common courtesy keep the game flowing much better than one might imagine. No one keeps score. Newcomers watch for a moment from the sidelines to determine the dominant team and then join the weaker side. The stuffy French yard owner lined the fence with barbed wire along the bottom to deter them, but they play on, making sure the younger kids stay clear of the danger. I'd like to join in, but I feel shy.

I know a lot of the younger kids by now. Daily, I offer treats, give them attention, and let them use my skateboard to glide back and forth in the alleyway on the other side of the fence. Their youthful energy and sincerity always gives me a boost. They've stopped calling me *madame*, to my great relief, and scream "Leeeeeeeez!" whenever I surface from inside *Swell*.

One afternoon my body badly needs to move. Today's soccer match is already going on. I finally walk out the gate and ask, "*Je peux jouer?*" (Can I play?)

"*Oui!*" they scream, delighted, assigning me to a team.

The street games becomes my daily release. I saunter out the gate, filthy and barefoot after a day of work aboard *Swell*, and sprint back and forth until it's too dark to see. Whether the clouds pour down rain or the sunset ignites the sky above, I feel grateful for the damp asphalt, the half-inflated ball, my callused feet, the warm salt-laden air, and the giggling, shit-talking, glowing faces of my new Tahitian friends.

In the tranquility of night, I often wrap up in long pants and a pareo to fend off the mosquitoes and go on deck. I don't really know how to pray, so I tell my worries to the moon. I tell her everything: that I'm lonely, I miss my family and friends, I want to find true love, and I hate being stuck in this noxious, filthy place. And I am doing my best not to whine, to see the opportunities for growth, but it's hard.

The first slender sliver of the crescent moon hears every word, gently reminding me to be patient and carry on with grace through the hardships. As the nights pass, she smiles wider and brighter and higher, as if it's all some hilarious cosmic joke. The waxing half-moon tells me of good things to come and to look at the half-full side of the story. As she nears her full grandeur, she encourages me to be brave—that others are struggling too—and I must use the light inside me to find my way. The waning moon advises me to stop resisting and try a different approach. I even feel the new moon through the dark starry nights, reminding me that light follows darkness—go inward, wipe my slate clean, start anew. Everything is perfect, she says, so perfect that you can't yet understand.

The Shaft Tube Challenge

The prop tube battle continues. I have a slightly larger steel cap made for the *extracteur* and use a hacksaw to cut the upper side of the tube level. Josh from the pearl farm I'd visited with Gaspar happens to be in the neighborhood and offers to help. He goes below the hull with the sledgehammer while I stay inside the cabin to make sure the steel cap is positioned correctly.

"My father always told me that your force comes from the *mula band-ha*—the area right between the sphincter and genitals. If you tighten it, you can find power you never knew you had," Josh calls up from below.

"Awesome!" I shout back. I'd just been reading about the yogic band-has, chakras, and nadis. Josh proves his father's words, because on the third try, he hits the steel plate with a force that severs the upper threads of the cap and sends the *extracteur* flying across the yard. But the tube doesn't budge.

I still can't find anyone else to hire to help cut out the tube. Storage fees for the yard mount each day. I have to find another solution ... but how? Who? As I wander aimlessly through the rows of masts on a Friday afternoon, Mike, a lively British cruiser with his boat in the yard, yells down at me from atop his shiny blue hull, "Hey Liz! We just got my rudder shaft out using a hydraulic jack. Maybe this is your answer?"

He passes it down to me. Never has a girl sprinted faster carrying a fifteen-pound hydraulic jack as I do back to the VIP yard. I haul it up the ladder, pull off *Swell*'s stairs, and place it into the space just in front of the tube.

"It fits!" I cheer. "I'll just have to remove the V-drive base and cut some wood and steel supports. Since it will have to work on its side, the jack might need some extra fluid," I tell myself.

I race cheerfully down to the Friday gathering in the garage to announce the good news. "I'm tired of seeing you walking around here looking like a lost puppy," Mike says. "I'll be at your boat at 10 am tomorrow. If I can't get that tube out in two hours, it's officially impossible!"

I roll over at 9:45 am, hoping that Mike wants to postpone our appointment for the Shaft Tube Challenge. I've only slept a few hours; Taputu had knocked on my hull at 3 am to warn of an approaching tsunami. I headed for higher ground with my friend Simona and her son, but thankfully the impact was insignificant. I'm about to douse myself with the hose when the British film director-turned-sailor rolls onto the scene right on time. In lieu of my shower, he sends me running about the yard in search of scrap wood and metal to brace the jack.

Tick, tock ... tick, tock ... he will give exactly two hours of his time, no more. The scavenger hunt continues. I'm exhausted, hot, and hungry while scavenging under the blazing tropical sun. The clock strikes noon and we've only just finished building a mish-mash of metal and wood scraps to brace and fit the jack properly against the small area of vertical fiberglass.

Just as Mike's overtime charges are about to begin accumulating, Adrian, the cheery six-foot-two Canadian aboard *Cassiopeia,* appears. He's been borrowing my bike to ride to town for parts to fix up his newly acquired steel sloop. I praise Mike for getting things started. Now Adrian steps in. He needs cash; I need help. We make a deal, and after a few more hours of setup, we're nearly ready to pressurize the jack.

I've borrowed a hefty, flame-spitting butane torch, and theorize with Adrian that if we heat and cool the bronze tube—without setting *Swell* on fire—we might be able to break the bond between the resin and the bronze. Adrian stands by with a bucket of water. The tube turns rainbow colors as I blast it with heat. When we agree that any more might cause *Swell* to spontaneously combust, Adrian throws on some water to induce a quick contraction of the metal.

After several rounds of heating and cooling, the true test begins. Back inside the cabin, Adrian pumps the jack's lever, placing twenty tons of pressure against that stubborn old shaft tube. I can hardly bear to watch—for my fear of exploding jacks since my accident at Georges and Marika's—and knowing that if this fails, the only solution is the lengthy open-fiberglass surgery. I decide to go down to ground level and survey the progress from the other end where I can see if it has moved: not a millimeter.

"Hit it with the sledgehammer!" Adrian calls from above.

"Great idea!" I holler back, slinging the beast of a tool over my shoulder, squeezing my *mula bandha*, and unloading a hefty swing on the exposed part of the tube. Wham!

"It moved!" he yells.

"REALLY?" I shriek back. Upon inspection, I confirm that the shaft tube has officially been pushed one millimeter in the right direction!

We carry on like this for hours, Adrian loading up pressure with the jack, and me swinging the sledgehammer. Millimeter by sweet millimeter, we make progress. When the tube finally nears extraction, the puzzling cause of the leak is revealed: a series of bean-sized holes corroded through the upper end.

Refugee Rescues on a Sea of Plastic

Swell hits the sea watertight after a series of miracles that followed the shaft tube extraction. When I emailed the news that the tube was out, Fin and Doug offered to ship me an epoxy replacement tube and cutlass bearing for half price, and cover the shipping! And then a willing glasser had appeared to install it. After two long years in and out of the yard, I can finally say that the leak saga has ended, but I feel depleted and a little lost.

The trade winds are out of breath today; I need to get back in the water. I have a hunch about a wave that might be breaking, so I grab my board and shove a pareo, a grapefruit, and sunscreen into my pack and jump in the dinghy. The worn-out hunk of rubber is barely hanging on, but again that day, it delivers me to the pass.

A few waves into the session, an enormous thunderhead swallows the high mountains behind me. Thunder cracks and cold rain pelts down so heavily I can barely see. I paddle back to the dinghy through the bullying drops and wait out the storm under my board bag.

By the time it stops, the squall winds have ruined the surf, so I slowly putt back toward *Swell*. As I turn the corner of the reef, the sight ahead is startling: a half-mile-long stretch of muddy brown water lined with drifting wood, leaves, and trash. The heavy rain must have opened the river mouth and flushed the debris into the lagoon all at once. I turn off the motor and row through it, collecting the scattered plastic trash.

As I pluck out bottles, bags, and wrappers, I notice movement among the flotsam. Creatures are everywhere. The geckos, lizards, grasshoppers, beetles, snails, and bugs must have been caught in the flash flood. They cling to logs, trash, and clumps of leaves. One by one, I catch them or offer my oar, and load them aboard. My dinghy quickly morphs into a refugee flotilla for life of all sorts—even a CD-sized cane spider. I spend two hours paddling like Pocahontas and loading my ark like Noah.

Amid the rescue efforts, a cockroach comes swimming frantically toward me, but all I can think of is that nasty family of roaches that had infested *Swell*. He struggles in the little whirlpool from my paddle. I look forward and try not to think about him. But how can I leave only him? I decide to turn back, but he's already gone.

When we reach the end of the debris patch, my new crew and I head toward the nearest islet. All sorts of little feet grip the dinghy's flexing, half-deflated hypalon tubes in the evening air; a salty gecko coolly tips its nose into the wind. I snap a picture of the amusing scene for Barry.

I set the creatures free, one by one, then collect even more plastic on the trash-covered islet. On the way home, the dinghy's floor seam suddenly parts from the port tube and the boat fills with six inches of water.

We limp slowly back to *Swell* just after dark, brimming with soggy plastic trash and a few straggling stowaways.

Money and Men

Swell's dock lines slacken and then tighten again. I watch them for a moment, the water droplets leaping off as the lines pull taut. Stepping onto the dock, I stroll around the Tahiti marina. It's a cloudy afternoon and the breeze softly animates the ironwood trees; rain sprinkles intermittently. I suck at the thick sea air and delight in the simplicity of watching my bare feet step rhythmically over the dirt, weeds, and puddles along the marina walkway.

It's good to be back in a baggy T-shirt and cut-offs. It's taken a few days to decompress from the rush and hustle of Southern California. I had flown back to finish up the book project, but despite the potential financial benefits, I ended it completely. It didn't feel right, so I returned the advance money. I also broke it off with a really great guy I'd started dating. I had been torn about both decisions.

Sometimes I feel like I don't fit in anywhere anymore. I've been doing this for five years now and friends have stopped asking when I'm coming home. Only when I'm aboard *Swell* or in wilderness do I feel a sense of true belonging. I try not to judge myself for still being single and nearly broke at thirty years old, but I constantly wrestle these irritating subconscious beliefs about needing a permanent partner and an accruing 401(k).

Of course, I want lasting love, but not at the expense of freedom. And a steady income would be nice, too, but only if it comes from doing something I believe in. Anything else feels like surrender, captivity. I'm now receiving offers to star in television shows and documentary films, but I cherish my anonymity and the purity of the experiences that come from voyaging like I do. The thought of constantly caravanning with a follow boat or film crew makes me cringe.

I feel committed to adhering to my truth, and making choices that feel right. I'm constantly working hard, but most of the time it isn't for money. I stay up late responding to emails, encouraging people to live their dreams. I write blogs to inspire, research environmental issues, connect people, help my neighbors—without any paycheck. But it all comes around. It seems the more I live from the heart, the more my material requirements show up when I really need them.

Patagonia pitched in significantly for the final round in the boatyard. Achilles just sponsored me by providing a new dinghy. A variety of small companies and individuals who are inspired by my voyage often help out with products or donations. Just when I'm down to a couple hundred bucks, I get a request to write an article or sell a photo, or a check just arrives in the mail. A sweet family from South Carolina sends donations from time to time, signed with "Be Encouraged. Love, The Seshuns."

I'm choosing this life adrift, even though it doesn't make it easy to commit to either men or money. I've found that guys with good jobs generally have too many commitments. But men with few commitments often don't like to work hard. Long-distance relationships are no fun, and language and cultural barriers have proven difficult with the few foreign men I've dated. Add the fact that my list of perfect man requirements just keeps getting longer. I've started to wonder if I'll ever find the Yin to my Yang.

In the past, I always liked to have a relationship brewing. I needed a friend to adventure with, and often it was easier to find eager guys than girls. I gleaned confidence from having a man adore me, too. I drove a few mad because they couldn't hold onto me. Other times I got clingy—my abhorrence of abandonment keeping me from leaving or making smart boundaries. Sometimes we both knew the romance was situational and purely for fun. There were excruciating heartbreaks too.

Whether it was just one date, a week's fling, or a longer connection, I've learned from every man I ever spent time with. Some taught me what I don't want in a partner, but most of them offered something positive. My first boyfriend taught me not to be a kook in the surf. A few others also helped me hone my wave-riding skills. The fisherman showed me the magic of generosity and nonattachment. The poet made me feel securely enraptured by his love. I had mad chemistry with the carpenter. The yes-man taught me how to have more fun. The lifeguard knew how to keep things light, loving, and simple. But these romances all ended for one reason or another. Paralleling paths are precious while they last, but holding onto a relationship for longer than it serves both parties does neither any good. Casual romance doesn't interest me anymore; I want the real deal.

When will a man show up who really complements my strengths and my lifestyle? I'd like him to be tough but sensitive. Strong and charming. A surfer. A thinker and a romantic. A nature lover and thrill seeker. Positive and funny. A dreamer and a hero. Spontaneous yet patient. Confident yet not too prideful. Spiritual but not a know-it-all. I hope he enjoys dancing. He'll have things to teach me, but also be willing to learn. Most importantly, he should make me a better person by setting my heart ablaze and forcing me to look at my blocks to fully loving and being loved.

While I'm waiting for him to appear, though, being single feels okay, spacious I guess. I walk on, watching raindrops hit puddles and finding great contentment in giving my whole attention to the present. My father is coming for Christmas. I have two months to get *Swell* dialed in, catch up on my writing, and enjoy some surfing and sailing.

Before long, while walking back to *Swell* after doing laundry at a friend's house, I see a bunch of guys I know sitting around a small dock they're building. A tall, handsome stranger is among them. They're finished for the day and offer me a beer. I have a sip or two to be polite, but I can't stay. I have things to get done before my departure tomorrow morning.

"Thank you, but I have to go put my dinghy on deck before dark," I say in the local mixture of French and Tahitian.

"*Tu veux un coup de main?*" (Can I give you a hand?) the new guy asks.

I look at the other guys for approval. I rarely take the help of a total stranger, but four hands would make it so much easier. They nod and encourage me.

"*Je m'appelle Rainui,*" he says, sticking out his hand respectfully. It closes around mine, strong and callused. He picks up my sail bag full of clean clothes and follows me to the dinghy. Together, we quickly get the dinghy and motor on deck. He is quiet and gentlemanly, and I thank him sincerely before he swims ashore in the coming darkness.

Tubes for Breakfast

Offshore winds rip over the stacked swell lines, blowing water droplets off the wave faces into hovering rainbows as the lips pitch and arc into glorious indigo barrels. My eyes bulge as the quiet girl with long, brown hair and a slender, athletic body drives gracefully through another deep tube and shoots out right in front of me.

"Yew!" I holler from the shoulder. "That was unreal!" She shrugs it off.

"Thanks," she says softly, "but you can totally do it too. You surf well. You just gotta commit early and swoop in behind it."

"I don't know," I mumble, following her back up the reef.

I have tried hard to master tube riding, but I'm still inconsistent. I have moments when everything comes together but I lack confidence, which often makes the difference between making the drop or getting pitched over the falls. I have learned a lot about falling, though—like how to "starfish" underwater, cover my head, and just relax to decrease my chances of hitting the sharp coral. I can't count how many times I've hit the reef. My legs, feet, and back are scarred with reminders.

I paddle for my next wave, get in early, and do some turns, but when it warps into a hollow section with jagged exposed reef sticking up only feet from the impact zone, I kick out like usual. Frustrated, I paddle back toward the lineup again, knowing I'm still missing out on the holy grail of surfing.

Kepi is a natural—smooth, powerful, stylish, and poised. She uproots my prior ideas of what a woman is capable of doing on a wave. Her reserve intimidated me when I first arrived in the bay, but since we both surf in the early mornings before the crowds, we've gotten to know each other. She was raised in California and Kaua'i, chose this South Pacific paradise over a high-profile surfing career, married a local surfer, and has two beautiful kids. I dig her simple, unassuming style.

The swell keeps pouring in over the next week. Not too big, not too small, offshore winds, and just the right angle to produce flawless wave cylinders.

I have no excuses not to step it up. We meet at the peak after she drops her kids at school. I study her every movement. Little by little I gain more confidence.

"Go!" my tube guru encourages.

"Are you sure? I'm not too deep?" I hesitate.

"No, you're good. You got it. Just paddle," she affirms.

Finally, it happens: a breakthrough. I start trusting myself and the wave. Instead of jumping into the face or closing my eyes when it looks like it's going to close out, I hold my line. I get clipped here and there, but falling inside the tube isn't as scary as I had imagined. I start to feel where to slow down, find the pocket, and then all I have to do is hang on while the lip falls around me and I shoot for the light.

"See?" Kepi cheers as I come flying out of a deep one. "You've got it!"

Short but Sweet

When I return from island hopping a couple weeks later, Rainui keeps appearing. First he's eating with friends by the waterfront and then he's near the pineapples at the open market. A few days later he picks me up when I'm hitchhiking to town and asks if I want to hang out sometime. I give him my number.

After I've spent a long day taking apart my corroded transmission lever, crammed in a stuffy compartment with a tube of grease and a pile of wrenches, Rainui calls. It's Friday and I feel like getting off the boat. He suggests walking to the lookout on the mountain above town.

"It's almost full moon," he reminds me.

"*J'aimerais bien*" (I'd like to), I agree. He picks me up and we drive to the trailhead, and start up the grassy path exchanging small talk. Soon we walk together in peaceful silence among the moon shadows, higher and higher above town. About three-quarters of the way up, I slip on a loose rock and plunge toward the ground. He lunges to catch me before

I hit, pulling me back to my feet. We both laugh and, as we take off again, he reaches for my hand.

It's a perfect fit. He holds it without hesitation—not too tight, not too loose. I feel safe; I would never do this walk at night alone. As a single female traveler I choose evening outings carefully, never forgetting the nights I've been chased by pit bulls on my bike or followed by lecherous or belligerent males.

We see each other several times over the next few weeks. He's not pushy when I tell him I'm busy, but he's available when I want to hang out. He's six years younger than me, speaks no English, and has no steady work, but he's polite and charming. Flowers and fruits appear in the cockpit some mornings, and I notice that our outings seem blessed—the wind turns offshore as we arrive to surf, a huge rainbow arches over the mountain when we find a waterfall, and on the next full moon together, we're sitting in *Swell's* cockpit intertwined, only to be surprised by a full lunar eclipse.

I have few obligations to take care of before Dad arrives, and I'm thrilled to have Rainui's chivalrous company to explore the island. He carries the heavy pack on a four-hour mountain hike to go camping. We set up the tent near a small waterfall among the lofty green peaks with a majestic view of the open sea to the west. The orange flames of our little campfire match the blazing colors of sunset, while we warm soup and munch on the guava berries we've collected. When the wind blows the tarp off the stake in the night, he leaps up to fix it. I relax and enjoy feeling like a princess.

Rainui calls one day, sounding troubled.

"What is it?" I ask when he arrives. We sit together on the bow of *Swell* and he takes my hands.

"I signed up for the army and I've been accepted to the parachutist program in the south of France. I'm supposed to leave in three weeks." He had recently returned to Tahiti after several years working construction in Marseilles when his dream of becoming a legionnaire was dashed.

The news takes me completely by surprise, but I hear his soul calling for this experience. I hide my selfish sadness and make sure he feels encouraged.

"Well this is great news!" I exclaim. "You must go. And tonight, we should celebrate."

The Dadmiral

A few days later, my father walks off the plane with an enormous smile on his face. We embrace for a full minute. He's loaded with all kinds of goodies, including a new refrigerator compressor to replace my dead one.

We are underway aboard *Swell* a couple hours later. Christmas Day has gifted us gentle trades, whisking handfuls of cumulus clouds across the grand ceiling of blue. Dad is in heaven; he has come from below-freezing temperatures in Michigan where he's recently been working. We're both glowing; this is the first time Dad has ever sailed on *Swell*. He's spent more than his share of hours working aboard, but today he stands at the helm, steering her smoothly through the lagoon with his grand perma-grin.

"She takes off like a racehorse through the water!" he exclaims as a gust accelerates us. I leap about trimming sails and making sure all is in order.

After dropping anchor later in the day, we can't resist installing the new fridge compressor, and an hour later he has a cold Hinano in hand. He works so hard; I'm thrilled he has this two-week vacation to enjoy the sea and nature with me.

We sail around the islands, and the ocean shows us a bit of everything—glorious fifteen knots on the stern quarter, some squally thirty-knot up-wind slogs, rain and rainbows, gusts and lulls, and even a waterspout. Every type of condition thrills Dad's pirate heart. He grows out his beard and relaxes into his favorite element.

I put up no resistance to his beer drinking. I don't want my wish for him to live a healthier lifestyle to cloud our time together. I want him to feel comfortable and enjoy himself as he pleases. He deserves it; I couldn't ask for a more loving dad.

I scowl out the porthole at the brooding sky, when we wake to pouring rain for the second day in a row. Dad cheerfully lights the teakettle.

"Oh Dad, I just wanted your time here to be so perfect," I moan.

"That's how it goes, honey. We can't control nature," he replies merrily. He breaks into the lyrics of a country song with a bold twang, "I love the rain, because the rain makes the corn, and the corn makes the whiskey, and I loooooove whiskey!"

He much prefers beer, but his point is clear. I hug him and we spend the day catching rain to fill the water tanks, then troubleshoot a problem with the bilge pumps, and enjoy a wet afternoon walk ashore holding hands and tromping through puddles.

After spending New Year's Eve with his family, Rainui and I say good-bye. Dad is there to hug me when I come back to *Swell* with swollen eyes.

I'm thinking about setting off on another voyage to the outer islands, now that my French has drastically improved and my visa is sorted for a while. But I'm having qualms about going alone.

"It would just be so much more fun to share it with someone I love," I tell Dad.

"I understand, Lizzy. Remember, you don't have to do this anymore. You can come home tomorrow if you want."

"I want to keep sailing," I reply.

"Well then, keep sailing. You can do it. You sail this boat like it's a part of you."

I'm certain that the confidence behind his ever-supportive words is a huge reason I have come so far. Looking back, it seems mad that he'd backed some of my choices, but through the years his profound belief in me always gave me the courage to choose love over fear.

15,851
Nautical Miles Traveled

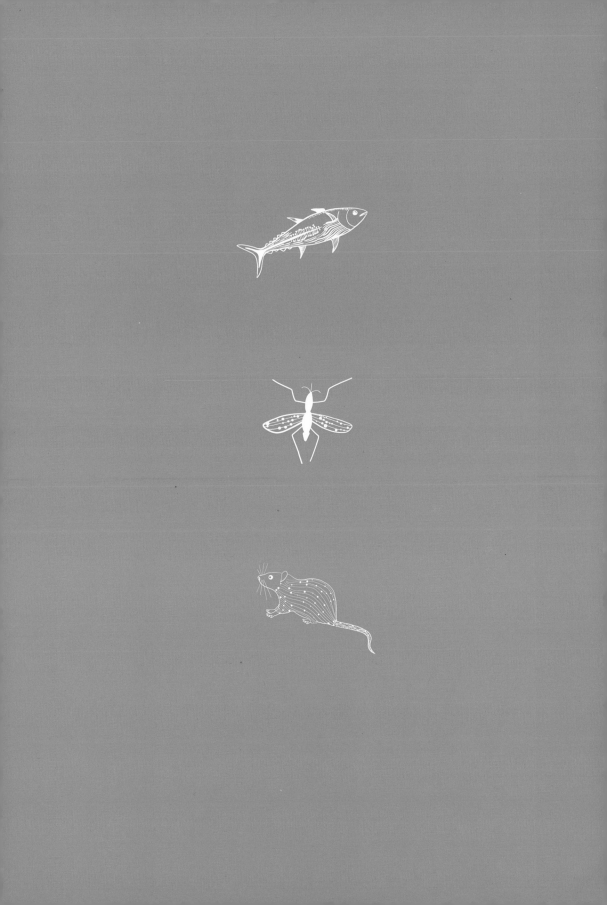

Om mani padme Om!

TAHITI

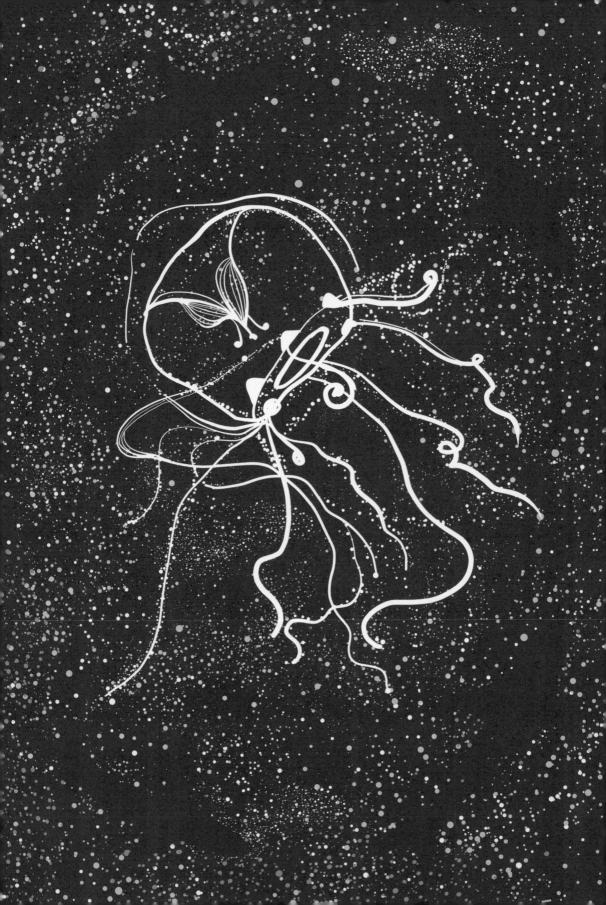

Revelations

Ripple Effect

On my own again, I lean back comfortably against the trunk of a slanted palm, and watch the waves still funneling through. "If it all ended now," I think, "that would be okay."

I made it through this afternoon's surf without a reef cut. A crew of good-vibes Tahitian guys was out, sharing waves and cheering each other's rides, and mine too. I'm relaxed and content after the thrill, camaraderie, and exercise. Pink hues begin to flash across a thick swab of clouds overhead and color the water's slick surface. A moment later, it begins to rain. When the fat, widely spaced raindrops hit the lagoon, circular ripples undulate from each drop.

Suddenly thousands of raindrops fall before me. The movement of the expanding rings through the rosy water triggers some kind of trance. I watch the droplets transform into mini-swells of energy—varying wave amplitudes crossing over each other from all directions. Dynamic, chaotic, brilliant. Both infinite and finite at once. Time freezes and it feels as if my consciousness is floating. I am the raindrop, and the cloud, and the sky, and the setting sun. On this unusual frequency, I feel the connectedness of all things, a sensation of deep belonging. All one and simultaneously separate. Feeling becomes understanding—this great dichotomy dissolves. In this strange, brief moment, I am expansive like the Milky Way, minute like plankton, powerful like the tides, as solid as the volcanic crater, fragile like a spider's web, patient like the trees, and empty as a cloudless sky.

Times and events flash through my mind like a sudden wind: happily joining my kindergarten circle; my auntie spreading fairy dust for my sixth birthday; capsizing in the bay in my little sailing dinghy; taking a taxi to gymnastics practice when I was grounded; beaten to the shore by the whitewater; sneaking out my bedroom window; pranking the lifeguards with my high school girlfriends; rolling in the hot sand; knocking on my first boyfriend's door to find another girl inside; accidentally eating a pot brownie before my classes at UCSB; my first wave at a point break; dancing with my mother; and curled up on the soft, blessed spot on my father's chest.

They all brought me to this mystic moment. All my knowing is unimportant. The facts and data have no relevance to this feeling of deep integration; oneness. There is no escape, but I don't want one. It's so peaceful here.

In another breath, I am back under the palm: The rainfall has lightened to an effervescent hum, the pinks are fading to grays, and the mosquito biting my toe reminds me that I am back in my skin. I slowly rise to my feet, wade out to the dinghy, and maneuver home through the coral heads before dark.

Conversations with the Clouds

I'm ready for big skies, open horizons, and wild islands. It's time to put some miles under the hull. My dad's reassurance helps me feel more confident about setting out on an extended solo passage again. I'm feeling strong and proud to see how my enhanced self-awareness and applied spiritual wisdoms have eased my day-to-day struggles. I haven't had a real bout of depression in more than two years. The more I feel connected to the world and beyond—through my expanded compassion, my "one love" experience by the lagoon, and the growing group of conscious people I've connected with through my blog—the more potential I see for myself and humanity.

But a new question burns in me: How do all these concepts I'm learning— Melanie's wisdom, karma, compassion, inner healing, oneness—how do they all fit into solving the environmental crisis? Everywhere I look, human greed, immediacy, psychological separation from nature and each other, and prioritizing profits and the present over the future are taking a toll on the planet. And despite all the technology and "progress," most people aren't thriving, they're just getting by. And now with global climate steadily warming, every aspect of Earth's life-support systems will be affected. There's no sailing away from it; in fact, long-standing weather patterns will shift and storms will get stronger. I want to stop participating in this madness, but even way out here, I don't really see how.

It's an uncomfortable feeling knowing that my light skin somehow links me to the erosion of Polynesian culture. The new god forced upon the native people since colonization—money—means nature is no longer respected here as it once was. An old man recently told me the story of Tahitian politician Pouvanaa Oopa, who mounted a movement against proposed French nuclear testing in the late fifties. At the height of his campaign, he was suspiciously accused of arson and exiled to France. By the time he returned home, a decade later, nuclear bombs were being dropped a few hundred miles from inhabited islands. Recently declassified documents show that only ten years into the thirty years of bombing, tests showed Tahiti was already contaminated with 500 times the maximum allowed level of plutonium fallout. *Is it okay to test bombs in someone else's backyard? Is it moral for corporations to sell their processed snacks here without informing Tahitians that it can hardly be considered food, and that the wrappers they arrive in will never biodegrade?*

Every day, I fish plastic out of the lagoons en route to and from *Swell*. Massive container ships arrive daily to offload fossil fuels, edibles, sugary drinks, and cheap plastic imports that quickly end up in the landfills. The coral is dying off in developed areas, and fish populations are clearly declining. People eat more and more imported meats, refined sugars, and packaged foods, contributing to high rates of obesity and rampant diabetes. The stores sell harsh pesticides to kill bugs and chemical soaps to wash our dishes, clothes, and bodies—all of it ending up in the waterways and oceans. Diesel generators run day and night to supply electricity, and leave behind barrels of used oil that's rarely disposed of safely.

Our fossil fuel–based economy means virtually everything we do releases carbon one way or another. The impact from climate change will be devastating here—the melting poles that cause rising seas may swallow the low-lying atolls and islets altogether. In the meantime, cruisers drop anchor on live coral, and our hulls release heavy metals from anti-fouling paint into the pristine waters. As much as I try to live lightly, I'm still part of the problem.

I write to Barry about these troubling observations. "It's overwhelming, really. I want to dedicate myself to a specific environmental cause, but it feels impossible to pick just *one*. They're all so interconnected and complex, and I know I'm up against huge forces of greed. All that's in my power right now is to change myself. I can further simplify, keep educating myself, buy less stuff I don't need, and vote with my dollar when I do make purchases. On this trip through the outer islands, I want to try to eat more from the local environments, instead of relying on imported foods with their high carbon footprint."

Barry writes back:

"Your observations are pertinent. ... The latest studies show that a rapid reduction in greenhouse gas emissions is inevitable for life to continue as we know it on our planet. Try not to be discouraged, though, Lizzy. What you're doing out there is important. I imagine you are eager to sail again; I'm much looking forward to your stories. I have hope that humanity can create the technology to provide modern living standards to all, while finding balance with nature. We will need to use our hearts just as much as our heads, though. I do wince to think of what may be lost in the meantime. ... Did I mention that a gas station up the street from the harbor sells biodiesel now? I bought some for *Freya's* engine. Every small step forward is exciting. Courage, my dear. Don't give up the ship!"

Swell is ready: dinghy on deck, gear stashed and stowed. My new leafy companions—basil, aloe, mint, lemongrass, and oregano plants—are wedged securely around the cabin. The night is eerily calm; the Milky Way explodes across the sky. *Swell* gently surges against the dock as I top off the water tanks. I make my preparations as if each knot and gear placement is part of a sacred routine—one lazy decision can mean losing everything.

I pull *Swell* away from the dock and head slowly toward the pass. I'm off.

I motor most of the night to make some solid miles of easting. The bright moonlight and slack winds ease me gently back into the rhythm of an overnight passage. The next morning, the sea is a regal sheet of blue silk billowing out in all directions. The calm weather has eased my pre-passage nerves. By midday a puff of east wind ripples the surface, so I put up all the sails and fall into a steady reach. With the engine off, the sounds of the open sea come alive. The high and low notes of waves lapping against the hull, the whispers of wind, the carbonated fizz of sea foam bubbling in our wake, the stretching sails and lines, and the cry of a passing seabird all harmonize into an ocean symphony.

I tell the sea of my sufferings in the boatyard, my distress about the state of the planet, and my loneliness since parting with Rainui. Last time

I spoke to him, he sounded disappointed. The army had deemed him too heavy to be a parachutist, and he had been shipped off to the freezing-cold northeast corner of France to become a regular infantryman with new, much younger recruits.

"Just give it a little time," I had told him. "Maybe it will get better." But I do miss him.

The cloud ballet coaxes me back to the present. The graceful wisps tell me to stop thinking about what isn't and appreciate what is. A sticky pang of emptiness clings to my chest. I tell the clouds I don't need to sail alone anymore, that I have proven to myself what needed proving. I want a lover to share the exploration, the workload, the sunsets, the meals, and the wild surprises with me. The clouds just keep morphing and moving—not resisting the winds that mold them. I get it, but it's not always easy.

After dozing off, I wake to the setting sun shooting a cluster of brilliant rays skyward. Scattered clouds above bathe in reds, pinks, and oranges. The colors grow brighter still, almost neon, then fade slowly back to grays. I watch until the day is only a glowing two-finger strip above the horizon. A thin layer of neon blue fends off the imminent darkness. Deep purple settles over the rest of the sky. Scattered planets appear. And then, like galactic candles being lit, the stars begin to glow one by one.

I can't remember the last time I watched a day's full transition to night. How have we become so busy that we hardly notice Earth's daily miracles?

Free as a Bird

"Skree, skreee, skree!" The birds' cries wake me from a dead sleep. I crack open my eyes and squint up at the flapping wings churning above me. *Where am I?*

"Skree, skree, skree!"

I sit up and wrap my sheet around me in the cool dawn air, relieved that I made it to a safe anchorage after two days of upwind slogging and a sketchy sunset run through the pass. The flock of hungry terns circles and dives around *Swell*. The baitfish hiding below are under full attack. A school of jacks and a lone needlefish dart at the school from below, sending them fleeing in all directions and erupting at the surface in frenzied leaps. This is exactly what I came for: thriving nature on full display right here on my turquoise doorstep.

"I MADE IT! I'm here!" I shout to the terns. They are more excited about the baitfish, but I continue bouncing up and down on the cockpit cushion.

After cleaning up *Swell* and emailing my parents and Barry to let them know I've arrived to the little island safely, I launch the dinghy, load up my rusty, no-brakes bike, and head toward what looks like the easiest place to land. My first moments in a new place are often my favorite; I hop on my bike excited to check out the island. With the trades now at my back, my lungs tingle and my legs thrill to push my weight after the passage. To my right, the brilliant blue ocean tosses itself dramatically upon the fringe of bare pink coral. I pedal a few miles through the shade of the coconut palms lining the road, past an airstrip, a hotel, a school, and a few stores and homes. Not a soul stirs; it's Sunday. I take my time, winding on through the empty town, and stopping to chat with a group of teens on their way back from a surf.

"Right up there," they point.

I come around the corner and nearly fall off my bike. Light offshores groom a set wave as it peels across the reef in the golden afternoon light. I smile in awe of the magical scene and then head over to say hello to some locals standing under a tree. They offer me a snack of *uto*—the spongy interior part of a sprouted coconut.

"You want to surf?" a guy asks, pointing to his yellowed, beat-up board.

"Really? Yeah! Thank you so much!" I say, jumping at the offer.

I grab the heavy old board, strip off my hat and sunnies with glee, and skip up the point in my clothes. A kid getting out of the water leads me through the maze of coral heads, then I paddle up the little coral point. Before I even reach the lineup, a wave swings wide, and I'm in position. I drop in and trim down the line of warping golds and pinks. The locals under the tree raise their arms in celebration. I relish a couple more waves while the sun melts into a tuft of clouds in the west. Seabirds soar through the magenta sky. One young kid is still out with me.

"*Regarde*" (Look), he says, pointing.

Through the palms at the top of the point, the voluptuous full moon glows rusty orange. I let out a wild howl; the kid yelps too.

Birthday Parting

I receive word via email that Barry isn't doing well. He had another shoulder surgery and the recovery has been tough. On the morning of my thirty-first birthday, a few days later, I learn that Barry—my dear friend, my environmental hero, the man who guided and empowered me to live my dream—has passed away at eighty-seven years old.

I walk the lagoon shallows that day, heavy with the loss, watching small sharks scavenge the shallow waters. Mourning Barry out in the natural world—where he always turned for inner strength and renewal—feels most appropriate. I toast him under the stars that evening with the last drops of a bottle of sherry he gave me. His parting comes so abruptly; I need some sort of goodbye sign—a shooting star, a whisper on the wind, a quick stop on his way to the other side?

That first night, I wait for a visit until well after midnight. Each night after, I look up at the heavens and think of him. I imagine him sitting at the wooden seat on the stern of my boat, wrapped in his black wool peacoat.

A week or two later, I sit in the surf alone after arriving at a new island. Since Barry's passing, there has been plenty of action: I dove with hordes of sharks, ran a tidal river in *Swell*, landed a yellowfin tuna, and swam with wild dolphins. Still no sign of him. Not even when I had to go up the mast at sea to retrieve the head of the furler because the stitching on the top of my genoa burst and the sail fell into the sea. The lineup feels lonely this morning. The sharky waters and shallow reef seem scarier than usual, and I let a few waves go by as tears flow down my face. I watch them drip into the sea off my chin.

Just then I notice something moving below the surface. A tiny jellyfish. All at once Barry is with me. On our last visit together, we went to lunch at the yacht club in Santa Barbara like always, and he gave me a book in which a tiny species of jellyfish called the *Lizzia blondina* is described. Edward Forbes—the humorous and passionate biologist, a contemporary of Charles Darwin—discovered the pretty little invertebrate, and named it after a crush. Barry found it amusing and had marked the page and saved the book for my visit.

He was in a wheelchair that day, and as I pushed him down the sidewalk near the beach after lunch, a large sand flea leapt frantically across the cement, desperate to find its element again. Barry leaned over to help the lost creature find its way, but before he could, a bird swooped down and picked it up, swallowing as it flew away.

"Well, we tried, Lizzy," he sighed. "There comes a time for all of us to get recycled back into the seams of life, my dear."

The little jellyfish dances and twirls just in front of me. Jellyfish are a rare sight in these waters, and never have I seen this sort of miniature, tasseled species. "*Lizzia blondina*," I chuckle. Something assures me the little creature is here to comfort me.

More tears fall as I tell Barry how much I am going to miss him—his scholarly wisdom, unfailing support, and thoughtful approach to life. His wit, philosophy, and tireless backing of people and causes he believed in. His efforts to make the world better. Our letters and lunches. I tell him that I wouldn't be who I am today if it wasn't for his foresight, encouragment, and generosity. The jellyfish stays close, pumping its many tentacles beside me.

"How can I ever thank you enough?" I ask him, "I often wonder what would have become of me if we hadn't met. I don't know how far I will make it, but you will live on with me every single day, on or off *Swell*. Thank you for believing in me. I love you, Barry."

When I finally stop gushing, I hear his voice clearly in my mind.

"Now, now, Lizzy girl. The pleasure was all mine. I will be with you on the darkest nights and wildest days. Carry on, brave one, and don't give up the ship!"

The dark line of a set wave lifts ahead of me and the little jellyfish disappears into the depths. "Don't go!" I say.

My instinct is to follow it, but I hear his words again, "My girl, I am in your heart."

I turn my board and paddle, smiling and crying as I drop in.

Fair Game?

The outer islands treat me well—aside from a few annoying men. It seems lately that men of any age find it perfectly appropriate to hit on me. Is this what happens to women in their thirties? I've dealt with it from men closer to my age throughout the voyage, but this is getting ridiculous. A middle-aged Frenchman is following me around like a puppy, an eighty-year-old doctor starts telling everyone I am his girlfriend, and a local fisherman's favorite fishing hole seems to be right under my boat.

Swell is tied to a town quay on an atoll with a population of two hundred, when a French customs boat bristling with mounted guns arrives around midday. They launch their tender, and a group of uniformed men comes speeding over. The captain scrambles out and storms over.

"What are you doing here?" he demands in French. "This dock is for cargo ships and official French vessels only!"

"I'm so sorry, sir," I reply. "The villagers told me that the next ship wouldn't be in until Thursday. I think we can both fit here if I move my boat forward."

"Where is your husband?" he demands. "Tell him he'll have to move this boat right now!"

"I don't have a husband," I reply.

"You mean you're alone?"

"Yes, sir."

His expression morphs from anger to surprise. Then his brow softens entirely.

"Yes, I believe you're right," he chirps accommodatingly. "We can both fit if we move you forward." He waves over the other men, who handle *Swell*'s lines while I motor her against the outgoing current, and the dark gray boat pulls in behind me.

The captain comes over with a clipboard in hand. I run down to get my official paperwork.

"You're welcome to join us for dinner on board tonight," he says. "And here's my phone number so you can give me a call next time you're in Papeete. I'd like to take you out for an evening on the town."

He tears a square of paper from the clipboard and slips it into my hand, squeezing my fingers for an uncomfortably long pause while looking me up and down. Without checking my paperwork, he turns and walks back to his ship.

I am tired of feeling vulnerable to men. I dress in raggedy, oversized clothes and try to send out the message that I'm not interested, but often it doesn't deter them. Once in the boatyard, and another time in a marina, I woke to young men staring down at me through my forward hatch in the night. Luckily, I'd been able to scare them both away.

A few days later I receive an email from Rainui. "My four-month trial period is ending. What if I come back?" he asks. "Could we try to be together? Could I live with you on the boat and find a way to make it work between us?" He isn't taking to the winter weather and doesn't like his commanding officials or his unit. His morale seems to be plunging. I am surprised by his proposition. I didn't expect him to change his mind about the army so drastically.

I have some trepidations about this—I love him, but living and traveling on a boat is a whole new level of intimacy, and I don't know him *that* well. But he's a fast learner, tough and hard-working. It will be another cross-cultural dating adventure, but Polynesians intrigue me—their laid-back style, generosity, and intimacy with nature. They don't hurry. They respect their roots, embrace their elders, and know how to live simply. All of this suits me. And cruising through the outer islands with him would be so much safer, easier, and more fun! It'll put these suitors at bay, too, and who knows, maybe it will work out for the long haul?

Reunited

Two months later, in a tiny outer island boatyard, I sit in the cockpit of *Swell* with Rainui. It hasn't been a smooth transition, but he's here.

We met up in California after I hauled out *Swell* to fly back and attend Barry's memorial service. I was so grateful to have found a way to be there to pay tribute to my legendary friend.

A few days after returning to *Swell*, I became gravely ill with ciguatera poisoning after eating some contaminated fish. As the symptoms came on in the middle of the night, I was reminded of Gaspar's description of the poison's effects. First, a sore throat and a fever, then I was spewing violently from both ends in the middle of the night, amongst the coral rubble and crab holes underneath *Swell*. I began to feel a strange aching and tingling sensation in my arms and legs as the poison took hold.

Rainui stayed by my side for the awful next few days—massaging my burning muscles where the pain was most intense. He had to hold me over the bucket in the forepeak to use the bathroom because my weakened, aching legs could not support me. I had my period at the same time, and cursed my horrid luck, as my new boyfriend disposed of disgusting buckets of my excrements. We consulted with a French doctor over the phone, and his advice to drink milk caused me extra days of suffering. When I wasn't improving, a local grandmother explained to Rainui that consuming any animal protein intensifies the toxin. Together, they made me the traditional remedy from coconut milk and pandanus root. I drank it twice a day for three days.

It's been almost two weeks now, and I'm feeling better, aside from the bizarre prickly and hot sensation I get from touching anything cold. While I gain back my strength, Rainui builds a shelf for cookware, dividers to organize the tools, and a stowable double bed where we can sleep side by side. Thankfully, the grandmother's remedy allows me to eat fish again right away, as not much other food is available among the sand and coral on this low-lying atoll.

Once I'm feeling strong enough, we launch *Swell* and sail away into the most remote, postcard-perfect corners of the islands.

The last time I was in this region, a few years ago, I wasn't able to do much in-depth exploring of the lagoons. It was too dangerous with the numerous unmarked coral heads and the treacherous fetch that can quickly build with a minor switch of the wind. But with two, it's possible. Rainui climbs the mast to direct me through the coral. We develop a technique to build our own temporary moorings, which allows us to tuck *Swell* behind some otherwise impossible sections of reef for protection.

Once *Swell* is secured, we dive or surf or wander on expansive white-sand beaches and bask in the sun. Even here, so far away from civilization, there is a staggering amount of plastic debris mingled with the driftwood in the high tide lines—empty shampoo and soda and oil bottles, lighters, toothbrushes, Styrofoam, and heaps of lost or discarded commercial fishing lines, nets, and buoys. We feel helpless to do anything about it. There is more than we can possibly collect, and even if we did, there are no facilities nearby to dispose of it.

Rainui shares my concerns about the environment and is up for the challenge of trying to eat primarily from what we can find around us. On days we're not sailing, we spend much of our time gathering food—fishing and spearfishing, we're careful to choose fish that eat plankton and have no chance of concentrating ciguatera poison. The mostly healthy reef systems mean sharks often lurk nearby, so we have to work as a team—one shoots the fish while the other keeps the dinghy nearby so we can quickly toss our catch inside. I am able to focus better since fishing in a pair feels much safer, improving my skills with the gun.

I become disciplined about saying a prayer when we take a life to nourish our own. And I feel a responsibility not to waste it, awakening my enthusiasm in the galley. Plus, cooking for two is much more fun than just for me. Meals become ceremonies, their ingredients sacred.

We use a bedsheet to collect tiny baitfish that come ashore by the thousands for a few days in a row, and forage the reef at night for lobsters. We harvest shellfish and urchins, too—but only what we can eat for our next meal. Heart of palm is a delicious vegetable complement to the seafood, easily extracted from a young coconut palm. Islanders often invite us to harvest coconuts from their land or join them in hunting, teaching us new skills. It's heartwarming to see how they consider Rainui family, always looking for ways to make sure our needs are met. An elder man shows us a small leafy plant that the Puamotu eat like salad. Rainui opens sprouted coconuts for the cotton candy–like *uto* on the inside, and we munch on the young shoots as well. We grate mature coconut meat, and wring the sweet milk out of the shavings, to pour over raw fish with a squeeze of lime for breakfast. On its own, the meat of a mature coconut makes an easy, filling snack when hunger calls. We sometimes even slice it thin and fry it.

Once in a while we find bananas or papayas or vegetables in a village. I sprout lentils and mung beans, make yogurt from powdered milk, bake bread, and haul out a bag of rice or pasta when we are desperate for extra calories.

Instead of using the watermaker, we haul water from land to fill *Swell's* tanks, kind villagers offering to share from their rain catchment. Each morning we leap overboard, to dive down and check that the anchor chain isn't snagged on coral. Boat maintenance, passage-making, meals—it's all easier with four hands instead of two. Sharing the workload and the simple wonders helps me fall in love with life afloat all over again. Through Rainui's enthusiasm, I rediscover little things that have become routine over the years. We sleep on deck under the massive atoll sky. The Great Shark—as the Puamotu people call the Milky Way—stretches magnificently over us. We even spot a moonbow one evening as I lie in his arms.

Occasionally we stumble upon waves with no one around, indulging in the surf until our arms can't move. On other days, we dive and hunt in the thriving passes or forage ashore. Gradually I feel as strong and wild as our surroundings.

I'm thrilled to have Rainui's chivalrous help with the heavy lifting, not only because of a nagging knee injury, but because it feels good to explore a more traditionally feminine role. Although I'd felt ready to be more feminine years ago, it made me feel vulnerable when I was alone, so I stuck to my tomboy ways. Now I feel free to wear my ponytail up a little higher, and dig to the bottom of the plastic storage bin that serves as my closet to pull out a skirt or dress. I finally feel safe in clothing that actually flatters my body instead of hides it.

Beyond my attire, I sense an inner transition, too—a letting go of needing to feel in charge. I've always been so intent on doing it all and showing myself and everyone else that I am as capable as a man, but nowadays, I don't feel as much need to show my strength on the outside. I know very well that it resides within me.

Bad Wiring

When all is well, Rainui and I make a fantastic team, but toward the end of our third month together, he starts acting like a light with bad wiring—occasionally going dark. It's like a short circuit occurs in his mind and he goes silent and inward, and then I can't connect with him anymore. He explains that he has a terrible mistrust of women because his first girlfriend left him for his best friend. We spend hours talking out his fears. With both my words and actions I try to convince him that I'm truly in love with him and want to make a life together. As situations arise to trigger him, I go into detailed discourses on the wisdom I have learned through books and experiences, about being present, staying positive, and focusing on the love, not the fear.

Sometimes the switch flips back quickly, and his wonderful, loving, talented, and fun self lights up again. Other times the blackness drags out over an entire day, even two. Every incident seems instigated by jealousy, or fear of losing me. Gradually, I stop calling my male friends. I go back to dressing like a tomboy. If I can just show Rainui how much I love him, maybe he'll feel more secure.

Part of the problem is that he doesn't have his own income, and it's killing him to use my money to continue voyaging. I explain over and over that all his help is actually earning us cruising money, because it frees me up to write blogs and articles, contact sponsors, and sell photos, in addition to allowing me more creative time for writing, thinking, yoga, and meditation. I teach him to use my camera and he takes photos for the blog and sponsors. He fixes, paints, hauls, fishes, and cooks, but it still doesn't feel right to him to use my money to buy dish soap or diesel.

After some island friends show us how to chop and dry copra, we come across an uninhabited islet perfect for the task. I help Rainui gather fallen coconuts and he splits them open and places them in the sun. After he dries six burlap sacks' worth, we haul the copra twenty miles across the lagoon to sell to a cargo ship headed for Tahiti. He earns 65,000 francs. But by and by, even with cash in his pocket, his darkness resurfaces. I start marking his bad days on the calendar to try to discern a pattern. I don't want to send him home, but boat life quickly becomes hell when you're sharing a tiny floating space with an unhappy human, no matter how heavenly the surroundings.

Underwater Neighborhood

I retreat into myself more often. On daily anchor checks I practice my breath holds and spend time with my underwater neighbors, dissolving into the liquid world. At one island, we build a mooring in a small false pass and I find myself in a living masterpiece beneath *Swell*. I kick down to the bottom each morning through the slicing beams of sunlight that dance across a myriad of coral forms. Invisible currents swirl while I hold the mooring line near the bottom.

At close range the detail intensifies. The blue spotted grouper comes out to patrol his zone, looking as serious as a nightclub bouncer. The yellow tangs waft over the reef together in a flock, grazing on algae like sheep at pasture.

"Lionfish! How do you fit in that hole with all those long delicate fins?" I ask him. He looks like he's stuck in an uncomfortable Halloween costume. I feel my diaphragm contract, look over the mooring line for signs of damage, and then jet back to the surface.

Rest, hover, breathe, relax ... then down again.

A school of nervous, black-striped jacks approach, looking like they just made a jailbreak. I reach the bottom, gripping rock. The shy red squirrelfish stay deep in the holes of the rocks, peering out curiously with one dark round eye. The butterfly fish and Moorish idols engage in a never-ending beauty pageant, flaunting their stripes and fancy fins. Anemone fingers flow in watery wafts of the current, and the corals—soft, hard, fingered, smooth, and purple to lime-green—stack upon each other like a colorful pile of dirty dishes in a kitchen sink.

My lungs burn and I shoot for the surface. The baby ballyhoos greet me, their long pointy snouts wiggling just out of reach as I catch my breath. From the top I notice a barracuda prowling. I fill my lungs with air, and go down again.

Parrotfish munch on coral. Gobies squat on their pectoral fins, chatting together like old ladies. A triggerfish bumbles by like a belligerent clown. A cowfish passes looking like she just left the salon with a bad haircut. From afar a great Napoleon wrasse, the king of the fishes, cruises slowly toward me with his thick lips pressed together smugly. The surface glistens above. I acknowledge my stinging lungs, let go, and float up through a scattered group of unicorn fish twirling their horns to gather plankton in the upper currents.

Deep breaths. Body renewed. Mind reset. I climb back into the dinghy tied to the stern of *Swell*, high on the incomprehensible complexity of the underwater world—its fervent, sumptuous stew of life the result of an unimaginable time span of evolutionary fine-tuning.

But what will be left here in a hundred years? Will this ecosystem survive the rising sea temperatures and levels, overfishing, and pollution? As remote as it feels in these islands, I shudder, thinking again about the inescapable impacts of climate change that will likely kill both the coral and the coconut palms. The atoll peoples will inevitably be displaced.

"When they go, we go," a Puamotu grandmother says to me one day when I ask her about the struggling coconut palms on her land.

Napoleon Breakdown

Much has changed since my first pass through the atolls a few years before. There is a surge of wealth among the local people because they are now selling fish to the more populous islands whose waters are fished out. Day after day, we watch thousands of pounds of fish harvested in traps, shot by spearfishermen, and caught in nets to be stacked in coolers and flown or shipped out. The local people have built stronger homes and bought trampolines and Xboxes for their kids, but at what cost?

The "tragedy of the commons" plays out before my eyes a few days later while anchored near a village. I watch a father and son fishing for Napoleon wrasse on handlines, hauling out fish after fish. These noble fish, which can grow to more than six feet long and 400 pounds, are highly sensitive to overfishing and have been completely eliminated from the more populated islands. This loss contributes to the burgeoning population of the crown-of-thorns starfish, which feeds on live coral and is destroying large areas of reef. The Napoleon wrasse is one of its few predators.

The great wrasses appear to be spawning in the pass, and for four straight days the father and son haul them out of the sea. On the way back from a dive, we stop to say hello. How can I explain the potential risk of overfishing them? I can't. It's not my place, nor can I judge their need for money. I need to get by just like them, and who is to say what my negative impacts are? As we drift beside their boat, they wrestle three gorgeous fish up from the bottom and proudly lift the floorboards to show us the eight or ten others they caught before we arrived. One is not even a foot long. An old man in the village explains that the father and son sell the fish to the passing cargo ships for the equivalent of a dollar a pound.

As the day goes on, I can't get the Napoleon wrasse off my mind. I learned in my Environmental Studies classes that the largest species in an ecosystem are historically the first to be exploited. The others fall victim to the next rung of human impact: habitat loss. If an animal isn't edible or valuable, we bulldoze its territory or poison its waters. For the first time, human activity is to blame as we near the sixth great mass extinction on Earth.

I've seen troubling scenarios playing out island after island. Rainui and I just came from an atoll whose entire population of lagoon fish are contaminated with ciguatera because a shipment of chemical fertilizer—left on the dock in the rain overnight—leaked into the lagoon. This caused a massive bloom of the algae that's linked to ciguatera in fish, cutting off the islander's main food source and bringing the local fishing economy to a screeching halt.

Here too, the Napoleon's plight is painfully tangible. I feel woozy over our loss of connection and reverence for the systems on Earth that give us life. For millennia, here and beyond, the natural world was seen as a dynamic, interconnected web of life in which humans participated fully, not just as an object of exploitation that primarily exists to meet our needs. But the islanders we talk to feel like there's no other choice—they must adapt to the new ways or be left behind. If they don't catch those fish to sell, someone else will.

That night I sit up on the bow of *Swell* looking up at the Great Shark stretching across the sky. I suddenly start to cry. My tears come first for the Napoleon. And then for the other reef fish that will be sure to follow. I cry for the next human generations, who might only see a Napoleon wrasse in a photo, and for the children, not only here on this tiny island, but those all around the world who will suffer from our negligent choices.

The next day I go to the local elementary school and ask if they would like me to do a presentation about my voyage and the environment. They agree eagerly, and I show up the following day with a bag of different sorts of local trash and explain approximately how long it takes for each piece to biodegrade. We talk about plastic pollution's effect on marine life, and I use my sailing trip to help explain where currents and winds carry plastic that finds its way into the ocean. I'm thrilled to find the kids highly enthusiastic. I leave feeling more hopeful, and vow to continue doing talks in schools at other islands we visit.

Simply Divine

It has been almost five months in the low-lying atolls with only sporadic Internet and infrequent phone use. Our bodies are lithe and strong.

There have been no hot showers, no fancy supermarkets or gourmet chocolates, no magical faucet spouting an endless flow of water. Provisions and comforts are modest, but my spirits are surprisingly high.

Amazingly, we've used less than a gallon of gasoline for *Swell*'s daily energy requirements, including refrigeration, lights, computer, music, and the water pump. The atolls have no mountains to block the sun or trades, so the solar panel and wind generator constantly replenish the batteries. We catch rainwater and wash our clothes by hand.

It's simple living and hard work, but this modest lifestyle awakens gratitude for even the smallest pleasures. If we exist in complete ease, with unending options, I think it's harder to truly enjoy luxuries and extravagance. "It's important to distinguish needs from wants," Barry used to say. Contrast helps develop gratitude. Even though Western society idealizes luxury, to me too much comfort is caustic.

Out here, simple things evoke such abundant gratitude—finding a safe anchorage after being at sea, savoring a just-caught fish, the rare real shower, sleeping in clean sheets, the unexpected kindness of a stranger, or finding a little wave to glide on! Moonbeams on the sea at night make me feel richer than any diamond ever could.

But by contrast, things with Rainui are far from simple. Some days he presses me to my limits, torturing me with words, and acting so unfair that I lash out. I can tell he likes it when I get upset, as if it assures him of my love. Sometimes when his foul mood crowds the cabin, I go ashore.

I try to meditate, or sometimes I cry a little, but usually I just end up sitting silently on a beach beside the lagoon or reef, watching the creatures around me: hermit crabs, bees, ants, circling terns, fish along the shoreline, flies, mosquitos, crabs, spiders, trees, vines, long-legged sandpipers. I realize that they all have messages for me—patience, hard work, perseverance, slowing down, relaxation, letting go, being still, or getting a higher perspective. They remind me that mine is one among the millions of life dramas going on all over Earth. Near them, I feel less alone. I hear a voiceless voice telling me that today is an exquisite phenomenon.

Urchin spines wave in the flow of the water over the reef. I watch flying fish wiggle free of the sea surface and hover a hundred yards with their wings glowing golden in the evening light. A baby humpback whale breaches nearby. Frigates circle and scissor in the tempestuous trades. Sharks patrol the shallows at sunset. Palm fronds dance on and on in the wind.

I don't know what it is about the direct contact with wilderness that nourishes me. Maybe it's what others feel in church or making art. I feel so drawn to its purity and unfathomable intelligence, its seemingly individual parts all working together as one. Its rhythms and extremes. Shadows and light. Serenity and chaos. Beginnings and endings. I recognize the same things going on inside my own little universe, and I know that I am That. *Namaste!*

Barry, too, knew the deeper value of wild places and the lessons they offer, returning to wilderness as often as he could. Like him, I cherish seeing the waters, the plants, the animals in a wild and free state—just how I love to be the most. They are perfect that way. Perfectly divine. Recognizing that we are all interdependent somehow makes me part of this grand and unexplainable miracle. All of us spark from the same Infinite Spirit, Source, God, Jah, Allah, Mana that connects everything.

If we can see everything as sacred, we may have a chance at healing the planet. Personal healing contributes too. And like Barry mentioned in his final letter, eco technologies could provide healthier ways to respect the planet while upholding modern lifestyles—electric cars mean cleaner air; grassroots movements like "permaculture" and urban gardens mean food production without the use of agro chemicals; wind and solar farms and bioplastics mean greener homes and cleaner living. Expanding compassion to include all life might mean less suffering, and might allow humans to live more meaningful lives.

Looking out at all the sacredness surrounding me, I fear that if we never have these sorts of close encounters with open spaces and wild creatures, if our only contact with wilderness and animals is through a television and our pets, we risk not caring whether they exist at all. We risk not feeling our spirits stirred. We risk losing a vital part of ourselves and a vital avenue to knowing this extraordinary feeling of connection.

"God" is no longer a distant mystery to me anymore. I feel the Divine within me and every time I look out my window.

Bait for Breakfast

As cyclone season approaches, we ready *Swell* to sail north to the safer latitudes in The Land of People. After a trying eight-day passage to the mountainous archipelago where Mom and I first arrived, Rainui and I straggle into an uninhabited bay to dry out, rest, and reorganize. It still amazes me how the thrill of landfall can so easily erase the misery of a difficult passage.

The tall surrounding cliffs, sprawling valley, and echoing bleats of mountaineering juvenile goats overwhelm our senses. While ashore to stretch our legs and explore, we find loads of wild food, and the locals in the nearest village assure us that we are welcome to help ourselves. After months on islands that can't support such tropical lushness, the wild oranges, papayas, mangos, limes, pumpkin, red bananas, grapefruit, guavas, and even taro and sweet potato are the sweetest treasures. We sit in the shade of a loaded mango tree up the valley, stuffing ourselves on golden flesh until it hurts, and then float down the cool river back to the beach.

But apart from the edible bliss and tranquility of the valley, there is an unmistakable aura of tragedy in the air. Remnants of the ancient civilization that once blossomed here are all around us. Stacked stone foundations of homes line the river for the length of the valley. The ancient Polynesians who lived here were skilled masons. Like Hiva's father had explained on my first pass through these islands, the Land of People supported an estimated 100,000 inhabitants before the catastrophic population collapse.

In the sixteenth century, the French took forceful claim to the islands in a spirit similar to European settlers' horrific treatment of Native Americans. The islanders lacked natural immunity to introduced diseases. Despite pleas from foreigners living here at the time, France refused medical assistance to the native peoples, taking them for "savage cannibals." But which is more barbaric, the occasional human barbecue or infecting an entire race of people and leaving them all to die? The population shrunk to under 2,000 by 1925. Today, many native descendants have moved out of isolated valleys like this one to be closer to schools, stores, imported supplies, and more opportunities for work.

We enjoy hopping around the islands, until one afternoon after chatting, an older local man scribbles down the name of a bay.

"You will like it here," he says with a convincing smile, and hands me the paper. We arrive a week later to find a deep bay with two nice waves, a big open-air copra storage area that's great for yoga, a shower spigot nearby with potable water, surrounding mountains to forage, and a quiet beachside community. Kids follow us on fruit-hunting missions and we take them out and push them into waves when the conditions are right. We pluck bunches of watercress from streams, surf and bodysurf, fish in the nearby waters, jump off the cliffs, and make friends with local families. They teach us to cook traditional delicacies and weave palm-frond hats. Rainui pursues wild pig and goat with hunter friends, while I enjoy peaceful mornings in the galley after a surf—making fresh juices and jams, fermenting vegetables, sprouting seeds, or baking.

After more than a month anchored here, we start to uncover more details about life in the bays, hills, trees, and rocks. It occurs to me that regional plant and animal knowledge was commonplace in native cultures worldwide, and now most of us don't even know that we don't know our local plants. I ponder the effects of this widespread alienation from our nearby environments. Could it be contributing to the increased rates of anxiety and depression? Chronic disease and staggering drug use?

Rainui and I don't go to the store with a list; we go to the hills with gratitude for whatever the earth has to offer. The beauty and the surprises found in the hills make me want to leap out of bed each morning. Rainui's moods seem more stable too. Again, the process of collecting food feels rewarding in itself: the sticky sap on my fingers, learning how to tell when fruits are ready to be picked, feeling that burst of adrenaline as I stretch out on a branch hoping to reach just one more mango. I see my food alive and thriving, versus buying it in a market. All of this reminds me of the complex processes and daily miracles that happen before the food goes in my mouth. That appreciation transfers into our meals, and food continues to take on rich new dimensions.

On an afternoon exploration, we meet Mami Faatiarau, a courageous seventy-nine-year-old woman living with her disabled grandson in an empty valley at a nearby bay. She's fit and spry—still hunting wild pigs, raising goats, collecting shellfish, harvesting her own fruits, cooking in the traditional underground oven, and walking four miles each way to the closest village. Maybe doctors should prescribe fresh air, nature, and gardens to treat more of our modern ailments?

As we stay on in the bay, algae grows thick on the anchor lines, and soon *Swell* has developed a little ocean ecosystem under her hull. Shrimp, crab, algae, tiny young fish, a seahorse, turning bait balls, passing tuna schools, and a roaming manta ray family make us feel part of the underwater party. We often wake to the sound of thrashing near the hull as tuna or other apex predators chase the baitfish into such a frenzy that some of them launch from the sea onto *Swell*'s deck. I run up and chase after their wiggling bodies, thanking each one for its life with a kiss of gratitude, then tossing them into the pan for a low-on-the-food-chain breakfast delicacy.

Jesus as a Black Boar

One day we head off to forage in a new area around the point to the east. I relish the clean, rich air and thank the trees as we walk into the open shade of the forest. I'm daydreaming of guavas and starfruits when something off the side of the trail grabs my eye. It's a battered old enclosure made of wood and rusty tin roofing. I wander over, curious, and peer inside to see a skinny, wiry-haired adolescent black boar.

He leaps fearfully to his feet. I jump too, and we both squeal a little. I move closer and so does he, sticking his nose out of the cage and grunting madly. He's hungry. I look around for a nearby home but see no signs of habitation or his owner. He stares out at me, hoping for something to eat. I apologetically explain that we are just getting started, but I will have something for him on our way back. His grunting quiets. We lock eyes for a long moment.

I see his suffering—his hunger for food, love, and freedom. Suddenly my emotions blindside me. He is so desperate and voiceless, begging me with his eyes to do something for him. I feel so helpless. I call to Rainui from the side of the cage.

"Can't we free him? Don't we have anything to give him?"

"He's not ours. We could have trouble if we let him out," he calls back. "Someone could be watching us right now. It's okay, we'll bring him some fruit on our way back."

No, it's really not okay. The boar continues staring at me with his deep, powerful gaze. I don't know why, but the image of Jesus comes into my mind. It was the same look that I saw on those crosses in my junior high years at Catholic school. Have mercy. How can we as humans not sympathize with the suffering of animals? How is it fair to treat them like property? It's obvious that they feel emotions and pain just like we do. I'm dizzy at the plight of the boar and all the animals around the world enduring enslavement for our food—especially in isolation or cramped enclosures, or even in a pasture where they have no real chance to feel freedom.

I walk away feeling like I've been punched in the stomach. Like all those years eating meat and drinking milk I had been tricked, not realizing what torture and suffering I was supporting. I've seen caged animals hundreds of times and felt sad for them, but never like this. I must have been too busy thinking about myself to pay attention—but this time the message is loud and clear. *I just met Jesus as a black boar.*

The Shadow Side

Rainui's darkness continues to resurface periodically, his jealousy provoked when I don't comply with the norms here—like not looking down when shaking hands with a man, or being too friendly. Each time, it's more extreme. In one dreadful incident, an older local man cops a feel of my backside, and Rainui blames me, belligerent and furious. "I love you too much!" he screams, and punches the walls while I huddle in fear.

I know it's time to break it off with him, but the problem is getting him off the boat here, where I don't have the support network I need. He is so charming with our local friends; I'm afraid they won't understand if I ask for help. To further complicate things, *Swell*'s autopilot and wind vane are broken. The autopilot is going to be a complicated fix and Monita needs a spring that we haven't been able to find. Without these two units functioning, the 1,000-some miles of passage-making to get back toward Tahiti will be nearly impossible on my own, so I have to be patient, try to keep him feeling secure, and stick it out until then.

My stress and anxiety start to surface in the form of injuries, illness, and bad luck. The bottoms of my feet have developed a painful condition; it now hurts to walk barefoot. My right knee is still weak from previous injury, my surfboard smashes me in the face, my big toe blows up with an infection from a small splinter, and then I strain the ligaments on the top of my left foot from, ironically, sitting too long in lotus pose to meditate. One night I awaken to the stings of a six-inch centipede on my bare belly; it must have come aboard in a bag or bushel of bananas. The ominous creature escapes behind the diesel tank before I can catch it.

Of the Stars

We begin to work our way south in the lush island chain as the five months of cyclone season come to an end. On our last stop, we harvest fruit to take to a tiny atoll where Rainui's father grew up, 250 miles south and not far out of our way. Rainui meets aunts and uncles and cousins for the first time, and they are delighted with our 200-pound delivery of bananas, limes, mangos, papayas, starfruit, and taro. We can't stay long due to the unsafe anchorage, and sail on.

With the wind behind us, it's smooth sailing. We could wait somewhere and order the parts to fix the wind vane or autopilot, but I prefer to carry on steering by hand so as not to slow my path toward freedom. We move quite quickly—covering over a thousand miles in two months with only four stops.

The obligation to steer has multiple rewards. Hands on the wheel, I'm engaged in every gust, every passing cloud, every lifting wave, as *Swell* and I surf down the following seas. I find the sweet spots in her old sails and learn more about her every day. Plus, maneuvering her through mile after mile of dynamic ocean, I become an active participant in the scene. As the waves pass beneath us, they pull the rudder right or left, and my arms strengthen in the long hours at the wheel. I gaze out at the ocean panorama: ever-changing, ever-wondrous. I follow wavelets on the sea surface, the teeny ones stacking upon the next, always in hot pursuit of their mates up ahead—until suddenly they are both overtaken by a much larger wave, and swallowed in a gurgle of white foam.

Subtleties surface each hour as the day progresses. At every angle of the sun, the rays play on the water and clouds in their own exceptional way. Sunrise and sunset steal the show, but midmorning's fresh rays up-lift, high noon's brilliance astounds, and mid-afternoon's bending yellows soothe and foretell day's end. When the last remnant of the sun's glow disappears, we are suddenly sailing through the unbridled heavens—perpetual, sublime, infinite, mysterious—always reminding me that no matter how much I think I understand, I know so very little.

I cover the GPS and practice steering by the stars, aligning them with the masthead or halyards—Taurus, Hercules, the Pleiades, Corona Borealis, or the Great Hook (as the Tahitians call Scorpio)—whichever star cluster lines up at that moment. Cloudy evenings hide my magnificent celestial guides, but I steer by maintaining our angle to the wind waves—checking the compass only now and then when I feel lost. When the winds are light, I lie back and steer with my feet to watch for shooting stars. When fatigue overcomes me, Rainui and I switch.

Applying my mind to sailing twelve hours a day, I develop an ever-deeper respect for the ancient Polynesian navigators and their intimate knowledge of the oceans, heavens, and universal forces. These masters steered all over the Pacific in seagoing double canoes with the sky as their only chart.

What a sad irony that the descendants of the Earth's greatest water travelers are now almost completely disconnected from their traditional form of voyaging. While sailing canoes are experiencing a small revival in the region, most people today can't even leave their home island unless they can afford a plane ticket or are able to secure a rare place on a cargo ship, making it difficult to gain perspective and feel pride in their great ocean heritage. I hope the revival continues. To test one's strengths on an autonomous sea voyage provides a chance to gain the self-knowledge, wisdom, and reverence for life that come from navigating the unfamiliar.

I imagine the ancestral navigators were intimately in touch with their intuition. Raw vulnerability makes one listen with every cell. The times when I have no guidebook, or Google, or any clue what to do—on or off the sea—I try to let my emotional guidance system lead. If I can quiet my mind and let go of my desired results, something deeper kicks in. That inner voice speaks up—the voice that is connected to the all-knowing, the omniscient—and damn, it's smart!

But even when I don't act upon the advice, the voice also assures me there are really no mistakes in eternity, that we are all of the stars, and that we all eventually find our way home.

18,685
Nautical Miles Traveled

Darkness
and
Light

T-Bone and a She-Hero

At 2 pm on a clear, breezy afternoon, *Swell* sits at anchor one short hop from Rainui's home island. I'm seated at my little desk in the cabin talking to my dad on the phone.

Suddenly I hear yelling and look out the window as a large catamaran barrels straight at us! Smash! The fifty-foot charter yacht T-bones *Swell*, ramming its port hull into her starboard side, just above the waterline slightly aft of the rigging. I hang up quickly and race up on deck.

The crash bends some stanchions, busts the lifelines, and kinks the forward lower cable of the rig. Rainui is yelling and cursing at a gray-haired American flailing his arms on the bow. The hull took the brunt of the hit. Its fiberglass wall gouged and flexed inward far enough to split and splinter the interior wooden siding, drawers, and bookshelf. I try to calm Rainui down while the captain, his wife, and a friend anchor behind us and then come over to assess the damage. They are less than apologetic, and even try to get me to sign a paper listing the evident damage.

"You know," he smirks, "just in case this turns into a pissing match."

My capacity for kindness hits the deck. He knows as well as I do that until the paint is stripped down, the rig is climbed, the closet emptied, and chainplates assessed, we can't know the extent of the damage. He doesn't care that he nearly just sank my home—he is only out to cover his own ass, knowing that his recklessness is going to cost him. The fact that the boat is rented further complicates the situation.

Rainui and I are both upset over the crash, but when Kepi, my tube guru girlfriend, comes to visit the next day, we try not to think about it and just enjoy hanging out. She's with some male friends on vacation from Hawai'i. I'm excited to see her after a year, so we chat and tell stories in English, just relaxing.

As soon as they leave, Rainui starts asking me what I said to them. I translate but he doesn't believe me. Maybe this is karma for the men I lied to, for all the hearts I sailed away from. Or maybe he senses that I'm pulling away as our trip is coming to an end.

He badgers me angrily that evening, but I have no more energy to give to his jealousy. I can't even respond. I have offered him so much love and spiritual wisdom and so many opportunities to get his fear under control. He's turned too many beautiful days gray. I have given him my heart, my soul, my body, and my possessions. I have pleaded with him and praised him, banged my head against the wall to get him to understand how much I love him. I am defeated. Nothing works.

My failure to react frustrates him even more. He starts drinking all the alcohol he can find and lashes out—pushing me around, hitting walls, and threatening to break valuables. I fight back at first, even try to punch him, but soon realize it's useless. He takes my phone away so that I can't call for help, and when I cower in my bunk, he harasses me, threatening more violence for hours.

When I open my eyes early the next morning, Rainui is sitting in the cockpit, still drinking, and having trouble holding himself upright. I can't believe I'm in this nightmare. I have to get away, but I know he will stop me from taking the dinghy. I sneak out the forward hatch, planning to swim for shore to get help. At the bow, I hear the whiz of Kepi's Jet Ski as she's taking her friends out for a surf. I wave my arms wildly to hail her without making a sound. I'm relieved when she makes a sharp turn toward *Swell*. Grief is written across my face.

"Are you okay? What happened?" she says. I can hardly speak. My words are stuck in the shock and sadness that clogs my throat.

"Help me …," is all I can manage to choke out. "I wanted to call you but he took my phone."

Without hesitation, she whips the ski around toward the cockpit and calls to Rainui in French, "Hey! Yeah, you! You're going to give back her phone right now. Then you either get on this ski and I'll take you to shore, or I'm going to get my husband."

He turns to me to defend him and I look away. "Get your bag together," she warns him. "You're getting off this boat."

Shattered

Alone among the reminders of the evening's hideous events, I wonder how on earth love can express itself in such an awful way. Our romance is shattered into Plexiglass splinters on the cabin floor from the cupboard door he smashed.

Kepi saved me that day, but also in the days to come—again and again—from sinking into a pit of painful memories, crippling emotions, regret, and self-pity. She picks me up to go surf early each morning, then brings her adorable kids over to swim and jump off of *Swell* in the afternoon. And each night, she invites me to join her family for dinner.

Over the next three weeks, living on my poor damaged *Swell*, I show myself that I can still do everything on my own. My injuries still annoy me, but like I did before Rainui, I find a way to take care of every task. Some days I lift the water jugs with tears in my eyes; other days I lift them with a fierce love of feeling free again. Some days I see the machete he left behind and feel sad; other days it makes me look away.

I don't want to go anywhere near him ever again, but there's one problem. The charter company that owns the offending catamaran is based near Rainui's parents' home. I have to go there for them to assess and repair the damage to *Swell*. I try to figure out an alternative, but there's no way around this. So with a ticket to fly to California in five days, *Swell* limps back to the rental base with her cracked hull and damaged rig. I figure I have just enough time to get her hauled, get the repairs going, and get the hell out of there.

A Pain in the Neck

I see a parking spot on my right and pull in. I sit there for a moment, watching California's morning sun glitter on the Pacific. Small waves trip on the shallows and spill upon the shore. I look out at the horizon and find comfort. This parking lot is closer to the ocean than any others I know in San Diego—if there is anywhere I can hobble to the water, it's here. My mother doesn't have to know.

Thanks to the stretched ligaments on my left foot that seem to be getting worse instead of better, I have been cooped up in my parents' condo for a month. I successfully completed a speaking tour through Patagonia's west coast stores right after I arrived, but since then I've been stalling my departure. I've massaged my foot. Iced it. Stayed off it. Gone to acupuncture. And rubbed it with Chinese herbs. But it refuses to heal. I can't surf, I can't do yoga, and I certainly can't go back to work on my wreck of a boat.

In addition to the damage from the collision, *Swell* accumulated quite a list of things to be fixed after the year of heavy use. The biggest job will be dealing with the decks, which are cracking and splitting. They need to be stripped and refinished to keep water from leaking into the sandwiched wooden core. It's a huge job and I'll be stuck working on it for too long and too close to Rainui to feel safe. I haven't shared the scary details of the ordeal with my family or friends, but maybe my subconscious—in the form of a sore foot—is keeping me from throwing myself to the lion.

The tide is dropping, and one particular sandbar beckons as the second consecutive right peels and spits. With an hour to kill and a bladder full of tea, a swim is in order. My doctor's appointment isn't far. A family friend has agreed to look at my foot—I have a handful of black pearls for him since I have no US health insurance. I wriggle excitedly into a swimsuit in the driver's seat; California has been the hottest I can remember this summer and fall.

I open the door, hobble down the rocks, and limp toward the sea. In six inches of water I fall to my knees and submerge my head. The chilly ocean feels like ecstasy in my pores, stinging and tingling. I open my eyes underwater to feel the cold on my eyeballs and then stroke out into deeper water.

I float inside the surfline for a bit, content to be lying in the sea's embrace again until a small peak outside grabs my attention. I swim out and push off into a clean little line, bodysurfing toward the shore, euphoric to be gliding again. I can't resist going back for one more.

I head back out and wait until a line spikes up. I swim into position and slide down the face as it sucks up under me. And then an odd warble suddenly crops up, tossing me head over heels as the wave closes out. My head hits the sand while the wave pushes my body toward the beach. I hear and feel a loud crack at the back of my neck.

"Okay. I'm conscious," I think, floating to the surface. I wiggle my arms and toes. "I'm okay." I let the water push me in to the shore, and I stand up. Pain grips my neck. I drive myself up the street to my sister's house, and use her phone to call my emergency nurse girlfriend, Chrissy.

An hour later, Chrissy pokes my left arm with an IV and checks to be sure my neck brace fits properly. "If it's nothing, we'll just go home, but it's your neck, girl. I'm really glad you called me." Luckily, she had answered and raced to pick me up.

Dr. Healy soon appears and points to the CT scan results. "See right there? You have a fracture at C3." Tears run down my face at the news. "You'll be fine in a few months," he says.

The director of the ER is a fan of my blog, and stops in to say hello. "I'm so happy to meet you, but so sorry it's here!" he says. He waives his personal hospital fee and explains how lucky I am. Had the bone cracked only a millimeter more, I would have likely drowned before someone found me.

Surrendering to Stillness

Mom is really upset with me the first few days after the accident, and I feel terribly guilty to be dependent on her for my every need, especially after all this time with my bum foot. Although I'm not excited to be bedridden in her tiny apartment, I know that full acceptance is my best refuge and will expedite my healing. I'm going to be okay, so I must embrace this and think positively. I must accept with trust if I am to understand why this has come into my reality.

I lie flat in my neck brace, staring at the ceiling, studying the plaster. I'm not going anywhere. Not returning emails, writing blog posts, completing shopping lists, or meeting anyone. I can't even watch a movie, unless it's projected on the ceiling. For the first time in, well, as long as I can remember, I just have to lie here and *be*.

In surrender, my mind feels more at ease; immobility has never been comfortable for me. On the upside: My foot will have more time to heal, and I don't have to go back and face Rainui or the boatyard yet. In the downtime I research bone healing, holding my smartphone up over my face. I learn about the benefits of nettle tea and that, contrary to common belief, dark leafy greens do more than milk and dairy products to build bone. Nothing in my horizontal Internet research points to needing meat, so I stay with the decision I'd made after meeting the black boar in the forest, to cut out all meat and dairy products and eat a plant-based diet (aside from the occasional fish).

While I'm healing, I cut out all caffeine, refined sugar, alcohol, and processed foods, too. Mom is slightly shocked by my new diet—for "the girl that lived on cheese and ice cream"—but she graciously accommodates my picky requests while I devour audiobooks. At my three-week checkup, my doctor is impressed by the rate of my healing and loosens my leash a little.

Shortly after, my favorite high school English teacher comes to visit, and she calls again a week later. Would I like to house-sit her friend's mansion in the pine trees for the next two months? Hell yes! Ironically, the beautiful home overlooks the beach where the accident occurred. Mom helps me get settled in and plans to stop by often, knowing it's a great healing environment, with its big windows, ocean views, back patio, and even a sauna. I can walk around for short periods, but otherwise must stay on my back, wear my neck brace, and relax.

Friends come to visit, and one gives me a pair of prism glasses that make it possible for me to lie flat but see horizontally. I can now read books and watch movies.

I devour a stack of suggested books. Each one offers important messages, links spiritual ideas, and provides insight into how to push past the blocks that keep me from becoming the person I want to be. My neck break doesn't seem like an accident anymore. When I made that list way back on the passage to Kiribati, I never expected to be here, but ask and you shall receive: *Conversations with God*, *Power vs. Force*, *Mutant Message Down Under*, *Autobiography of a Yogi*, *Journey of Souls*, *The Sculptor in the Sky*, and the *Tao Te Ching* all provide new tools, perspectives, and wisdom.

When I'm tired of reading, I throw on one documentary after another, and learn volumes about animal husbandry in America—the horrifyingly inhumane living conditions and undignified slaughter the animals are subjected to, the appalling life of slavery of a modern dairy cow, the incredibly costly environmental effects of animal agriculture. I'm shocked to learn that raising animals for meat and dairy is a significant source of the greenhouse gases that are causing climate change. And that clearing land for pasture is directly linked to deforestation, habitat loss, and a large majority of land-based species extinction. Or that it takes hundreds of gallons of water to produce the meat in a single hamburger!

I don't understand why these issues aren't better known, until I think about all the money involved. It becomes clearer why plant-based diets aren't being promoted as solutions to heart disease, high blood pressure, arthritis, cancer prevention, digestive issues, and more—despite plenty of research clearly pointing to their effectiveness. I watch stories of people winning triathalons, weight-lifting competitions, and a variety of endurance sports all on a diet of strictly plants—this myth we've been sold about needing meat for protein just isn't true.

As I gain more mobility, I spend more time outside. I drink tea with my feet in the dirt, or lie on my yoga mat and meditate under the sky. It's a miracle I get to heal and expand my mind in such a peaceful, therapeutic setting.

Nowhere to Hide

After four months of healing, and seven total months in the United States, I hop a plane back to the South Pacific, hoping that Rainui has moved on. *Swell* is unlivable—covered inside with black mildew—and I'm still not strong enough to deal with all the work needed to put her back together. Plus the charter company is giving me the runaround about properly making the collision repairs.

I'm lucky to meet a girl about my age who tends to a mountain property with a large home. Poana invites me to stay with her and we become sisters overnight. She's fun and loves nature and adventure. Plus she's going through a separation with her husband, so we help each other grieve.

Since *Swell* isn't insured, the yacht charter service isn't required to report the accident to their insurance company, and the miserly division manager makes a weak effort at fixing the damage. I eventually give up on being fairly compensated and finish the smaller repairs myself. Afterward, *Swell* spends more and more time in the yard untouched. I rest my neck a little longer, catch up on months of emails, meditate, harvest fresh fruit, do yoga, play in the sea, cook healthy food, and help Poana plant a garden. Putting my hands in the dirt feels so right. I seem to need the energy of the land. I'm safe and blessed. When I'm sad, Poana lifts me up, and I try to do the same for her.

The jungle paradise is almost too good to be true, until one day I hear a car pulling up the long driveway. It's Rainui. I tried to keep my whereabouts from him, but someone in the village told him where to find the house "with the surfer girls." I hide in a room and tell Poana to say I'm not there. All at once, the hillside home is no longer a safe oasis. A few days later, I hear the car coming up the driveway again. Goose bumps rise on my skin. Poana isn't home, and I'm working in the garden. He speaks gently, telling me he wants us to try to work things out. But when I keep my head down, pulling weeds, uninterested in talking, he storms into the house, and takes my computer and phone, and drives away.

I nearly call the police, but his mother promises to return them to me the next day. Over the next month, while I try to get to work on *Swell*, things steadily go from bad to worse. The more I resist, the more Rainui persists. The island becomes very small. He's unpredictable and always watching me. Since I don't feel safe alone at Poana's anymore, I stay aboard *Swell* one night in the yard when I know she's out with friends. I lock myself inside and turn out the lights to go to sleep, but soon I hear someone coming up the ladder. It's him. He must have seen the car I'm borrowing from Poana parked in the yard. He's drunk and angry and wants me to open the door.

Realizing the cabin is locked from the inside, he smashes on the door, breaking the outside lock, then beats on the forward hatch and rips off its canvas cover, yelling that he knows I'm inside and he's going to "break my face" when he gets in. I desperately call for help, shaking like a trapped mouse. The local police prove worthless, but I quickly get in touch with the yard owner and Poana. Rainui hears me and after a last violent attempt to get the door open, he slinks away into the dark, letting the air out of my car tires on his way. The yard owner and Poana show up shortly afterward. Lying next to Poana in her bed that night, I toss and turn with nightmares until dawn.

Submission

What the hell should I do? I don't want to fly away. Where would I even go? I don't want to leave my boat alone with him around, now that he's certain I don't want to get back together. I can't think of anyone I can ask to fly down to protect me. Kepi is on another island and Poana has her own life to live. There is only one way to get out of this situation. I know what I have to do, but it won't be easy.

The next morning, I call Rainui and tell him I want to work it out. I'm ready to come and live with him at his family's house, as he has asked me to repeatedly. This way he'll feel control over me, which will calm him down, and I will be in less danger because his whole family will be around.

His mother, father, brother, sister-in-law, and nephew welcome me graciously. His mother shows me to a room Rainui and I will share in an abandoned house right next to theirs. There is no electricity or bathroom, but it doesn't matter. There is a bed and a roof, and someone will always be in earshot. His family is warm and generous, and I pitch in with various chores. Rainui insists on helping me with the deck job on *Swell*, threatening that I'll be sorry if I hire someone else. His family encourages him to help too, and they have meals ready when we return after a long day at the yard.

The next few months seem eternal. The back-breaking deck job lags on. With so many nooks and crannies to contend with, the only way to strip the paint is sanding by hand, which takes forever. Knowing I can't get away until *Swell* is relaunched, I push myself through long days of intense labor when the weather allows. Rainui helps tremendously, although his behavior remains erratic. Even when he doesn't feel like working, he comes along anyway, not wanting to let me out of his sight. I can't talk freely to the people in the yard for fear he'll be jealous.

I pray that they and the others I interact with during that time won't judge me for my unfriendliness. This teaches me not to judge other people's behavior either, since it's never possible to fully understand its roots. Rainui's frightening mood changes have me living in constant fear. He doesn't hesitate to confiscate my belongings, or threaten me with violence when something flips his switch. Even the sunniest days seem stripped of color.

One day Rainui gets angry with me and pulls the car into an empty lot, yanks me out by my shirt, and says he's going to hit me. I look him in the eyes. "Go ahead. Do it." I seethe. He throws a punch at my face, stopping close enough to shear the hairs on my nose. My knees buckle in fright, and I cry out for help, but he puts his hand over my mouth and tells me to get back in the car. I plead with his mother that night, but there's not much she can do, either. I become muted, docile, and compliant—a role I've never known—and I try to stay around his family on the bad days.

Once the topsides are finally sanded, they must be washed down and taped off for primer. More sanding after the primer coats, then a coat of white, then I work my way around the boat, hand-rolling and filling each area of nonskid with sand particles for grip, then another two coats of paint over the sand. Week after week I do nothing but work during daylight hours. Then just when I think I'm nearing the end of this nightmare, I discover one entire side of the rudder is delaminated. The whole thing must come off and be reglassed.

Another dark month goes by. I am so far from the moments of oneness and connection I have felt over the years. My confusion and frustration and isolation are excruciating. I hunt for a silver lining, but instead feel increasingly hopeless, betrayed by the Greatness that I once felt so near. I'm broken, lost, invisible. I don't even look up at the moon.

When I am able to quietly share my story with other women on the island, I'm surprised to learn that many of them have dealt with similar situations—threats, bullying, psychological and physical abuse. I cry silently in the night at times, grieving with them. How can these women possibly pursue their talents and passions under such stifling circumstances? I know I will eventually get to sail away and have my life back. But here, and in so many other places in the world, women have nowhere to go, no money to get there, and no one to protect them. They must remain in these kinds of situations, constantly fearing for their safety.

The Great Escape

Finally, after more than four months under Rainui's rule, it's getting close to the time for me to make the final break. *Swell* is lowered back into the sea with beautiful new seafoam-green decks and topsides.

A boat with two young men is tied up near *Swell* in the slipway, and Rainui is instantly jealous. I watch his mood unravel and placate him as much as possible. That night I hear him come in and lie down on the other side of the bed. For many months he has stopped being affectionate, and rarely pushes to be intimate. I wait until he is sound asleep, then slip quietly out of bed to pack my few items with trembling hands, and carry them out to the car.

The next morning Rainui is still in a terrible mood and doesn't want to come to the yard with me to move *Swell* out of the slipway. This is my chance. I leave some clothes in the room to throw him off, but notice that he's hidden my favorite surfboard. I eat breakfast like nothing's unusual and while he's showering I'm able to find my board. I load it up and drive off with my heart beating wildly.

I spend the morning doing the bare minimum to get *Swell* off the dock, but there is a ton of stuff to shift and sort through to find what I need after so many months of work. When I turn on the motor to back out of the launching slip, I hear water leaking: There's a crack in the plastic base of the strainer that filters the seawater before it flows to cool the engine. Miraculously, the yard owner has a replacement. I buy it and change out the broken piece immediately, knowing that Rainui could show up any moment. Instead, he calls around lunchtime and says he's working on something with his cousin. He must not have noticed I took the surfboard.

"That's fine," I tell him. "I'll be home later."

By the time I'm ready to go, it's almost dark. I'm exhausted and can hardly think about moving the boat. But when Poana and another friend, Aymeric, come by on their way back from a surf, they offer to help me—tying up their skiff behind *Swell* and climbing aboard for the crossing. The three of us sail away under a lopsided waxing moon.

Broken Open

Things don't get easier right away. Rainui is livid and hunting me. He leaves crazy, threatening messages on my phone. He wants money and surfboards. I'm only one island away and worry terribly that he might find out where I am and come looking for me. And then, I wake up to find that half of my face has gone limp. Aymeric rushes me to the hospital, and I'm treated for Bells palsy, brought on by the last few months of high stress. I realize how far I have pushed myself, and the toll it's taken on me.

I need a place to heal. Fortunately, Monique, Aymeric's recently widowed mother, insists I stay in their guest bungalow and eat with them until I'm better, which the doctor says will take about three weeks. I have the local police listen to Rainui's threatening phone messages. They warn him to stop, and that I can press charges. On top of the temporary facial paralysis, I develop a case of shingles that the doctors attribute to my severely weakened immune system.

I stare at my limp face in the mirror; I can't believe I've let myself reach this state. I loved Rainui with all my heart, but I should have been loving my own self just as avidly.

I start doing small, nice things for myself every day. I sleep in, lie in the sun or soak in the shallows near the bungalow, not leaving their large, lush property. Feeling safe makes simply waking up a wonderful thing. I eat beautiful meals with my new adoptive family, take naps, meditate, reflect, and read. My face gradually returns to normal and the painful shingles dissipate.

After being forced to hide my body and my beauty, I want to cherish my feminine side like never before. Back on the boat, I cut my T-shirts into crop-tops, fringe the edges, and wear what I feel accentuates my body. I enjoy taking an extra five minutes to braid my hair or choose my outfit. I start surfing again, walking barefoot, and dancing.

I was naïve and self-righteous to think that I could get Rainui to evolve faster than he was ready for because of my advice. Every soul is undergoing its own unique journey at its own pace. I resolve that the only expectation I will have of a future relationship is that both of us feel happy, free, and fulfilled. Love means supporting each other to grow into the best versions of ourselves. What Rainui hated about me—my openness and compassion—are parts of me that I love, and I'm thrilled to feel them reawakening.

As I heal over the next few months, I begin to feel outrageously liberated and stronger in mind than ever before—as if my heart is no longer broken, but broken completely open. Two fun-loving Spanish girls, Paula and Lucia, arrive to stay with Monique and Aymeric, and just being near them helps revive my playful spirit. As I remember what it's like to be me again, I indulge in that me-ness like never before. I'm like a coiled spring that was pushed down flat, and I now shoot skyward in my freedom— bursting with inspiration and ready to completely love myself.

The deeper healing will take time, though. I'm still fragile. Gradually, I piece myself and *Swell* back together. I even begin to bless this dark experience, as hard as it was. I know I would not appreciate this heightened feeling of safety and freedom without the fear and oppression that I went through. In polarity, there is perspective. I have gained valuable compassion for women (and men) in similar situations. And lifted a few of the subconscious veils I was seeing life through. Maybe I also needed to know the depths of Rainui's darkness in order to totally free myself from my hopes for his transformation.

New Crew, New View

When I'm ready to take to the sea again, my new friend Simon accompanies me back to the house I shared with Poana to pick up a few items I left in the garage. The house is empty and the garden full of weeds. Poana is no longer living there. As Simon and I step out of the car, a skinny adolescent orange-and-gray striped cat comes out of the bushes crying like a young child who skinned her knees. She rubs against my legs and tells me how lonely and hungry she has been, and how much love she needs. I scoop her up and cuddle her. I remember seeing her as a tiny kitten before I moved out.

After gathering my belongings, Simon and I walk the property. We met before my time with Rainui but only recently became friends while he was working in the bay near Monique and Aymeric's house. The little cat follows us up through the banana forest and into the open field below the waterfall. She bounds like a gazelle through the high grasses and dashes after us as we head back toward the house. I'm taken by her commanding air and carefree bravado. As it nears time to go, I hesitate to leave her.

I can't count the forlorn cats and dogs I've longed to adopt over the years, but it never seemed fair to drag them into my nomadic lifestyle. I'm not sure that I can properly care for a pet. But something about this cat's spirit touches me.

"She's all alone here and it seems like she needs love. I can at least try to find her a good home," I tell Simon.

"Or you can keep her. She's a cool cat."

"I doubt it. The boat is too small. She'll get bored. And I have to travel from time to time," I reason. "But she seems lonely, don't you think?"

"Definitely. Don't you think love is just as important as freedom?" he asks me.

I ponder for a minute. I've had extreme freedom with no love. And extreme "love" with no freedom.

"I think she needs a balance of both," I tell him.

Adjusting to boat life isn't easy for her. Life on a slippery, forty-by-eleven-foot hunk of fiberglass surrounded by water is a radical contrast to the lonesome jungle mansion. She scours every nook and locker of *Swell* for anything that moves, then resorts to ambushing flies. She nuzzles her food dish, watches sunsets from atop the dodger, and spends twilight dawns on the dinghy eyeing fish below. Her high-flying, over-the-water acrobatic routines soon lead to a few "kitty overboard" incidents. She quickly learns to dread the sea, but despite her distaste for swimming, she is amazingly good at it, and masters the art of clawing her way onto the rubber dinghy when necessary. Amelia seems like a good name for her, since her courageous, unbounded spirit reminds me of the esteemed pioneering pilot Miss Amelia Earhart.

I ask everyone I can think of who might give Amelia a good home, but find no takers. In the meantime, she's quickly growing on me. I do my best to make life as fun as possible for her aboard, devising toys and dragging strings for her to chase. I worry she might fall overboard when I am away, so I make a ladder from a long strip of old towel and hang it over the side. It dangles aft into the sea so she can grab it easily. I come back from surfing one morning to find her wet and madly preening; she obviously made good use of it.

Simon becomes a dear friend. He's as optimistic and sincere as a kindergarten teacher. The idea of starting a new relationship completely freaks me out, but he is happy to just be close and philosophize about life, love, and the mystic. We read Rumi aloud, perform underwater ballet, take long, slow walks, and feel a closeness that supersedes attachment. His kindness helps rebuild my faith in males after my great romantic fail.

"Hypothetically," I ask one afternoon. "What if we were in love, and then one day I fell in love with someone else?"

"I would be happy for you," he says. "Sad for me, but so happy for you. True love is wanting for the other person what they truly want for themselves."

I never thought of it this way before, but it makes perfect sense. Is it love if you love someone only if they are going to love you back? Wanting someone to be happy, regardless if it means that you are in the equation—that sounds like true love to me. It sounds full of room for growth, changes, imperfections, and opportunities.

Simon watches Amelia and *Swell* when Patagonia invites me to join the surf crew on the North Shore of Hawai'i. I leap at the chance, knowing I'll also get to see my sea sister, Anna, who lives there in a house full of surfer girls. Upon my return, Simon graciously accompanies me on the first long passage since my "great escape." We head two hundred miles northeast to the atolls, and then he flies back home.

The Sisterhood

"It looks a bit tricky ahead," Léa calls from halfway up the mast, scanning for coral heads from her perch on the spreader. We have been dodging them for a few miles across the lagoon, but now they're becoming thicker.

"It's getting harder to see with the afternoon glare. Let's just stop here for tonight," I reply.

I circle back to drop the anchor. Léa helps me locate an area with a sandy bottom, then climbs down while I pay out the chain and set the anchor. When I shut down the engine, we find ourselves in perfect silence. We look at each other and grin; it's magical. It's real. It's all ours. The ocean lagoon is calm and there isn't another boat or human in sight.

"The beach across the way looks divine," she says in her endearing accent. She's a French surf adventurer, and a fellow Patagonia ambassador.

"Let's go ashore," I reply. "We can bring the soap and bathe in the shallows."

"And cook over a fire!" she adds. The miles of deserted sand call. We enthusiastically prep for an evening ashore.

Amelia rides eagerly on the bow of the dinghy as we motor toward a patch of palms. Approaching the beach, the cat makes an enormous leap over the shallows to be first on the rosy-pink sand. A turquoise ocean rivulet flows through the reef from the open Pacific into a variety of sand-lined pools, and then gushes out into the lagoon. Léa and I quickly unload the gear and anchor the dinghy. These are the most gorgeous bathing pools imaginable!

We strip down to bare skin, grab the eco soap, and slip into the water. I can sense that Léa also feels that this moment is holy. As sunset dyes the whole sky pink and red, vibrant reflections dance around us in the pools and saturate the evening scene with rosy light. Amelia races up nearby palms and stalks crabs, while we exfoliate our skin with the fine sands and massage our scalps with soap, laughing and joyful. There couldn't be more royal baths for two mermaid queens.

We don't want it to end, but we set out to collect firewood before it's too dark. Léa lights the fire, and once the leaping flames have settled, we cook some local sweet potatoes and the fish that Léa had speared. With full bellies, we throw more wood on the fire and lounge in the sand nearby to stare at the broad night sky and the mango-orange flames. Amelia chases the leaping shadows. The campfire of my heart is ablaze, too. Ever since I left Rainui my immediate world has been overflowing with strong, spirited, open-hearted women—of course Kepi the brave; then gracious matron Monique and the Spanish goddesses, Paula and Lucia; then my wild and righteous sea sisters Anna, Leah, Leane, and Lauren, at the Hen House in Hawai'i; my hilarious and loving blood sister, Kathleen, who put me up en route; and now Léa and Kimi.

Patagonia had kindly arranged an outer island rendezvous with two of my fellow female Patagonia ambassadors to shoot photos. It took some scrambling to prepare *Swell*, and then seven days and two island stops to arrive at the remote locale where a sleek catamaran hosted Léa and Kimi and the crew. But after only a few hours, it felt as if I'd known them in another lifetime—maybe as lions or seabirds, warriors, brash maids, or "witches" burned at the stake.

When the Patagonia crew headed home, Léa hopped aboard *Swell*. She'd like to buy a sailboat, and hopes to learn a bit while she's with me. Amelia and I are delighted to have her company. She shares my unquenchable thirst for adventure and wild places. The way that she looks out at the open horizon, it's clear that she gets why I do this. It feels good to be so deeply understood.

In contrast to so many female relationships that are implicitly based on competition—for attractiveness, men, talent, and status—these ladies are pure love. They are fearless, confident women who want the best for others, and consider themselves part of a great, unlimited sisterhood. They are honest and direct and too busy bettering themselves to gossip. They feel more, think less, and are not afraid to seek their own truth—and manifest big dreams. They know their power and use it wisely. While they don't settle, they do compromise. They are stewards for Mother Earth, ready to make sacrifices for her, and explore new ways to love her. They can pee in the bushes, and often prefer to. They embrace their femininity however it feels right. They focus on loving others better, more than how to be loved more. With them, as with my best old girlfriends and *Swell* crewmates, daily life is a celebration. Lying back in the sand near our dying fire, I wink back at the stars above, grateful for all my beautiful sisters.

In the coming days, Léa and I make no plans—just flow with the weather and swell. We howl at the moon and don't brush our hair. We find ourselves backflipping underwater with manta rays, breathing in sync through morning yoga, and hooting each other into waves.

On a two-day passage to another island, Léa, Amelia, and I slog through the first night of sloppy seas and relentless rain—all of us seasick. Throughout her misery, Léa smiles and makes sure I know that she's deeply contented despite needing to puke at any second. When a downpour arrives, I hop up to install the canvas tarp over the cockpit to shelter her makeshift bed from the heavy rain. She can't even contemplate leaving the fresh air to go below. She lies flat, indifferent, immobilized by the daemon of motion sickness while the rain pummels her lower half. I struggle to get the zippers lined up in the tugging wind, blinding rain, and darkness.

"I'm so sorry I can't help you. I can't move," she says.

"Don't!" I tell her, not holding back my laughter.

Normally, she wants to help with everything. But even now, her determination to love voyaging refuses to surrender, exhibited by her unrelenting grin. I love her for that grin. I understand all too well. No matter how awful the seasickness feels, the adventure, the freedom, and the wildness feel better. I finally succeed at installing the cover, and go back to my soggy position at the wheel. We giggle at each other's plight off and on through the night. When one of Monita's steering lines breaks, I hang over the stern, topless, trying to run a new line in the bucking seas. Now she's the one laughing. Our mutual discomfort—both nauseous, wet, cold, exhausted, and hungry—is simultaneously hilarious and glorious. *We're way out here, all on our own!*

From the corner of my dive mask a few days later, I see Léa reaching out for me. I kick my fins harder to catch up and take her hand. She knows I've been dreaming of this moment for years. As we swim across the surface of the translucent blue, the sun's rays shoot light pillars into the depths of the dropoff. I peer down in excitement, but see nothing unusual. Then Léa squeezes tighter, pointing. To our left a female humpback whale is watching us only a few meters below the surface.

Her pectoral fins hang softly by her sides. She hovers in stillness as if evaluating us. Léa and I both instinctively relax, breathe slowly through our snorkels, and gaze back at her earnestly, motionless. A full minute passes until, with a slow, effortless push of her tail, she glides across the canvas of blue underneath us.

Léa squeezes me again, this time pointing down as two enormous males approach. We clutch each other, exhilarated. The girth of their bodies alone renders me instantly breathless. All three whales meet in the middle like it's been choreographed, then together they glide majestically toward the surface. Grace, intelligence, humility, power—all conveyed without a word.

"Pssssshhhhhh! Psssssshhhhhh! Pssssshhhhhh!" Their mighty exhales vibrate through us. My mind turns inside out; the whales are only a few meters away. Léa and I look on with sheer awe.

They observe us for another moment, then descend to forty feet below, where they hover horizontally—heads in the middle, tails out—forming a symmetrical, three-pointed star. Every cell in my body thrills!

Léa's whale specialist friend, who's holding onto my dinghy, swims over to explain that the whales are resting. "If they didn't approve of you, they wouldn't have surfaced beside you like that," he adds. We're completely honored.

Léa and I dive among the plunging rays of light, until the whales surface again ten minutes later. One of them nears, making eye contact while passing slowly. Boundless respect stirs my spirit. I'm suddenly reminded of my purpose: the Earth, the kids, the plants, trees, cows, corals, and whales need my voice.

19,935
Nautical Miles Traveled

Vahine

Tits in the Wind

Amelia and I settle into a quiet, spacious bay—there's a market, a few waves nearby, and good holding in nine feet of white sand—perfect for living on the hook. It's August 2014. I've signed a book contract, and must leave the anchor down for a while in order to wrap my head around writing my story. It actually feels good to think about staying put, but the task ahead is daunting. I begin by sifting through eight years of journals, sea logs, and blogs. There's Internet in the bay here, so I can also spread inspiration and environmental messages on social media. Being connected has other benefits too. I've been battling recurring staph infections for months, and after unsuccessful rounds of antibiotics and supplements, I sign up for Wim Hof's online breathing course in hopes of strengthening my immune system.

As a kid, I was often sick. During the voyage I suffered through numerous fevers, rashes, bladder infections, sinus and skin infections, sore throats, and other bouts of bedridden illness. If it was catchable, I would get it. Spending lots of time away from medical facilities, I've realized that I have to take a proactive approach to my health. No vitamin or immunity-booster compares to simply changing the way I eat.

Since I embraced a mainly organic, whole foods, plant-based diet, my nagging injuries disappeared, my joints feel better, and the persistent acne on my face vanished. Colds and flus are less frequent. The stable flow of strong energy I have through the day cannot be compared to my old ups and downs. Alongside my personal health benefits, the animals and earth rejoice too.

I eat fish only rarely now, for two reasons: First, much of the coral is dead here, and there are noticeably few edible fish species around, and, second, after experiencing the fear and helplessness that I felt at times with Rainui, I can't bear to inflict the same on any being—even a fish. It triggers me to relive those feelings. Fortunately, plant food is abundant here. I don't judge others for what they eat, as this has been a long, personal process, but it's clear that for me, a diet in alignment with my beliefs is as nourishing as the food itself. I do struggle with how to feed Amelia sustainably, though.

In monitoring my patterns, I've noticed that illness and injury often follow bouts of negative emotions or times when my inner world is out of alignment. The episode with Rainui was the worst, but it was far from the only case. I see that forgiveness, positive thinking, and making choices that support my deepest truth also contribute to maintaining my health. I try to do more meditation, more exercise—releasing stress in between bouts of accruing it. Less stress not only seems to benefit my health, but it's also easier to be self-aware—in other words, I realize more quickly when I'm being an ass.

I putt slowly in the dinghy and appreciate the scenery. Amelia and I take long walks on the beach or in the mountains. I can spend half a day doing errands in town, moseying down the main road and practicing Tahitian with friendly older ladies. I think twice about who to spend time and energy on, often opting to be near kids. I enjoy cooking too—it used to be that eating was a necessity that got me back to surfing, sailing, fixing, and whatever else my packed days entailed, but now my nourishment is sacred. I spend a lot of time naked, appreciating every lump and freckle of my body. (Plus, it's hot, and wearing clothing only means more laundry.) I often sit up on deck, enjoying the breeze on my tits, and wishing every woman could revel in the same delicious feeling.

When I'm not writing, there's music playing—while I do dishes, clean the head, check the waves, sew repairs to my clothes, cook. Or while I prep extra line, chain, anchors, and shackles for the possibility of a big storm during cyclone season. When I'm finished with a task or just need a break I play with Amelia and dance ... I dance a lot—sometimes while chopping veggies, sometimes in the rain, in the wind, or after dark—my body and the moonbeams moving to the beat. I dance to connect to myself, and the heavens, and to ask for my continued safety through the cyclone season. I plan out a strategy for several different storm scenarios, because I'm scared at the thought of riding out a powerful storm alone aboard *Swell*.

Although at times I feel lonely, being single at this stage is giving me the time to explore who I am more deeply. I seek other ways to stay in balance and listen to my body: tracking my female cycles, rarely overeating, saying no to invites that don't resonate, and fasting occasionally. When my Auntie Julie Ann sends me a vibrator and a harmonica for my thirty-fifth birthday, all I can do is embrace my crazy cat-lady tendencies, make that harmonica and my own body sing, and keep holding out for the man who will love all of me.

I continue seeking practical, immediate solutions to making a positive difference in a world where the mightiest powers seem stiffly resistant to bending from our destructive trajectory. I focus on what I *can* do, examining my daily choices and actions. Solar and wind power provide my energy needs, although I still cook with propane and use gasoline and diesel to power the dinghy and *Swell* when needed. I purchase a small canoe to paddle ashore when I don't have a heavy load. I bring reusable shopping bags to the store, refuse unnecessary plastic, recycle, pick up trash, repair instead of buying new, and research the sources and ramifications of my purchases. I buy only eco-friendly soaps, and begin collaborating with a sunscreen company that uses only non-nanoparticle, mineral UV blockers. My Spanish girlfriends introduce me to a menstrual cup, and I can't believe I'm only now discovering this amazingly comfortable and wasteless revolution in dealing with periods!

Food choices seem to pack the most punch, though. Three times a day, I can support organic farming, animal welfare, and local options. Eating this way is activism, and I feel empowered with each bite. It doesn't matter that the opposing forces are immeasurably bigger than I am, the problems endlessly more complicated than I can comprehend. My efforts need not be measured or compared; I feel their benefits in the fabric of my own integrity.

After cooking lunch one afternoon, I pile my plate with steamed sweet potatoes, fried red bananas, and local greens, then bring it up on deck to eat. Amelia rouses from her midday nap, and follows me up the stairs. She curls up on the life raft as I sit down near the bow with my meal and gaze up to where the surrounding mountains look like the form of a woman. Maybe she is part of a Tahitian legend, a goddess; I don't know for sure. I just know I like being near her. The *Vahine* (Tahitian for woman) gives off a feeling of grace, strength, wisdom, patience, and power. Today she accepts the gusting winds and gray, moody sky with equanimity.

Looking up at her, I say a little prayer before taking my first bite.

Her magnificence reminds me that despite all my efforts toward self-improvement, I haven't really changed that much. I am clearly aware of my weaknesses, though, which means many opportunities for improvement. The effort alone has earned me the self-respect and confidence I hadn't found in other ways. Sometimes I go backwards, but I realize this is a lifelong process. As Melanie pointed out, there will always be more adversities and precious teachers to help me practice. With persistence and repetition, it's getting easier. I'm a hell of a long way from perfect, but I think I understand what works for me, and which way to keep walking.

AWOL

"Come down, Amelia," I coax. "It's okay. The dogs are gone." She looks down at me and then away; she's unlikely to descend from the tree anytime soon. "Just go ahead without me," I call to the surfer who drove us to this spot on the other side of the island.

I walk over to sit on a log where I can see the water. Amelia looks quite comfortable where she is.

Two local guys are checking the surf, too. One of them heads out with his board; the other stays back. "*Tu ne vas pas aller?*" (You're not going?) he asks.

"Well," I sigh and reply in French, "My cat is stuck up that tree. And I was hoping to bring her to the break with me, but I didn't realize I'd have to cross the lagoon to the islet to get there. So ..." my words trail off. Spit it out, crazy cat lady! You could have just said, "No, I'm not going surfing."

"Would you like me to help get her down?" he asks.

"It's all right, thank you though. She'll come down eventually. And when she does, I'm not going to make her paddle with me on my board out to the islet. She hates water. I'll just wait here for my friend to finish surfing."

I'm not sure if the look on his face is pity or wonder. "Well, I could bring her over in my canoe if you'd like."

"Wow, really? *Māuruuru* (Thank you), that would be fantastic."

While he sets off to his home nearby to get the canoe, I think of how my life has changed since Amelia came on board. In the several months since we dropped the hook, I still hadn't found a better home for her. It wasn't that I wanted to give her away, but she's a wild thing and sometimes boat life doesn't seem enough for her. I wrapped a yoga mat around the mast so she can climb, and tied up strings for her to play with around the cabin. But she still seemed bored. I worried that she missed climbing trees and feeling adrenaline; stalking and pouncing; and sharpening her nails in tree bark. Still, I wasn't sure about bringing her ashore.

But one afternoon I decided to take her with me to a secluded beach. I figured if she really disliked life afloat, she'd seize the opportunity to run off and do her thing. She thoroughly enjoyed herself that day, and stayed nearby. Gradually we expanded to sharing mountain hikes and afternoon paddles. Soon, she started coming along to the outdoor restaurant by the water and to friends' houses, other boats, and parties. She's now accustomed to riding in the dinghy, canoe, cars, and even on a scooter.

She isn't always thrilled about the means of transportation, but once we arrive, she loves to explore. She roams and hunts every nook for something to kill. If she were big enough (or I were small enough) she would probably kill me, too. She might regret it afterward, but that's her merciless nature. Since our land adventures began, she seems happier back on the boat. I cherish having her furry little heartbeat near.

Tropicat, as she has been nicknamed, charms most and ignores the others. She's the star of her own never-ending mystery movie, until she's exhausted—and then she finds the most luxurious place possible to nap.

So far I have done more procrastination than writing, but a semblance of routine has formed—a contrast to the past eight years. I surf early, write until midafternoon, and then let the local kids jump and swim off *Swell* or take Amelia ashore. She climbs trees while I do my breathing, meditation, or yoga on a beach or in the nearby mountains.

But with all the recent rain and my increased efforts to focus on writing, our afternoon excursions have been less frequent. When a visiting surfer asked me to join her this morning at a spot I've never surfed, I thought it might be fun.

"Bring your cat," she said. "It's a perfect place for her to run around. I'll pick you up at 7:30 am."

She somehow forgot that the break is on an islet, separated from the main island by 300 yards of water. I refuse to leave Amelia behind. She's still sprawled out royally on the same comfy branch above me.

When the kind local guy returns, he leaps straight onto the trunk of the tree, and gently plucks Amelia into his arms, then passes her down to me. I hold onto the squirming furball, and we set her on the back of his canoe.

He tells me to lie on my board and hold on to the *iato*, which connects the hull to the outrigger. "She'll be more comfortable with you near," he surmises. I agree. He sets off paddling the three of us toward the islet with smooth, conscientious strokes.

But Amelia remains nervous about the whole thing. Instead of staying where she's safe in the middle of the canoe, she walks out onto its thin tail and slips off the smooth fiberglass surface into the water. I quickly scoop her up, but she's horrified and obviously wondering why the hell I thought this outing was a good idea. It's definitely all my fault and it doesn't help when I giggle at her skinny, drenched body.

I towel her off when we reach the islet, and she follows us out a palm-lined trail to the surf spot. I drop my bag and spread out my pareo so she'll have a notion of home base. The waves are small, but the water will feel nice, and I haven't surfed much lately. So I paddle out for a couple of quick rides.

When I come in twenty minutes later, Amelia is gone. I spend the entire afternoon tromping around the half-mile-square islet, calling her name and apologizing for laughing at her earlier. She never appears. It gets late. At least there are no cars or mean dogs on this speck of land, and there are plenty of rats and lizards for her to hunt. The sweet guy who helped me bring her over promises that he will ask the people living on the other side of the islet to keep an eye out for her. I return to *Swell* alone.

I go back the next day and numerous times afterward. I camp out where I last saw her, leaving my stinky clothes for her to smell, along with piles of cat food. Not a sign of her anywhere.

Back aboard *Swell*, I try to resist exploding into emotional smithereens, feeling painfully alone. Sadness overwhelms me, my abandonment issues triggered. Having recently learned about regression therapy, I decide to try it to address the deeper memories that might be linked to these feelings. Using a guided online video, I dive into traumatic memories but instead, imagine what I wish had happened in those moments. I feel instant relief, but I still can't move on from the loss of Amelia. The litter box sits empty and her toys are still scattered about. Weeks become a month, and my longing to see her again pushes me to call an animal communicator or pet psychic as they're often called.

Five weeks go by. No one has seen her, and I tell myself I must let go. I never owned her; the time we shared was precious. Her untamable spirit will always stay with me. I must stay true to the belief that true love means wanting for Amelia what she desires for herself. I wish my furry friend great freedom and fulfillment.

Unlimited

And then, forty-two days after she ran off, my wild feline friend reappears. The animal communicator was right: She was alive and well the whole time, just wanted the freedom to roam on land for a while. Since her return, I take her needs more seriously.

Today she stands precariously on the bow of our canoe as I paddle toward the shoreline across from *Swell*. She hops off and waits for me in the shade of a small palm that cuts the heat of midmorning. After I unload and secure the boat, she follows me across the street and we start the hike up to my new office on the mountain. When Amelia returned to *Swell*, the same guy who helped us over to the islet the day she went missing offered to build a desk in the forest so I can work on the book while Amelia climbs trees and chases chickens.

"Hello, mango tree," I say to the gnarled old beauty that shades my open-air office. "Hi, wasp."

I clear away the fallen leaves and debris, then heave my backpack onto the split branches that make the desktop. I pull out my laptop and hop up into my seat made of lashed branches. As the words hit the keyboard they feel healing, showing me how far I have come. I haven't made it all the way around the world and I still don't have that perfect partner, but it doesn't matter. I have so much to be grateful for. The breathing technique beat the staph infections for good. And, after watching my health transform, Mom and Dad are now eating mostly plant-based diets and are both healthier than they've been in years. Mom has happily relocated to the Big Island of Hawai'i. And with the help of medical cannabis to ease him through the first few weeks, Dad has quit drinking! Miracles have never seemed more possible!

Two hours later, my stomach gurgles. I pull out my lunchbox. It's been hard to find time to cook, between writing, hauling water, handling emails, juggling work projects, and constantly maintaining *Swell*. I mostly get by on fruits, nuts, coconuts, cooked roots, and a weekly bag of organic veggies. Friends drop off dinner once in a while, too.

I type until the mosquitoes start biting, around sunset, then pack up to head down the trail. Amelia leads. I've been *in* nature, but now I want to be *with* her. We near the bottom of the trail and stroll toward the water.

My bare feet thrill to touch the sand. I stop and feel the earth rejoice to be appreciated. Loose hairs tickle the back of my neck in the breeze. Inhale. Exhale. I gaze up. The highest mountain surrounding the bay says, "Think big." The sky laughs down from above, and says, "No, think even bigger!"

We continue along the beach. Amelia dashes under my feet in pursuit of a crab. She's clever, relentlessly determined, sensitive, daring, sometimes unpredictable and other times just plain terrible. She is wonderful just as she is, and so am I.

I've fallen countless times, only to rise again, cloaked in new strength, and determined to find my way to a mental horizon of unlimited potential again. I have wrinkles around my eyes and sunspots splotch my skin, but I feel beautiful. I still have little money in the bank. I only own three pairs of shoes, all of my clothing can fit in one duffel bag, and I still flush my toilet with a hand pump—but I feel rich. I have spent the most energetic years of my life testing my physical, mental, and emotional capacities in pursuit of a dream. I have done it on a blank canvas, in a variety of backdrops, and with more time than most. We all deserve this kind of chance to spread our wings and learn to fly.

I have proven, at least to myself, that with plenty of hard work, choosing love will never lead to lack. It takes courage, but once the decision is made, doors open that seemed forever shut. Walking through them feels hopeful, exhilarating, and full of purpose. I am not the best sailor or the best surfer, or the most credentialed at anything, but chasing my dream has taught me that fulfillment and self-love don't come from being "the best." They come from pursuing our passions and connecting to our own spirits, communities, and world. Being the best, or richest, or strongest, or sexiest—without feeling connected—doesn't sound heavenly at all. The times I've stepped on people to reach the top, the view was chilling and lonely.

Connection brings me the most joy. It is communion in a wink from a resting tern a thousand miles from land, and comfort in shared laughter that transcends language barriers. It is the gratitude felt for a tree that offers shade, and a high-five with a stranger in the lineup. It's noticing the signs and going with my gut, feeling *Swell* in perfect trim or making it out of a deep tube. A momentary meeting of eyes that needs no words. The first bite of a hard-earned meal. A transcendent moment of meditation. It is feeling sorry for the barnacle that must be scraped off the rudder, long-distance video calls with my sister, and earning Amelia's trust. It's picking up a kid who's fallen down with the gentleness of his own mother, and the dignity that follows small victories in self-improvement. These are moments that make me feel close to the Great Spirit that unites us all.

Bugs and beauty queens, immigrants and indigenous, rich and poor, furry and scaled; we are all struggling, striving, loving, and breathing on this green-and-blue ship flying through space—each with a purpose that combines to form the incomprehensibly beautiful mandala of our collective meaning. Feeling closer to every being that struggles in the coarser, chillier, riper, naked, more startling layers of existence has made the whole planet feel like home.

I stop occasionally to pick up scattered chip bags, plastic forks, and empty bottles along the shore as the sun touches down on the horizon. It doesn't matter that it isn't my trash; it's my Earth. And that's the beauty of Oneness: Love has no borders.

Emotional isolation and separation cause most of our problems. We're capable of creating a system that allows humans to live in harmony with each other and our planet, encourages our uniqueness, and makes us feel whole and united—it's time. May we find the fortitude to heal ourselves from within, because doing so heals the world. May we understand that our health and the health of the planet are inextricably connected. May we find a way to accept that we are multidimensional beings—separate, yet at the same time, energetically, socially, ecologically, spiritually interconnected and dependent on everything else. Everything.

Even out there alone in the middle of the sea, I am connected to everyone who shaped me and my vessel. Barry is still with me through my every triumph and folly, and I feel his pride for my sailing accomplishments and for carrying on his environmental torch. I'm connected to both my grandmothers who left their hometowns in Kansas and Virginia alone to head to California in the 1940s; their courage meant I was raised near the ocean. My great-uncle Jim taught my father to sail, so his spirit sails with me, too. The children who gave me bracelets off their arms and unasked-for hugs kept me hopeful when I doubted. Countless people offered a warm meal, an extra hand, or let me fill my water jugs and do my laundry—without any expectations. The dolphins singing to me from under the hull on night passages while I lay in my bunk convinced me that I was never alone.

We can't do it all on our own. And if we think we already know everything, we shut ourselves off to unlimited possibilities and potential. If we leave it all up to the experts, we give up our power. There is more going on in this universe and beyond than humans have yet learned to measure. And more things with value than the Western world has put price tags on. It's up to us to stay curious, keep evolving. And let go of what no longer serves us. It's up to us to work together and use our unique callings and skills to get our planetary spaceship back on course.

The top of the sun melts across the horizon. The breeze has softened. I reach down to untangle nylon fishing line from under a rock. Amelia hauls a sea cucumber up from the shallows, leaping and batting at it. It lies in listless protest. I pick it up gently and toss it back to the sea.

"Good luck, buddy," I call. Empathy warms my inner world.

I don't know what's next for me, but know I must keep one ear to my heart to stay in life's sacred trim. I set out on this voyage with the goal of sailing around the world, but the truth is that I've found what I was looking for inside myself. It would be wonderful to complete the whole dream someday, but I don't feel like that's the objective anymore. Being true to myself was Barry's only real expectation. I've learned that adventure is an attitude, not a destination. So, whether on land, at sea, or in line at the DMV, I'll always be on an adventure. And whichever direction the calls of my inner voice lead, I know I'll be taken care of. Faith is not inborn in all of us, but it can be built like muscle, living from the heart.

My trash bag is full. I set it down and lift my hands to the sky to move through a few sun salutations while evening's purple curtain falls upon the luminous strip of horizon. I lie in the sand in *savasana* and let a few mosquitoes have dinner at my expense. When I sit up, it's nearly dark.

"Amelia! Kitty! Let's go home," I call into the night. I retrieve my bag, dispose of the trash, and carry the canoe to the water's edge.

The slow rise and fall of the sea on my ankles feels like the ocean breathing. *Swell*'s anchor light sways, shining boldly out into the darkness. Amelia appears, mewing and pleased with her evening's escapades.

I load her into the canoe, and paddle us home through the morphing reflections on the dark, glassy sea. Once we're aboard, I strip down to bare skin, then leap into my sublime, starlit bathtub and float on my back, dreaming.

20,065
Nautical Miles Traveled

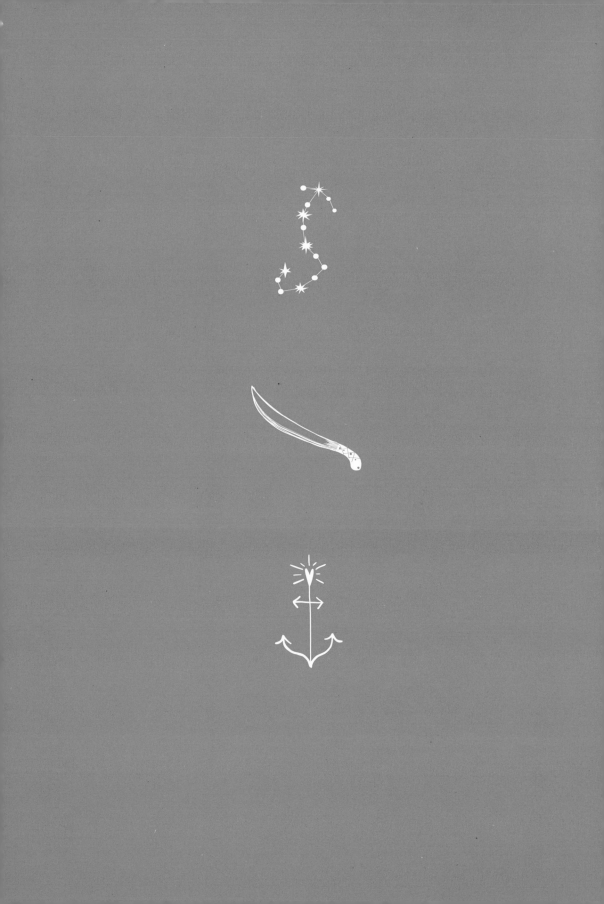

ACKNOWLEDGMENTS

Meeting Dr. Arent H. 'Barry' Schuyler was like catching a shooting star. Without his encouragement and generosity this voyage would not have happened like it did. Barry and his wife, Jean, quietly empowered innumerable other individuals, as well as actively backing an endless stream of projects for environmental and social good. These two remarkable human beings are still my dearest role models.

My parents, Russell and Melissa Clark, also had a huge role in making this dream possible. They raised me to believe I could do anything, and their support of my pursuits has been unfailing and inexhaustible. I love them more than anything.

The unparalleled expertise of Marty Spargur, James Lambden, and Mike Jansen transformed *Swell* into a dynamic, ocean-going vessel. The care and foresight they employed in each detail of their work on the boat has kept me safe and enabled me to reach each new landfall. New friends along the way also helped make repairs and upgrades to *Swell* when my expertise or muscle fell short.

I'd also like to thank the numerous businesses and private donors who have offered product, discounts, or dollars to keep this adventure going through the years. From the beginning Patagonia believed in helping one of the first female captains to sail off in search of surf. The people who make this company so extraordinary have my utmost gratitude for their support and their diligent efforts to protect our planet.

Hundreds of others also contributed to my voyage in countless ways over the years, including support for writing this book. Whether we crossed paths in an anchorage or you cheered me on via the Internet, whether you gave me a lift, lent a hand, published my writing, or offered a warm meal, a good idea, a dock to tie to, a hot shower, a care package, encouraging words, the use of your washing machine, a place to sleep or write, a good luck charm, fresh water to fill my tanks, a prayer or hug when I needed one—thank you. Your kindness and generosity have become a part of me, and I look for ways to pay them forward every day.

ABOUT THE AUTHOR

When Liz Clark was nine, her family spent seven months sailing down Mexico's Pacific coast. After returning to land life in San Diego, she dreamed of one day seeing the world by sailboat. While earning her BA in Environmental Studies from UC Santa Barbara, she fell in love with surfing. After college, she turned her voyaging dream into reality, sailing south from Southern California through Central America and the Pacific Islands. For more than a decade, she has kept her nomadic ocean lifestyle going through writing, blogging, photography, representing conscious brands, and earning recognition as a surf adventurer, environmental activist, and captain. She hopes to inspire people to live their passions and reconnect with nature and our inherent oneness. She was featured in the film *Dear and Yonder* (2009), and nominated for National Geographic Adventurer of the Year in 2015.

ABOVE JIANCA LAZARUS

PARTING SHOT Like a swell traversing the ocean to crash upon a distant shore, may we push on towards our dreams and realize that we are both the wave and the sea all at once. MORGAN MAASSEN

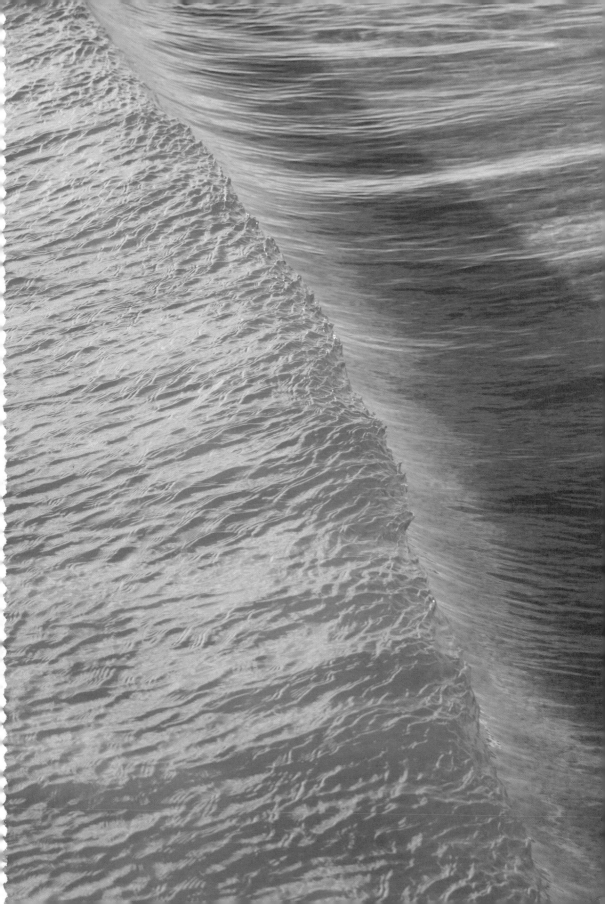